My Celtic Soul

Our Year In the West of Ireland

Patricia O'Brien

This Book Belongs to:

Susan Otterbacher

Writers Club Press

San Jose New York Lincoln Shanghai

My Celtic Soul
Our Year In the West of Ireland

Published by Writers Club Press
an imprint of iUniverse.com, Inc.

For information address:
iUniverse.com, Inc.
620 North 48th Street
Suite 201
Lincoln, NE 68504-3467
www.iuniverse.com

ISBN: 0-595-00519-5

Printed in the United States of America

To Mike

That Ireland which we dreamed of, would be the home of a people who valued material wealth only as a basis for right living...and devoted their leisure to the things of the spirit...

Eamon de Valera

Contents

Preface

My Celtic Soul was inspired by my first visit to Ireland, when I was struck by an overwhelming sense of *deja vu*. Everything felt familiar, as if I had already known this land of my ancestors in a previous life. This powerful, spiritual connection made me feel as if a part of my soul had forever dwelled in Ireland and my return had awakened the Celtic soul within me.

From that time on, I promised to someday live in the land my great-grandfathers had reluctantly abandoned. *My Celtic Soul* is the story of what that experience might be like. In this romantic adventure novel, Irish Americans Pat and Mike O'Brien give up their comfortable American lifestyle and move to Ireland in order to discover the roots of their ancient Celtic ancestors.

In the tradition of Irish story telling, *My Celtic Soul* is a mixture of history and myth, fact and fiction. I have created most of the main characters and situations wholly of my own imagination. However, those that are based on real people and actual situations have been altered for obvious reasons. The locales are portrayed faithfully and the reader may depend on all historical facts, details, places, myths, customs and traditions as being accurate. The depth and drama are real.

My greatest thanks go to the Irish people, the real soul of Ireland, and to my husband, Michael, who added his enthusiasm and humor to our Irish escapades. He taught me to treasure our Celtic heritage, and better yet, how to tell a good story.

Thanks to Vic, a dedicated teacher and mentor.

Arriving in Shannon

"Look, there's Galway Bay!" Mike exclaimed, tapping the window with his finger.

As the pilot asked the flight attendants to prepare for landing, Mike peered out the window. " Can you believe we made it to Ireland in less time than it would take to bake a turkey? And in a few minutes," he said as he squeezed my hand, "we'll finally be home."

"*Home*," I whispered. The comfort of the word enveloped me as I thought of finally realizing our dream of living in the land of our ancestors. It had been an unusually quick trip, six and a half-hours from Chicago. We had visited Ireland many times before, but this trip, the final trip to live a whole year in our ancestral homeland, had been up until this point, an elusive dream. Now it seemed too quick, too easy

Our plane banked sharply on its final descent into Shannon Airport. Suddenly, a sprawling patchwork of green squares emerged beneath us. It resembled a massive quilt bordered by a row of rocky cliffs and blue ocean.

"If that's Galway Bay, then those must be the Cliffs of Moher," I said, leaning forward to look over him.

"A sight for sore eyes," Mike sighed.

"It's more beautiful than I remembered," I said, but I was suddenly overcome by an overwhelming feeling of anxiety. Whose idea was this anyway? Did I *really* agree to this crazy notion of living in Ireland for a year? Okay, we had been over this a million times since we promised each other that someday we would live in Ireland. But it had been so easy to promise *then*—fifteen years ago—a few glasses of wine with a candlelight dinner overlooking the shimmering Lakes of Killarney. But that was then, this was now. What if our romantic scheme somehow went to hell in a handbag?

Mike leaned over and kissed me lightly on the forehead, his way of reassuring me when he knew I was about to become unglued. His strength and calm always seemed to soothe me even when his adventurous spirit made me take chances I wouldn't have taken without him. I was the romantic one but he was the gutsy one. We were here, weren't we?

I had stubbornly set certain conditions before agreeing to leave my comfy home in the Chicago suburbs. After all, why give up my four bedroom custom built dream home for a dilapidated farmhouse?—although the farmhouse had a breath-taking view of the River Shannon. Why would I exchange my computer-controlled central heat for a drafty fireplace?—even *if* the fireplace had warmed families for two hundred years with hand-cut peat taken from the bog. Surely we would miss family, friends, and everything else we were giving up for this impetuous romp in the West of Ireland.

In the end, Mike had met all of my conditions and it became increasingly difficult to come up with any more excuses not to go. He had secured a one year leave of absence from his job, rented our home to responsible tenants, and found what might be an ideal situation in Ireland: We would be overseeing a quaint Bed & Breakfast farmhouse located in the west of Ireland. Wasn't that exactly what we had dreamed of? The plane descended lower and lower and I braced myself for the *thump* and the skid of wheels. It was too late to turn back now.

"We made it!" Mike shouted, barely able to contain his excitement.

Minutes later we were disembarking. As I looked out over the crowd in Shannon airport, I felt an overwhelming sense of *deja vu*. The Irish faces about me looked as familiar as family, yet they were perfect strangers. I felt as if I had done this all before, a routine practiced over and over in my mind, the day we would move to Ireland.

In contrast to the familiarity of the people around me, the airport seemed foreign, dated, as if it hadn't been touched, or retouched, since the 1950's. Orange vinyl seats filled the waiting areas, with worn brown tiles covering the floors. The entire airport seemed smaller than the square footage of our local Wal-Mart. It was hard to imagine how an international airport could manage with this size. Well, wasn't that Ireland's allure, being familiar, small, manageable? And now we had committed to a year of calling this home.

My eyes tried to focus on the myriad of rent-a-car signs. The well-known American companies Hertz, Avis and Budget were surrounded by names that sounded like they came from an Irish telephone directory. O'Shea, Donahue, Lynch and Foley. But no Dooley sign appeared. We had specifically booked our car with a local agency so that we could save a few Irish pounds.

"Why don't you go find the car rental," Mike said, "and I'll get the bags. Meet me over at carousel number three."

"Don't worry, I'll find you," I said, knowing how easy it was to pick Mike out of a crowd. At six foot four inches tall, he stood a head above everyone else. I watched him walk away. For the first time I noticed that his thick black hair was beginning to gray at the temples. Unlike myself, who had inherited the typical Irish coloring from the Vikings and Celts, both fair and blonde, Mike was what the Irish would refer to as *Black Irish*. Black Irish were those who could trace their ancestry back to 1601 when the Spanish came to the aid of the Irish against England at The Battle of Kinsale.

I inquired as to the whereabouts of the Dan Dooley Rental Car Agency at the Avis counter. A slim young redheaded girl in her early twenties, leaned over the counter to point to the opposite side of the room. She was dressed in a navy blue pleated skirt and white blouse with a print silk scarf tied neatly around her neck.

"Now then," she said. "As you can see, your man Mr. Dooley doesn't believe in spending money on airport space like the rest of us. You'll have to be chauffeured to the 'out lot.'" She pointed toward one of the exit doors. "See the fat man by the door over there," she directed. "He'll be happy to assist you."

I approached the man with some hesitation. Perhaps this was some sort of scam we had seen in other foreign countries. The scheme involves an unlicensed taxi driver who lures unwitting tourists from the airport with the promise of a discounted fare. Halfway to the destination, he stops and removes the passengers and their luggage and demands money in exchange for calling a legitimate taxi to continue the trip. Confused tourists sheepishly pay up rather than be left stranded and learn a hard lesson in bargain hunting.

It struck me that this could be something even worse. I imagined a set-up, where terrorist disguised as car rental agents might kidnap us directly from the airport, as had happened to Americans in in other countries. When I get tired, my imagination runs away with me.

The portly man wore an ill-fitted gray tweed jacket, which hung open. His wrists were crossed over his ample belly. This stance made him appear anything but daunting. Dangling from his hand was a cardboard sign with big, black block letters printed in magic marker: "**O'BRIEN.**"

It comforted me slightly that either he or the car agency knew how to spell our name. This was unlike our local Blockbuster clerk who, after asking me to spell out what I considered our common surname, demanded to know where the apostrophe went.

"We're the Yanks with a year's worth of luggage," I said, introducing ourselves. Mike was returning from the carousel with our bags and his golf clubs stacked precariously on a luggage cart.

The fat man shook our hands and gestured for us to hop into a van. It was a hot day even by Irish standards. Beads of sweat formed on the chauffeur's brow as he slung the bags into the back. I wondered why he was wearing tweed on a hot day like this. Soon the van bulged with the three of us, our luggage, and my husband's new set of golf clubs which he had received as a going away present. Through the van windows, the flat green landscape rolled past us. The sun shone through billowy white clouds above, casting sharp shadows onto the ground. Hot air blew through the dashboard vents.

The van stopped in a large gravel lot in the middle of an empty field, some two miles from the airport. My irrational fears started to slip away, as we were greeted by none other than Mr. Dan Dooley himself, who emerged from a trailer that served as his office on the corner of the lot. Dooley was gregarious and red-faced, and he greeted us with the warmth we would soon come to expect from all Irish people. He, like our portly chauffeur, was also unseasonably dressed in a tweed sport jacket *and* a tweed cap.

"Michael and Patricia O'Brien, is it?" Mr. Dooley asked. He shook our hands enthusiastically and told us that he, in fact, had Dooley cousins who lived in the Chicago area. Did we know them? We told him we probably did. His heartfelt welcome was so genuine that I was ashamed to think that until five minutes ago I was afraid we were being kidnapped. To add to my shame, he upgraded us to a larger car at no extra charge.

"You'll be needin' a minibus with the size of ya'," he chided Mike.

Mike was thankful, but I was tired, sweaty and hot. We still had two hours of driving ahead of us. So with my most polite voice, and my most lyrical but affected Irish accent, I gently inquired, "Now Mr. Dooley, would you be havin' a car with air conditionin' for us Yanks?"

He threw his head back in laughter and flippantly tossed the keys over to Mike. "Mind ye, you're in Ireland now, ya' know. If it's the air conditionin' you'll be wantin', just get the car up to thirty miles an hour and roll the windows down! Ha!"

Mike laughed, as he caught the keys in midair with one hand while saluting good-bye to Mr. Dooley's with the other. "We are thrilled to be here," Mike said. "It's taken us a long time to finally get home."

"Home?" Dooley asked.

"Yes," Mike said. "Well, really, our grandparents'. Our return to Irish soil is a symbolic gesture to our grandparents who were forced to leave Ireland three generations ago. We're hoping our moving back to the Old Sod will take the place of their finally coming home."

Dooley grinned. "Well, I hope we can all make you feel welcome. Now, get on with yas before ya get me all misty-eyed." He waved us away and turned toward the trailer door.

Although I wouldn't be getting my air conditioning, I was heartened by the fact it would be a long time before anybody would ask me how to spell "O'Brien."

Mike pulled the car out of the gravel lot and headed for the highway. A half-hour later, we came to a "T" in the road. Two white trapezoid signs with black lettering pointed in opposite directions. The signs gave us two clear choices: *Limerick* or *Other Destinations*. I glanced at the index card which was perched in my lap and instructed Mike to make a sharp right for *Other Destinations*. In spite of jet lag, hunger and free floating anxiety, we were getting more excited with every mile to be finally seeing our new home for the next year, the Farmhouse at Castleconnell.

The dream we had been planning for fifteen years was finally starting to look like it might be coming true. As Mike had often reminded me with his gentle nudging, "What's the worst that could happen? A year of total bliss?" To which I always shot back, "Or a year of our lives wasted on a cocka-mamie scheme! Can you imagine our returning with our tails between our legs, lying to our friends about what a wonderful experience it was, and learning not to try anything adventurous again?" He always responded to this with his quick wit, "No, that's the *best* that could happen!"

No wonder I could never say "no" to the guy. So here we were.

Both sides of the index card were covered with directions. Each line contained references to some landmark or another. *After turning toward other destinations off the Nl3, drive approximately two miles until you see a little gray stone church on the left. Don't turn there. Wait until the next inter-section that veers left, it's not really a fork in the road but a slight veer, stay left and continue until you see a brown brick schoolhouse. Don't turn here either.*

Was this somebody's idea of a joke? It resembled a road rally puzzle, as there were twenty lines of details without one street name. The directions continued on in a more and more inane fashion. Stay on, go on, stay right, stay left. After meticulously following every twist and turn for at least a half-hour, we found ourselves completely lost. Then we did what at the time seemed like the most logical thing to do, which was to retrace the directions backwards so we could find where we went wrong. This of course, only worsened our plight. We ended up back at the little stone church, where luckily there was a telephone booth across the street. After I fiddled with the unfamiliar coins, and dialed what seemed like an inordinately long set of numbers, the phone on the other end rang and rang.

Finally, a breathless male voice picked up. "Hello?"

"Hi, it's Pat and Mike O'Brien, from the States," I said. "I'm afraid we're lost."

"Now, Pat, where the hell are ya? We've been waitin' for yas for hours!"

"The gray stone church," I said.

"Stay there, we'll come and get yas. God bless your tiny little brain!" He hung up before I could explain.

What a great first impression. They probably think we're total idiots! How would they trust us running the place if we can't even *find* it? Tiny little brains, that's for sure.

Soon an old, rickety, red jalopy pulled up in front of the church. A tall, lanky, dark-haired young fellow jumped out. He extended his hands and grasped ours vigorously. "Welcome!" he exclaimed. "I'm Kevin. You must be Pat and Mike. Just like you Yanks, not to follow the directions!"

"We followed the directions *you* sent us," I protested, countering to his ridicule.

"Maybe next time we'll have to read them first," Mike added good-naturedly. Then, Mike and I looked at each other and broke up in laughter. His friendly chiding took the edge off of our embarrassing situation of needing to be rescued from the side of the road.

As he climbed back into his car, he yelled to us, "Come on, Yanks, would yas please be payin' attention this time?"

We followed him as he kept us in his rear view mirror the whole way. We continued until we came to where we had given up and turned

around. There was one more half-mile and then a sharp turn in the road.
We came to an incline and then another bend in the road. There, before
us, emerged one of the most beautiful sights I had ever seen.

It looked like something out of a fairy tale. The wide, yellow stucco
house stood nestled in a thicket of green climbers that embraced the entire
facade. It was massive, but charming at the same time. It looked as if it
could have been seventy-five feet wide, with rows of double-hung windows lined up symmetrically on either side of gray wooden doors. A shock
of brown thatch crowned the roof. I could see and hear the ripples of the
River Shannon flowing behind it. For the first time in my life, I was dumb
struck. I could barely gather the energy to get out of the car.

"Home," I whispered, "our Castleconnell Farmhouse…"

With that, a large brown dog that had been sleeping on the front stoop,
stood up, looked at us and yawned.

"Now, what have I been telling you the last fifteen years?" Mike said.
"Just look at this place!" He put his arm around me as we gazed at the two
hundred-year-old farmhouse.

The dog sauntered gaily toward us, wagging his entire hindquarters as
if we were long lost friends.

"Now, see, what did I tell you?" Mike said as he stroked the dog's snout.
"What's the *worst* thing that could happen, *this*?"

I leaned over to pet the dog on his oversized muzzle. "You could be
right, dear. This might be the *best* thing that could happen!"

Barnyard Tour

The sound of a cock crowing woke me out of a sound sleep. For a moment, I had no idea where I was. Through the open window, cows and sheep rhythmically called to each other in alternating mooing and bleating. It was heavenly to think that this natural chorus would be our daily wake-up call for the next twelve months. It was our first morning in Ireland.

This morning, Kevin, our resident farm hand, would take us around and give us the so-called "lay of the land." As I tried hard to recollect what time we had decided upon, I could smell the strong scent of coffee wafting in from the downstairs kitchen. Mary, the housekeeper, whom we hadn't met yet, must have been alerted as to our arrival as I could hear her clanging around the kitchen. I decided to look alive and scurry downstairs to introduce myself to her and show her how delighted we were to be the new proprietors at Castleconnell Farmhouse.

"Well, if it isn't herself!" Mary extended her hand cheerfully. She smiled as if she not only knew *of* me but actually *knew* me. "How was the first night's sleep for ye? Did Tarzan wake ye up?"

"You mean my husband, Mike?" I answered half-incredulously.

"No, but that woulda been a bit better I'd say," she giggled.

"That Tarzan has been wakin' us up at the crack of dawn for the past ten years. He's makin' us all age beyond our years. We're all hopin' he'll soon be joining the ranks of other roosters, in the big chicken coop in the sky." She pointed to the ceiling. "Maybe then we'll have ourselves some peace and quiet."

"Considering that was the first time I've ever been awakened by a rooster instead of an alarm clock, I thought it was actually quite charming. I feel like I'm on a real live farm. I can't wait for Kevin to show us around. Have you seen him this morning?"

"Oh, he'll be comin' around soon enough, my dear." Mary poured me some coffee without asking. "Would ya be takin' some sugar with this sludge?" she added with charming yet self-effacing humor.

"I have some Sweet 'n Low in my purse in the room," I answered. Although I knew now was probably not the time to think about dieting, I wanted to get Mike up just the same. "I'll be right back."

I raced up the stairs and found Mike still fast asleep. He could sleep through anything. I shook his shoulder as I passed by the bed. "Honey, wake up, the barnyard is waiting."

"Be there in a minute," he responded half-asleep.

I skipped down the stairs with my Sweet'n Low.

"That stuff will be givin' ya the cancer, ya know," Mary said with the authority of a doctor as I poured the white powder into my coffee.

"How about cream?" Mary asked. "Ya don't use that powdered fake stuff too, do ya?"

"Oh, never." I lied trying to be agreeable. I really *had* used it most of the time to avoid the extra fat calories of milk or cream.

She reached in the frig and pulled out a white porcelain creamer in the shape of a cow. "This is compliments of Nettie, our very own best milker. You'll be meetin' her soon enough, no doubt."

She poured the creamy froth into my cup. "What time did Kevin say he'd be round?"

"I wish I could remember, but I'm afraid the jet lag has gotten the better part of my brain," I said.

With that, a little bell jangled at the side door. The screen door burst open and in sauntered Kevin. I didn't remember noticing last night just how good looking he was. He was lean, about six feet tall, with muscular shoulders. He had deep set crystal blue eyes and brown short-cropped hair. He could have been a Marlboro Man, but his jeans and work boots looked more construction worker than cowboy.

"How are ye?" he grinned exposing perfectly square, white teeth.

"Great. Although I have to admit I don't remember much about last night, it's all a bit fuzzy."

"That's what all the pretty girls tell me," Kevin replied with a sly smile. "Ya know it's startin' ta give me a complex."

"Oh, go on, ya big blaggard," Mary yelled. "Don't be givin' her any of your lip just. Ya haven't even givin' her a chance ta know ya."

I was assuming this was all done in friendly humor to make me feel at home. It was either that or the two of them were ready to go at it with each other. Kevin poured himself a cup of coffee and helped himself to plenty of Nettie's best.

"I'm really very excited to be here," I said as politely as I could to keep the two from starting an argument. "Mike'll be down in a minute, I'm sure. Oh, here he is now!" I was relieved to see him lumber slowly through the kitchen door, half-asleep.

"How about a cuppa', Michael, you look like you could use one," Mary said as she introduced herself. "And of course you met Kev*een* last night." She accentuated the "een," the Irish term of endearment for "little," although he was far from that. Kevin smiled broadly and shook Mike's hand, perhaps a bit too hard. Mike shook it back harder still. Mike asked, "So when does that tour of yours start? We city folks can't wait to learn how to milk a cow."

"Right now if you'd like. You can take yer coffees with ya." He pushed the screen door open ahead of us and nodded back to Mary. "I'll be makin' farmers outta these Yanks in no time."

We trudged along the gravel driveway as dust kicked up over my sandals and onto my feet. I wondered why it was so difficult for people to walk three abreast and talk at the same time. Maybe we were just a bit nervous. I made sure Mike and Kevin walked next to each other. Perhaps it would ease the apparent awkwardness. Also, I worried about looking like an overly assertive or flirtatious American woman if I walked in between them.

"I guess I'll start with the cows," Kevin began his discourse. "How much do you know about cows?"

"We only know that milk comes from them," Mike quipped trying to be clever. "Doesn't white milk from the light ones, and chocolate from the brown ones?"

God, I hated it when he tried too hard to win people over with his repertoire of sophomoric jokes. I looked down at his shoes. I couldn't believe he was wearing his good wing tipped business shoes with his jeans. I felt a little embarrassed by him in front of this cool Celtic cowboy. The term "Ugly American" must have been coined by somebody who recognized American businessmen by their shoes.

"Yeah, that's right, Mike. And the black and white cows give light chocolate." Kevin didn't miss a beat as he tried to one-up Mike on the humor scale. "Did you ever hear that the bravest man in the world was the first one to try drinking from a cow's udder?"

Well, I thought, this just might prove to be a bit more interesting than just a barnyard tour. He was awfully cute, *and* he proved he had a sense of humor, my number one requirement after looks. At least, for the next year, I would enjoy the scenery.

"Okay, let me introduce you to Miss Nettie. She is the queen of all cows. She's good for a few gallons a day…minimum. That's with two milkings."

Nettie stood complacently while she eyed us up. She didn't seem to bothered by the fact that it looked like her udder was about to burst.

"Gosh, she's huge," I murmured absentmindedly. "That's how little I know. I thought only bulls were this big."

"The heifers always grow big when there aren't any bulls around," he winked at me.

I blushed.

"Speaking of bulls," Kevin responded, "here comes Norman, lookin' for his breakfast. He's our prize bull. Do you remember him from *City Slickers*? We named him after the movie. Don't yas think there's a powerful resemblance?"

It was difficult to associate the well-known Hollywood movie filmed in New York and the American West with these surroundings. "Of course," I responded. "One of my favorite films." I thought that would further endear myself to him.

Norman, the calf, was almost the size of Nettie. He had a beautiful golden tan coat with white markings splashed symmetrically across his gigantic muzzle. As I was admiring his graceful countenance I tried to get another look at Kevin's without looking too obvious. Norman bolted right past us. That's what I get for flirting. Because I hadn't been paying attention, Norman almost stepped on my foot in his eagerness to get a hold of Nettie's teat. This startled me, as he must have weighed nearly three hundred pounds if he weighed an ounce.

"I guess he's hungry," I stammered, trying not to sound like a frightened urban cowgirl. "Isn't he a little old to be her calf?"

"Oh, he's not hers," Kevin explained patiently. "His mother won't feed him so he's takin' to Miss Nettie. Come on, Norman, get on it."

Kevin pushed all of his weight on Norman's left flank trying to get Norman in position. In defiance, Norman reared back and almost knocked all three of us over. Mike bravely stood his ground but I backed up a safe twenty feet away. I'd be darned if my first letter home was to inform our friends that I had been trampled by one of our own bulls, on our first day on the farm, no less.

"Come on Normie," Mike said. Now Mike was getting into the act. I could have sworn he was competing with Kevin's well-practiced bull nudging abilities.

Norman eyed Mike curiously, probably trying to figure out who this wing-tipped-clad-stranger thought he was trying to push *him* around. Norman approached Nettie again, this time he was getting closer to his goal. As he nudged his face between her legs, Miss Nettie gave a strong side kick and placed her left back hoof squarely onto Norman's surprised face. She didn't want any part of him. Kevin continued to push and pull a now reluctant Norman back into a good suckling position.

"Do you think this is such a good idea?" I heard myself ask.

"Oh, Miss Nettie's a typical female. She always plays hard to get at first. She'll take to 'im eventually. She just needs a little coaxin'."

With that, Kevin heaved himself against Norman until Norman again nudged his way under Nettie's belly. Miss Nettie landed another hoof on poor Norman's head, this time grazing his eye. The big, beautiful bull was starting to look pathetic, as his search for a little nourishment appeared nearly futile.

"Hey, Mike, could ya give me a hand with 'im?" Kevin asked. "Try gettin' on the other side and we'll work 'im together."

Oh, good. Now they were in collusion, perhaps even *cooperating*. Men could be so weird. Maybe they really *weren't* cooperating. Maybe they were really *competing*, just showing off for each other or better yet, showing off for *me*.

"Between the two of us pushin' someone's gonna get some milk," Mike called to Kevin, as he eagerly stepped forward to prove his strength. "We can't let a couple of cows push us around."

After much pushing and shoving, Mike found himself precariously wedged between Miss Nettie and the frustrated bull. Knowing politics can always be called upon when physical force failed, he suddenly changed tactics. That is, he decided to work on Nettie instead of pushing Norman any further.

"Come on, Miss Nettie," Mike cooed. "Be nice to poor Norman whose own mommy won't give him a drink."

Miss Nettie gazed at Mike with her huge brown eyes and lashes. She listened. She blinked. She suddenly seemed to understand. She tilted her head and listened attentively as Mike told her how sweet she was, what a nice girl she was being. The guy should have been a politician.

While Mike held Nettie's undivided attention, Norman seized the opportunity to nuzzle his way in, grab onto his prize and take a grateful gulp. We stood back in amazement as this enormous bull sucked happily and feverishly off his adopted mom who resignedly munched on some hay. I looked at Kevin and my would be cattle rustling husband, who again proved himself the quintessential hero in the face of a challenge. Maybe, *he* could show *Kevin* a thing or two.

Maybe, with a little help, we *could* learn to be competent farmers. We might actually be good at this. After all, we loved animals. I looked down at my sandals which were now, not only covered with dust, but with cow dung as well. I'd have to learn how to dress properly if I were going to be a good farmer.

Next, we made our way to the chicken coop. This time, I walked behind Kevin and Mike letting them relish in their victory over Nettie. We stepped out of the sun into an enclosure, which housed the laying hens.

It took awhile for my eyes to focus in the dark, but eventually I made out three rows of chickens, perhaps a dozen in all. Their feathers were a reddish brown with little white tufts on their tails which, were edged in black. I had never been this close to unplucked chickens before, let alone *live* unplucked chickens. They sat quietly in each of their individual wooden boxes which were filled with hay.

Kevin bent over and picked up a small metal bucket lying on the ground next to the rows of contented hens. "I'll just be collectin' tomorrow's breakfast for Mary to fry up with some rashers."

Mike's face fell. He looked directly at Kevin. "You're not going to disturb them, are you?"

"Oh, I won't be disturbin' them. I'll be pullin' those eggs out from under these girls so fast, they won't even know what hit 'em."

Mike refused to be mollified. I could see Kevin's irreverent reference to the would-be mothers bothered Mike even more. He had always been a bit oversensitive, but that's what I liked most about him. However, I was not about to stand there and let us look like naive Americans known for over sympathizing and empathizing with animals of any kind. Mike was clearly overreacting, and I was starting to feel embarrassed by him again.

I whispered out of earshot from Kevin in a soft, but firm tone. "Now, Mike, just where do you think eggs come from, egg factories?"

"Well, yes, of course!" He whispered back. "This is a real farm, not an egg-laying factory. How do we know these eggs wouldn't turn into chicks if we left them to incubate under their mothers?"

Maybe he was right. I didn't know how to answer him as I really didn't know the answer myself.

Kevin reached under the first hen and pulled out a brown colored egg. I could tell Mike was getting more disturbed as Kevin carelessly tossed the still warm egg into the bucket.

"Let's see," Kevin said. "We'll be havin' six guests and so we'll be needin' at least a clean dozen."

Mike looked at me, aghast. "That could be a dozen little chicks he may be destroying!" he whispered in my ear desperately.

I had to do something to mollify Mike. I put my hand on Kevin's arm to stop him from reaching in for the next egg.

"Kev, how do you know which eggs are for cookin' and which are for hatchin?" I asked.

Kevin looked at me like I was speaking Chinese.

"I'm not quite sure I'm gettin' ya, Pat."

"Well, I'm sorry if this sounds a bit naive, but I'm just concerned that maybe we're collecting and eating eggs that could possibly hatch into chicks if we left them alone."

Kevin looked at the two of us blankly, if not a bit impatiently. "You two are goin' to make great farmers! I can see that. What do you want me ta do with 'em, put 'em back?"

Knowing Mike's sensibilities were at stake, I groped for a response.

"Well no…" I stammered. "I guess we just want to know how the whole thing works. I mean, how many eggs do these hens lay? Can we afford to dispose of a dozen chicks in one fell swoop? And how do we know which eggs should be left to become chicks and which should end up on the plate next to the bacon?"

By now, Kevin was doubled over with laughter. "Yer kiddin' me, now, Pat aren't ya? It's a great joke on me if ya are! If yas ask me, it sounds like yer both better off up at the house than in the barn."

Kevin's sarcasm seemed to hit a bit below the belt. I looked to Mike to save me. After all, I was just trying to save *his* feelings and had only succeeded in setting both of us up for ridicule by Kevin.

"Hey, we're not wimps or anything," Mike said strongly, now defending our virtue. He turned the whole scenario around. "My wife just happens to be a bit on the delicate side, as you can obviously see. Couldn't you just explain what she needs to know to make her a bit comfortable with this egg-to-chicken thing, you know, like a gentleman would?"

Kevin sighed heavily. "I'm afraid that if I've gone and offended ya, Pat, I'm truly sorry. I didn't realize yer the sensitive type. That's usually why we keep the women out of the barn yard."

I couldn't tell if his speech was heartfelt, or if this was another put down. It felt like he was using the opportunity to throw a little chauvinism in on top of his previous insult.

"Let me be puttin' it to ya this way, Pat. Each hen lays one egg every other day whether they want to or not. These are yer *breakfast* eggs. Occasionally we'll let Tarzan have the run of the place. When this happens, his job is to fertilize any one of the eggs *before* they're laid. These are yer *chicken* eggs. So ya see now, we're not doin' anything cruel or inhumane, nothing the Lord himself didn't design."

"Thanks for explaining that, Kevin. We *both* feel a lot better now," as I looked over at my sensitive man who appeared relieved now that we had gotten the whole explanation.

Feeling our consciences cleared, we walked out of the shed and into a large dirt yard enclosed with chicken wire. Hundreds of hysterical hens ran around it, running endlessly and stupidly in circles. It suddenly dawned on me just how demeaning it would be to be called "a chicken." They clacked nervously and ran from one side of the yard to the other in a single wave. As soon as the first few ran to one side, the rest would follow.

Once they raced to one side, they'd turn around and head for the other side. They seemed frantic, as if they were acting in a riotous attempt to get out of a fire.

"They're gettin' excited," Kevin explained. "Tarzan must be comin'." With that, a big rusty colored rooster the size of a turkey came charging out of the barn and tore into the middle of the flock. The hens separated into two wild groups running for either side of the yard. Tarzan's bulging red crown jiggled up and down and back and forth as he searched for his selected mate. He spotted her. Feathers flew. Hens screamed. Now the chickens were frantically running into each other in an effort to escape the headstrong rooster.

Kevin snickered, "Well, now, here's himself, Tarzan, the cock we love to hate." Kevin winked at Mike. Oh great. Now, not only were they united in this Farmer John thing, but they were going to start making macho sexual innuendoes together.

To add insult to injury, Kevin continued his chauvinistic line of chat. "Those crazy hens will run 'round and 'round until one of them decides she'll let him catch her."

"That's an oblique way of saying it," I responded somewhat stiffly. I couldn't tell whether I should have been offended or humored by this remark.

"Now, my dear *sensitive* Pat," putting the emphasis on "sensitive," as Kevin knew he was getting me riled again. "This is the same Tarzan who woke you at 5:00 a.m. this morning and will continue to do so until ya want ta snap his neck with yer own two hands." He snapped his two fingers together for effect. "And I don't care how sensitive ya are, you'll want to do it yerself just like everyone else does, after a few sleepless mornings!"

I chuckled to myself at the unlikely thought of my breaking a chicken's neck in half.

"So Pat," Kevin continued. Now don't be worryin' yer pretty little head anymore. And you do get pretty when you're riled up."

I blushed again. Although I thought Kevin was a sexist, he thought I was pretty. His flattery made me consider telling him that it was actually his new bull-wrestling buddy *Mike* who was worried about the unborn chicks, not me! But Kevin interrupted me.

"With Tarzan around," Kevin assured us with bravado, "there will always be plenty of eggs *and chicks* to go around. That is, if the hens eventually let him catch them."

The Farmhouse

Our contract to manage the B&B had been consummated by Fax. All that we knew about the Castleconnell Farmhouse came from a hand drawn illustration on a brochure cover, and some glossy but dog-eared photos sent by the owners. The couple who owned the place wanted to take a year off, a kind of maternity leave, to have their first child. The hired help, Mary the housekeeper and Kevin the farm hand, would stay on in their absence.

All we'd have to do was run the B&B itself, keeping charge of the reservations and financial matters. Thank God, since we had never owned a hammer in the twenty years we'd been married. In spite of this, we were confident that what we lacked in practical qualifications we made up for with our financial astuteness. After all, we came equipped with our laptops and were computer literate!

The farmhouse had six rooms, the magic number for a successful B&B. Two of the rooms were suites and the other four were doubles that ranged from closet-sized to palatial. A full house in high season could bring in six hundred US dollars a night. This could be our retirement plan made in heaven. Never mind waiting for the corporate pension to kick in. We could be raking in thousands a week without much effort. After all, what could be easier money? Mary would have the cooking and general house-cleaning tasks. This included preparing a full Irish country breakfast for the guests each morning, making up the beds with fresh linens and wiping down the baths. She would be responsible for all of the dirty, unromantic tasks. We, on the other hand, would be living out our dream as king and queen of an authentic Irish farmhouse.

The thirty acres surrounding the house would be overseen by Kevin, who had taken care of the property since he had been a teenager. He would provide all of the outside and inside maintenance on the farmhouse. As most of the land was leased out to crop farmers, his farm skills were mostly limited to tending to the farm animals. All we had to do was make sure our guests were thanked and escorted out by the 11:00 a.m. checkout time, which was discreetly posted on each guest room door. We would have the whole day to relax.

That's what we *thought.*

But when we got there, it was a different story.

What we'd neglected to note was that someone had to be home all day and all night to take calls for reservations, not only for the current day but for dates booked months in advance. Also, many guests were walk-ins, lured by the charming trellised gate adjacent to the welcome sign boldly scripted in ancient Gaelic, *mille faillte.* Another thing we didn't realize was that almost every guest ignored the little sign on their door regarding checkout time. No matter how many gentle reminders were given by phoning their room, knocking on the door, or shoving their guest bill under their door they left whenever they felt like it. They just couldn't take a hint. And, of course, training to become the consummate Irish innkeepers, we wouldn't think of politely asking them to leave.

This could be worked out, we thought. We could take turns keeping vigil.

First we decided that my husband would leave the morning supervision to me, while he worked on his golf handicap at one of the many local courses. After 18 holes, he would take over the afternoon vigil of check-ins and reservation making. This would allow me to spend the entire afternoon shopping, running errands or otherwise pursuing my own interests. We took turns every other evening making dinners and tending to the phone.

It turned out to be a pretty equal division of chores except for handling the unhappy job of late arrivals and phone calls after midnight. Although these middle of the night intrusions happened sporadically, they happened. Since this job went by default to the one who could least endure the sound of bells ringing, it usually fell upon me. Many a night I dragged myself bleary-eyed to the phone to hear the inevitable perky voice of an American on the other end who didn't have a clue as to what time it was. I knew that I had scared away many would be guests with my not-too-cheery response at 2:00 am.

Mike never felt compelled to take a turn, as he could sleep with a band of bagpipers marching through our bedroom. This wasn't fair. We needed a new plan. So, I secretly decided to figure out a solution which worked in both our favors.

Luckily for me, Mike suffered from the universal male malady of *golf guilt* for each and every minute spent on the links. He would return from each golf outing trying not to appear too happy about his most recent round. I magnanimously allowed him to wallow in his guilt as I quizzed him about every one of his chips, putts, birdies and pars. He would start to get excited as he relived each and every shot, until it all seemed to be replaying itself in front of me by videotape. The two missed birdies, the perfect chip in, the ever elusive hole-in-one that was thwarted by that pesky tree or bush that had jumped in front of him at the last second.

I always wondered if men didn't have more fun reliving their golf games than actually playing the game itself. He did have an uncanny way of remembering every exact detail, including how many shots were made by the other players at each hole. No wonder no one ever tried to shave strokes or kick a ball while playing with him. He didn't miss a thing. He was so delighted with every recalled shot, I'd let him go on and on.

"And that wasn't even the best shot of the day! You should have seen my second shot on number eighteen."

"Gosh."

"I faded it around a tree and over the pond and onto the green. It stopped eight feet from the hole. It was a downhill putt that broke to the right, which I had to make to break ninety."

"Did you?"

"Not only did I make the putt, but I won that two dollars back from Tom Kelly!"

Suddenly, he became a little self conscious about his theatrics, which were becoming more and more animated as he approached what I hoped was the end of the story. Perhaps he was beginning to realize what a sweet kind wife he had who had spent the better part of the day working while he was trying to be another Arnold Palmer?

After all, how many wives would cheerfully send their husbands off to the links every day without complaint? Never mind that I actually *enjoyed* the fact he was able to get out every day and do something that he loved for exercise and general psychological well being. Forget that this was a great way for us not to be bored by too much togetherness. Never mind that I didn't feel one pang of jealousy, as I would rather watch grass grow than pick up a golf club.

He was relieved when I finally gave him the opportunity to release the grip his guilt was spreading over his happy countenance. I simply suggested that if he wanted to make up for all of the hours I was left alone while he was on the links, he could take phone and door duty after midnight.

You would have thought I had given him a million dollars. He looked at me thankfully and incredulously.

"That just doesn't seem fair!" he said. "It seems like I should be doing more!" "Don't worry, Arnie," I replied. "I'm sure I'll get my fair share out of this."

We could both be satisfied with this new arrangement. In the wee hours, I would be getting my beauty sleep all night, every night knowing he would be the one that would have to take the late phone calls and arrivals. Mike could play golf all day, every day, guilt free. Now all I had to do was to collect my fair share out of this golfing agreement, by spending the whole day, any day working on my favorite sport, shopping.

I reached for my wallet on the sideboard and checked to see if all of my credit cards were still arranged alphabetically in their respective plastic slots. There were so many quaint, charming shops awaiting me in Adare. I was off to practice my favorite stroke, credit card swiping.

Ballybunnion

"Hey, hey, ya'll!" shouted a burley American with a thick Southern drawl. He wore a neatly trimmed graying beard and carried a generous belly which forced him to turn sideways in order to squeeze through the front door. "Anybody here watchin' the fort?"

Mary yelled down from the top of the stairs, "I'll be comin' right down to ya."

"You just take your time, young lady," he boomed. "Sorry to tell you, we have a lot of bags. We don't know how to pack light."

"No mind," Mary said cheerfully. "We're all like that. If yas don't bring it with you, you'll be needin' it." She bounced down the stairs to meet him at the registration desk.

He bowed slightly, removed his golf cap and said in an exaggerated Southern drawl, "How do you do, Mam, are you the little lady of the house?" He took her hand and kissed the back of it.

Mary blushed.

"They call me the Colonel," he announced. "My boys are coming right behind me. They're doing all of the lugging, since I'm doing all of the driving, organizing and *paying*. Ya'll are having some pretty fine weather this week we've been told."

"I've been told it never rains on the golf course. I think you'll be havin' a good time no matter what the weather. Nobody comes to Ireland for the climate."

"Well, we brought our rain gear just in case. Are you ready for this? We call our little group *The Masters,* you know, after the Master's Tournament in Augusta, Georgia." He continued assuming Mary knew what he was talking about, and pointed to the Master's logo on his golf cap. "We played there in 1995."

"Did ya now?" Mary asked.

"They're still talking about us down there," he bragged. "We really tore up the place. I hope you can put up with us. We've been known to get a little rowdy, especially when we do well on the course! Or should I say *links*? Isn't that what you people call your brand of golf course here?"

"Yes, I believe we people do call them *links*." Mary couldn't help repeating the detested reference to the Irish as *you people*. "Is this your first time playing in Ireland?"

"It sure is, Mam, and we're mighty proud to be here. We're starting with the best. We're scheduled to play Ballybunnion this afternoon, and then onto your other great courses of Waterville, Port Rush and Port Marnook. We're sort of working, or should I say playing, our way across the country from Shannonside to Dublin."

"Let's get you up to your rooms," Mary said as she reached for a bag he had dropped on the foyer floor.

"No delicate Irish lady is going to carry bags when the ol' Colonel is around," he insisted, as he grabbed the bag away from her.

Mary ignored his flattery but let go of the bag. "Did you say *Colonel*, as in Colonel in an army?"

"Not a *real* Colonel, but that's what the boys have gotten used to calling me, ever since my little victory at Augusta National."

"A military victory?"

"Oh, no, nothing like that!" He guffawed and slapped his thigh. "It was a much sweeter victory. I shot a 76 with a six handicap *at Augusta*. Why, to some people that's even *better* than winning the Civil War!"

Mary knew little about golf terminology but knew enough to realize that this Southern gent was serious about his game.

"Here, let me get the boys to carry these bags." He excused himself and walked out to his rental van where he supervised seven young men climbing out and unloading their baggage. He came back into the house, with one of the men trailing behind him laden with luggage.

Another one of the men dragged an oversized golf bag through the door. "I think this is yours, Colonel." He leaned the bag up against the wall. It almost toppled over from its own bulky weight. It was enormous, the size of two average sized golf bags put together. The woods were protected by red and white knit golf club covers whose pattern mimicked the red and white stripes of American Confederate flags. Each cover was topped off by an enormous red pompon.

"Hey, will ya'll take that upstairs to my room like nice boys? I have to make our arrangements with this charming young lady," the Colonel shouted to the two young men now standing in the foyer. They, as well as the rest of the group, wore neatly pressed khaki twill trousers, red golf shirts and coordinating golf sweaters. The whole group also wore matching green golf caps. Each article of golf clothing displayed the U.S. Master's Tournament logo with a miniature map of America with a golf flag sticking into where Augusta would be located.

"How do you like our outfits?" The Colonel continued, turning again to Mary. "We got them in 1995 at the Masters. That's when we vowed we would come here and play Ballybunnion, over a few Southern Comforts, of course," he boasted.

"That's just grand." Mary humored him. "At least no one will lose sight of yas on the course with all yer colors."

The Colonel beamed.

Mary pointed to the hallway off the foyer. "I'm sorry, gentlemen, but the golf bags aren't allowed up in the guest rooms. You can just leave them right there. Nobody will be payin' them any mind."

The Colonel hesitated. His face grew red with embarrassment as he searched for a genteel form of protest. "My dear lady," he started to argue with her, "I must insist that I be able to sleep in the same room with my golf bag. I need to keep my eye on it. It's a very expensive bag, custom made. It's irreplaceable! Why, someone might take off with it if we leave it down here."

Mary was mortified at his suggestion that anyone allowed under her roof would be inclined to steal anything, especially a golf bag as hideous as his. "I'm sorry," she insisted as she eyed the monstrous golf bag. "How does anyone carry that thing anyway? It looks like it weighs twenty stone."

"Oh, it's quite heavy, but that's what golf carts are for. Anyway, that's why I have the boys carry it for me. It's made out of one hundred percent handcrafted leather from South Carolina. You won't be seeing one like it again soon, that's for sure." The Colonel thought he was winning her over with his Southern charm, hoping that she would let him bring his beloved bag up with him.

"Sorry, Colonel," she replied, keeping her resolve. "It's the house policy. Ya see, the bags tend to nick the paint on the walls and can scratch the wooden floors. Don't you be worryin' about yer precious bag. Nobody has stolen a golf bag from this house in twenty years that I know of. Besides, it's such a grand bag! It would take at least two strapping thieves to lug the likes of it out of here. Besides, anyone who laid eyes on it would know it's not theirs, what with *The Colonel* emblazoned in red letters on the side of it and all of those American Confederate flags wavin' in the breeze!"

The two younger men chuckled softly to themselves as they started back into the parking lot to retrieve the rest of the suitcases and duffel bags from the van. "Where should we put these, Mam?" one of them asked.

"There are eight of yas, right?" Mary confirmed. "You'll be takin' the two rooms at the top of these stairs and the two next to them. I tried to keep yas together. If yas will be wantin' a smoke, drink or a deck of cards for yer late night poker game, you can find all of that in the parlor." She waved over to the living room adjacent to the foyer. "You'll be findin' every kind of liquor at our little sideboard just there and I'll be gettin' yas a bucket of ice if ya want. The drinks are on the honor system. Just write down what ya took."

"Honor system, " the Colonel repeated. "It's good to know the Irish are carrying on a Southern tradition." The Colonel bowed gallantly to Mary. "We appreciate your hospitality, Mam. It's just like the Southern

Hospitality we're used to. Now, if you'll kindly excuse us, we'll just go on up and take a quick shower and nap, it's been a long flight."

"Do yas want me to be waking yas up at any particular time?"

"Well, we do have our own travel alarms, but we wouldn't want to miss our three o'clock tee times," he said thoughtfully, rubbing his chin. "Ballybunnion! I still can't believe we're really here, the oldest golf course in Ireland. They say it's even better than St. Andrew's!"

"Well, I have heard that claim myself more than a few times, Colonel," Mary said. "Now you'll be havin' the opportunity to judge that for yerselves."

Mary gestured up the stairway. "Now get yerselves all settled in and don't yas worry. I'll have yas up with plenty of time to practice on the puttin' green," she added good-naturedly. "You can be dreamin' about all of those holes-in-one you'll be makin' at Ballybunnion." She giggled to herself. The poor lambs. At least they could dream about it, before they realized just how formidable a course it could be, even to the best golfers in the world.

The group obediently lugged their luggage up the stairway. They resembled a small team of furniture movers with their matching green outfits and caps humping up the stairs.

Several hours later, Mary knocked on the bedroom doors and the golfers began to stir. They called out to each other from room to room in eager anticipation of their first attempt at Irish golf.

A short while later, Mary appeared at my door. "Where's the Mister?" she asked. "Do ya think he's available for some golf this afternoon? The Americans can't seem to get one of their jet-lagged teammates out of the hay. They want to know if I can come up with a fill in."

"Tell them *yes*. I'll find him somewhere," I replied, as I got up to search for him outside. "You know Mike would play Ballybunnion every day if he could."

"I thought that's what you'd say. But they're leaving in twenty minutes. At least they can save some time drivin' over there if Mike's in the car with 'em!"

Mike entered the yard just as I was approaching the gate. "I heard, I heard. I'll be ready in ten!" He dashed into the house.

Five minutes later, Mike met the group out by their van as they were looking at a map discussing the best way to get there. He walked up to them, thanked them for their invitation, and offered to drive the group since he was familiar with the route. Relieved by his offer, the Colonel gestured for Mike to climb in behind the wheel, and he and the Masters climbed into the van.

Mike called to the group in the back seats. "We'll take the short cut through Listowell. We'll be there in less than two hours. Your first time playing in Ireland?"

"We've been talking about this trip for as long as I can remember," the Colonel answered, acting as spokesperson for the group.

"What happened to your eighth guy?" Mike asked.

"He must have had a bit too much to drink on the plane. You know those pretty stewardesses like to ply you with booze in first class! That, combined with jet lag did him in. I think he'll be awfully sorry when he finally does wake up."

"Well, at least he'll have the rest of the week to play," Mike said. "Aren't you fellas playing golf all over Ireland?"

"Well, not all over, just the best courses. We're the Masters! You ever been to the Master's tournament, Mike? You're American, aren't you?"

"I sure have! One of my old customers was a member. That's how I was lucky enough to get on. How about you, Colonel?"

"I played by a special invitation. You see, I'm president of a club in Atlanta. It entitles me to certain privileges." He stuck his chest out proudly.

"How lucky. You must have a lot of friends!"

"I do now. Look at all these guys." He turned to all of the green-capped boys in the back. "They're my little following, my little groupies."

"Well, I'm sure Ballybunnion will be everything you expected, maybe more," Mike responded. He continued to humor the Colonel. "It's my favorite course in the world, that is, *outside of Augusta*. I have to warn you, though, it's a bit more challenging than Augusta."

"Impossible!" the Colonel argued.

"You'll see," Mike said.

"Are you a betting man, Mike?"

"Sure, what are you playing for, Colonel?"

"We have a little system of betting on each hole. It keeps things interesting, but we only play for small change. Frank, here, takes care of all that," the Colonel explained.

Frank nodded to Mike. "We also play twenty dollars a man for the match," Frank added. "Why don't Joe and I take on you and the Colonel."

"I'm in," Mike committed, turning into Ballybunnion's modest parking lot.

The Colonel gazed out at the rolling course, bordered by blue-green ocean. Huge waves threw themselves roughly onto the shore. "It's magnificent," he drawled. "Just like I imagined. Just like all the pictures. In fact, it looks more wild!"

The van came to a stop and the group climbed out, but as Mike helped them pull their golf bags out, the Colonel said to him, "Why don't I find out how we go about getting us some carts. You boys can wait here with the bags and I'll meet you back here."

"Carts?" Mike asked.

"Yeah, carts. We don't want to be dragging these bags up and down all of those hills." He pointed to the hilly bumps and moguls which made up the golf course.

"Oh, there are no carts," Mike said. "Each person is assigned a caddie."

"Good Lord, boy, we don't need caddies!" the Colonel protested emphatically. "I'm my own man on the golf course. I don't believe in caddies. They distract me."

"You *have* to," Mike said. "It's the Club rules. Carts are not allowed on the course." Mike tried to make him feel better. "Besides, these caddies are experienced, they're pros. They can really come in handy, reading each hole for you. They might even be able to shave a few strokes off your game!"

"I don't know if a caddie could carry this thing." He looked down at the huge monstrosity which laid on its side on the gravel parking lot. The red pompoms had started to droop and slide off of the clubs from all of the bouncing around they had taken in the van.

"Don't worry, these caddies are as strong as bulls," Mike assured him. "I'll let the starter know we're here." Mike left them to go into the clubhouse.

Several minutes later, Mike returned with four caddies in tow. "Who wants to be in the first group?" he chirped, but the Colonel studied the four caddies. Their median age appeared to be sixty years old. Their faces were weathered and they were small in stature. They wore Irish tweed caps and they sported worn wool blazers over their faded blue jeans.

The Colonel leaned over and whispered into Mike's ear. "You've got to be kidding! Why, they're old men! At least twenty years my senior! And besides, the way they're dressed, they look more like groundskeepers than caddies. What good could they possibly do me?" He yelled to Frank, loud enough for the caddies to hear him. "Tell them we won't be needing their services. Now, go get us some young boys who can handle these clubs."

Mike tugged at The Colonel's golf sweater and whispered into his ear. "These are the caddies the Club *assigns*. You must take whom they give you. Maybe you want to be in the second foursome. Perhaps they'll be more to your liking."

"Never mind," the Colonel replied in an exasperated tone. "I'll be in the first group if you want to. What do you say, Mike?"

"I'd be honored, Colonel."

The Colonel directed Frank and Joe to follow him and Mike. "We'll go on ahead, boys," he said to the remaining four.

"The other caddies will be out shortly," Mike assured them. He then lead the Colonel, and two of the Masters towards the first tee, then checked in with the starter. The caddies trailed behind them. It seemed the smallest caddie was stuck carrying the Colonel's bag.

It was a brisk, windy day. The foursome gazed reverently out over the panoramic ocean view. The waves slammed violently against a sandy stretch of beach. The course was rough, with tall grass swaying in the salty sea air. There were undulating mounds, brush hills and deep rough covering the entire course. There seemed to be no logic as to the sequence of the holes, which appeared flagged hither and yon in all directions, punctuated by enormous sand traps that resembled un-excavated beach. Several seagulls hovered over the golfers and gazed down mockingly at them.

The Colonel was cheerful in spite of being forced to rely on the ancient caddies. "I still can't believe I'm here," he confided in Mike, while looking around in amazement, his hands on his hips. "I've been wanting to come here my whole life. My granddaddy used to talk about this place when he took me golfing my very first time, God rest his soul. I was just a kid. Now I'm here, and it's better than what I expected. Now," he turned inquisitively to Mike, "where's the fairway?"

Mike stifled a chuckle. "That's why they call these courses *links*. The links are supposed to be wild, no different than cow pastures, unkempt and raw, therefore, making it more difficult to get a golf ball in the hole. That's the fun of it. They're not perfectly manicured fairways surrounded by artificial fountains and flowers like the American courses. You'll love it. Actually, you'll prefer it, once you get the hang of it."

The starter signaled them to begin, so Mike added, "Why don't you go first?" He stepped back ceremoniously to allow the Colonel to address the ball.

The Colonel went to reach for his favorite driver from his bulging bag which hung over the caddie's shoulder. But, the caddie slid the strap down his arm, stood the bag in front of him and grabbed the head of the three wood. He pulled the confederate-flag club cover off, and carefully handed it to the Colonel, as if it were a precious antique.

"I want to use my trusty driver!" the Colonel yelled to the caddie.

"I respectfully suggest the number three, sir. This hole has quite a grade."

The Colonel ignored the caddie's advice and reached into the bag for his first choice. The caddie looked at Mike and shrugged his shoulders.

The Colonel then stooped belly over, pinched his tee into Irish soil, took a few practice swings and then wound his body up like a corkscrew. His club came down with incredible velocity and struck the ball with a loud and satisfying *thock*. The Colonel had taken his first shot on the links of Ballybunnion.

It looked like he struck the ball solidly, but the wind proceeded to lift the ball higher and higher as it traveled. The ball hung in the air for several seconds. Suddenly, a gust of wind threw the ball to the right until it plummeted like a rock, hitting a burme. The ball bounced off of the burme and dribbled into a sand trap.

"Shit." The Colonel said evenly. "See what happens when you're distracted?" He glared at the old caddie.

Each of the others in the foursome took their tee shots but each gratefully took the advice of their caddies and faired much better. They all walked to the sand trap to see if they could help locate The Colonel's ball.

"There it is," Frank, the golf bookie, said, pointing toward the edge of the sand trap. "At least you have a pretty good lie," he said, encouraging The Colonel.

"Don't patronize me, boy," the Colonel barked back at him. Frank looked at Mike and rolled his eyes. The Colonel reached for his nine iron.

The caddie placed his hand over the club to keep The Colonel from taking it all the way out and said, "I respectfully suggest that you use your sand wedge on this particular trap. You'll be needin' the lift of the wedge. You're awful close to the lip."

The Colonel responded defensively. "I'll play whatever club I choose to play. Do you understand that, *boy?* His choice of the word "boy" seemed ludicrous considering the caddie was old enough to be his father.

"Yes, sir," the caddie replied softly. "Here's your nine iron." He handed it over.

It was a tricky shot as there was only about an inch of space between the lip of the trap and the ball. The Colonel bent his knees, straddled near the ball, and inched forward to get a good angle, one foot in the short grass, the other in the sand. Finally, he took a half swing, and topped the ball. This caused the ball to hit the lip and roll back into the sand trap. A tiny, narrow furrow trailed behind it.

"*Now*, at least you have a good lie," Mike said sarcastically but good-naturedly.

The Colonel growled. "Give me that sand wedge. What the hell good are caddies if you don't use them?" This time he gave his shot the minimum back swing and the ball bounced easily out of the sand. The Colonel gave the club back to the caddie. "Looks like you were right on that one."

"No prob," the caddie responded nonchalantly.

His next shot placed him on the green where he got off a fair putt, ending up with two over par on the first hole.

"I think I'm warmed up, now," the Colonel called out to the others with a new burst of energy as he retrieved his ball from the hole. "Now, I'm on a roll."

He looked down at his ball. Then he looked around, almost turning in a complete circle, searching for the flag.

"It's over there," the caddie told him and pointed out a yellow flag which flapped furiously in the wind from behind the next hill of knee-high grass. The caddie handed the Colonel what he thought was the appropriate club. The Colonel accepted it.

The caddie, taking this as an indication that his advice actually meant something to the Colonel, offered a few words of advice. "There's a bit of wind for ya at this hole, and it's coming right at ya from the ocean. Give her all you've got."

The Colonel did what he was told. The ball took off, hovered in the air and dropped somewhere behind the hill.

"Very good, sir. That was perfectly straight."

"Thanks." The Colonel beamed. He looked around at the rest of the foursome to make sure they were paying attention to the best shot he'd had all day.

The group admired the shot and for the rest of the afternoon, the Colonel's game improved. By the back nine, the Colonel sought and received valuable tips from his obliging caddie

"I love this place!" he gushed.

As the group approached the seventeenth tee, Mike and the Colonel found themselves even for the match. They came upon a threesome who were playing in front of them.

"What the hell is *that*?" the Colonel turned to his caddie.

"Why, it's a dog, sir, a collie," he responded.

"I can see it's a dog. What the hell is it doing on a golf course?" the Colonel demanded.

"It must be with the group in front of us." The caddie squinted at the group to get a better look.

"They allow *dogs* on Ballybunnion but *no carts*?"

"Why, yes, they do," the caddie responded hesitantly.

"What kind of crazy country is this?" the Colonel burst out irritatedly. He brushed aside the club the caddie held out to him and snatched another club out of his bag, not paying too much attention to which one it was. "Now I've seen everything! You're right, Mike. It certainly is a far cry from the Masters!"

When the Colonel approached his tee shot, the rebuffed caddie offered no advice. The Colonel proceeded to take a huge backswing and came down on the ball as hard as he could. The ball was hit perfectly straight and landed a hundred yards out. When it came down, however, it struck a rocky edge and ricocheted off of it, bouncing backward toward the Colonel at an increasing velocity. The ball continued to bounce gaily towards him. It then took a long roll, trickled down another hill, and picked up speed as it continued to roll backwards towards the tee.

"I don't believe this!" the Colonel muttered through tightly clenched teeth. "This is the most humiliating thing that's ever happened to me. Get me back to my Augusta!"

The ball kept on rolling as if some mysterious force were drawing it back to the Colonel. It finally stopped just three feet from the tee. The Colonel stared at the ball he successfully hit 100 yards and now it had managed to bounce backwards 99. The four players and their caddies stood silently in disbelief. They avoided looking at the Colonel by continuing to stare at the petulant ball.

The Colonel's caddie finally broke the silence. "I've been caddyin' this golf course for the past fifty years, and I've never seen anything like that before." Now *he* was glaring at the Colonel. "If I had a gun, I'd shoot ya'!"

The Colonel stared back at the caddie incredulously. "What did you say to me *boy*?"

Mike stepped in between the two. He put his hands up solicitously. "Now calm yourselves, gentlemen." He looked at he Colonel. "May I have a little word with you over here, Colonel?" He motioned to the other side of the tee.

The Colonel begrudgingly obliged.

"Look, Colonel. You might not know this, but most of the money the caddies make out here is from betting on their own golfers, on good golfers, like yourself. You probably just cost the poor guy fifty pounds. That's probably double his hourly wages for the past two days. So, why don't you give the guy a break, shake hands and show him what a good sport you are. After all, it's a compliment he bet on you at all. And you let the old guy down. We might not be able to recover point wise from this hole, but at least you can save face for him in front of his buddies as well as yourself."

"See what I mean about playing with a damn caddie?" the Colonel cursed under his breath. "Not only do I have to worry about playing well for *myself*, but now I have to worry about playing well for *him*, too!" The

Colonel tried to regain his composure as he marched angrily back towards his ball.

As he walked up to the tee for the second time, the caddie came up to him and extended his hand in a handshake.

"Sorry," the caddie said softly, "but just like you, I hate to lose." The Colonel shook his hand firmly.

"Think nothing of it, sir. I deserved that for showing poor sportsman-ship. My Granddaddy would be ashamed of me."

As he released the grip of the caddie, he called out to the rest of the foursome. "Any of you boys up for pressing our bet?"

"Sure," they all replied simultaneously.

"Thatta boys," the Colonel responded cheerfully. "I've got to win back the money my caddie lost because of *me,* and I only have two holes to do it in. Frank, note that we're doubling all bets!" The Colonel then turned to his caddie. "What do you suggest?"

"I'd play a three wood followed by your five iron. This hole has a nar-row approach which requires a rollin' shot up to the green," the caddie eagerly offered.

The Colonel took his shot and hit it somewhere towards the seven-teenth hole.

Everyone clapped. It was a tremendous shot. Next, the Colonel lofted a beautiful five-iron shot onto the green, and sank a twenty-foot putt, tying the hole.

Reaching the eighteenth tee, the match remained even. "I feel awfully good about our chances on this, our last hole at Ballybunnion," the Colonel said to the caddie. Then he turned to Mike. "Let's show them, partner."

The Colonel proved he played better under pressure. He drove the ball just off the fairway and made a scrambling birdie, winning the hole and thereby, the match.

After triumphantly plucking his ball out of the hole, he raised his arm into the air in a gesture of victory. Then, he put his arm around the caddie's shoulder. "Now we're both winners! I hope this makes it up to you for blowing that other shot. You helped me win at Ballybunnion. It was an experience I'll never forget." His eyes teared up. "I just wish my Granddaddy could have been here to see it. He was a great player *and* a great sportsman, and *you* reminded me of the importance of being *both*. Thanks." He grabbed the caddie's hand and shook it vigorously. "If you ever get to Atlanta....I'd be honored to take you out on the course where my Granddaddy taught me how to play and how to always be a gentleman, win or lose."

The caddie smiled as he placed the Colonel's club back into the bag with all of the Confederate flag-covered clubs.

The Water Bed

"Now, Pat, haven't you ever seen a cow before?" asked Kevin as he slowed the car down.

Ignoring his remark, I leaned out of the passenger side window to get a good photo. If I hadn't known better, I'd have thought his sarcasm a bit biting. But the friendly and always cheerful Kevin was becoming a cherished friend, and as my mother used to console me, *guys wouldn't tease you if they didn't like you.* I squinted through the lens of my camera. "Yes, but I never saw cows like these."

As I said this, a dozen big, beautiful shiny black beasts came clomping down the asphalt towards us. They were enormous, magnificent, something to behold. By the time I finished shooting, most of the cows surrounded the car as they lumbered toward the neighboring field by the only passageway they knew, the street. We had seen them before, but only from a distance. Now they were within arm's length.

Today Kevin was acting as both an escort and chauffeur. He was driving me to Galway, which despite arguments to the contrary by many natives, is the most American of the cities in the Republic of Ireland. Mike's birthday was coming up and I wanted to surprise him with a waterbed. He had always talked about getting one since we were first married. But because I didn't want my mother to see it when she would come to visit, and conclude that under my new husband's influence I had become some kind of pervert, I had said no.

Now that we were married for twenty years, I decided she probably wouldn't care and finally agreed with Mike that perhaps it *was* a good idea. But I'd ended up always putting it off, waiting for our good ol' faithful and original double sized bed to completely break down. The practical side of me also argued that they were expensive, they were a

41

luxury, and might be bad for your back. In the meantime, Mike had completely forgotten about the notion.

After our move to Ireland, I reconsidered and decided getting a waterbed was a great *and* practical idea. After several weeks of being forced to share an "Irish" double bed, which is a euphemism for two twin beds pushed together inside of one frame, I now thought it was not only a terrific idea, but essential to my well being.

At first, I thought the twin bed arrangement was going to be a great improvement over our lumpy, bumpy bed we had left at home. Many a sleepless night I had spent feeling the bed quaking from Mike's movements as he tossed, turned and kicked his way through the night. It was as if he were doing the Irish jig in his sleep. He was also prone to taking one of the pillows, usually mine, and wrapping himself around it in a tight bear hug. This left me not only pillow less, but with little bed surface to stretch out. He was also a blanket hog.

It wasn't as if he were a classic blanket hog, one who pulls all of the covers off of me and onto himself. Rather, because of his overactive internal thermostat, which would kick into high in the middle of the night, he would kick all of the covers off of himself and off of me ending up in a pile on the floor. I would often awaken in the middle of the night freezing without even a sheet to cover me. On top of all of this, he almost *never* stayed on his side!

So it would seem that our new Irish bed arrangement would solve my sleeping problems. Together, the two twin beds gave us almost fifty per cent more sleeping area. Another advantage was that each twin bed had its own spring mattress. He could do a three-hand reel and never wake me up. Also, the sheets and bedding were fitted to each bed. I would awaken, undisturbed, every morning neatly tucked into my own little cocoon. The fact that the two beds were now separated by their ridged edges meant that he could never steal my pillow or come onto my side without falling into the one-inch moat between the two beds. It was too good to be true!

The problem was, I couldn't sleep. The hot body that used to envelop me as we spooned our way to sleep felt like it was a football field away. The neatly tucked sheets and covers were never dislodged and therefore made me feel slightly mummified as I awoke every morning predictably paralyzed in the exact spot in which I had fallen asleep. Since I never had to move around in the middle of the night, searching for my pillow or the covers, I often woke up stiff and achy. I found myself actually *missing* waking up several times a night to find him sleeping with his hand tucked under his chin and drooling on my pillow. It was time for the waterbed.

Having spent the better part of two days trying to locate a waterbed supplier, I finally found a little shop in Galway which imported waterbeds directly from New York. As Kevin and I made our way into the outskirts of Galway, I was struck by its contrast of old and new. The fringes of the city were lined with large, American style houses which couldn't have been more than ten years old. The town itself, however, looked quaint with old, cobblestone streets and narrow, meandering walkways.

Unfortunately, quaint towns mean few parking spots. While circling the block looking for a place to park, I checked the addresses for the bed shop. I expected to find a mattress store, but, instead, found a shop with its windows filled with *sex paraphernalia!* Could I have gotten the wrong address? We circled the block again. No, this was definitely the place. Maybe this wasn't such a good idea. I thought of how I could explain it to my mother. I looked in the rearview mirror and noticed that my crow's feet had grown into crevices from lack of sleep. I *needed* that waterbed.

Kevin and I finally found a place to park, and we walked hesitantly into the shop. I could have sworn the clerk was giving me the eye, or at least looking at me strangely. He probably thought I was some kind of lewd woman. And to top it off, I wasn't even with my husband, but another man. How was I to explain this?

I cautiously introduced myself and quickly explained who Kevin was in case there was any doubt. "I came to pick up my order which is a surprise present for my *husband*," I said, maybe a little too emphatically.

The clerk smiled. He obviously didn't believe me. I felt like running out of the place, but before I could, he told me he had my shipment which had just arrived from the states yesterday. Unfortunately, though, there was a problem with the order. He was very sorry.

For a second, I thought I wasn't going to get my waterbed. Now, what was I going to do? How would I ever think of a more perfect gift? His birthday was only two days away. Now that I thought I wasn't getting it, I *really* wanted it. Furthermore, if I didn't get some sleep soon, I might not survive to see his next birthday. After two months of no sleep, I was desperate.

"Now don't you be worryin', Mrs. O'Brien," the clerk said. "Mr. O'Brien will still be gettin' his birthday gift." I blushed at the idea that he was actually thinking of me on a waterbed with my husband. Perhaps he was still questioning the fact that Kevin was indeed my farm hand. The clerk turned and entered a dark back room behind the counter. "I'll be right out."

I turned to Kevin and said, "Kev, get me out of here. I'm absolutely humiliated. I don't care if I ever sleep again. I'll make Mike a birthday cake instead."

Kevin patted me on the shoulder. "Now, Pat, let's see what the lad has to say." His calm, cool, big brother demeanor seemed to reassure me until the clerk emerged with a huge box. He slit the box open and unveiled a large lump of clear blue plastic. He heaved it onto the counter and I was taken by how much plastic there was in this bundle. It must have weighed fifteen pounds!

"I'm afraid the problem is," the clerk said haltingly, " that they sent the *jumbo* instead of the king. The good thing is that it's eight inches wider and six inches longer than the king. Do you think you'll have the room for it?"

I thought of the twin beds that we were, by this time, occasionally sharing. "No problem," I said. "This is even better."

"Oh, by the way," the clerk responded, "I'm afraid that the heater they sent just won't do. It is suppose to go with the king size. It's not sufficient for the jumbo. Do ye think ye could be gettin' by without it for a week until the proper one arrives?"

I thought about my hot-blooded husband. "No problem," I said confidently. "Wrap it up. He'll love it."

The clerk rang it up. He told me he would call as soon as the heater arrived. As we left the shop, I tried not to glance at the sex toys on display. What would my mother say?

This was going to be the perfect gift. We sped home so Kevin and I could start putting the bed together for Mike's birthday surprise. Mike was in Limerick buying himself a new guitar, which he thought, was his real birthday present. We thought that would give us enough time to set the bed up and fill it.

After removing the two twin beds from our room, we started unfolding the bulky plastic cube. As we were unfolding it, a small sheet with directions fell out of the folds. *After you have the wooden frame assembled,* it started. I began to panic. What do they mean, "wooden frame?" I read further: *Next, place the liner and then the waterbed itself into the frame.*

"No prob," Kevin assured me, "I can build anything."

It was a good thing. The jumbo bed, after we spread it out on the floor, measured nine feet long and seven feet wide. It nearly took up the entire room! Kevin took off his measuring tape, which was attached to his belt, and measured for the frame. He assured me again. "I'll just go over to Murphy's lumber and get the wood we'll be' needin'. We'll have the frame built in no time."

I was pleased he included me in on the "we" stuff. If it were only up to me, the entire plan would have been dashed at that moment.

Two hours later he arrived with the lumber. It looked like it was enough wood to build a small shed. I decided the only thing I could do at this point was to make him some tea. Kevin set up the wooden planks and started hammering them together.

By the time I came back with the tea, the frame was up. I was delighted. We rolled the liner out and then unfolded the waterbed into it. It was definitely a jumbo bed.

Kevin looked over at me. "I'm afraid you're going to have a little problem gettin' into your closet over there." He pointed to the far end of the room.

Because the bed stretched from one wall to the other, there were only a couple of inches between it and the closet. From now on, the closet would have to remain permanently closed. You couldn't stand next to the bed, open the door, and get into it.

I shrugged, then said to Kevin. "I guess we'll have to use another closet. Let's fill her up!"

Kevin attached the hose to the adjacent bathroom faucet and stuck the other end into the circular opening of the waterbed itself. He turned on the faucet full blast. We stood over the sixty-three square feet of plastic lying limply on the floor. "Ya know," he said, "this might take awhile. I better be gettin' on with my *real* chores."

His sarcasm made me feel a bit guilty that I had asked him to spend so much time on this crazy personal project. He good-naturedly waved through the bedroom door, leaving me to the ignoble task of watching the bed slowly fill with cold tap water.

Five hours later the bed was less than one quarter full. My worry about Mike returning before it was set up was now replaced with the question of just where we were going to sleep for the next two nights. Luckily, there were two sofas downstairs in the sitting room which could be used for temporary beds, although I was sure this meant another couple of sleepless nights for me. No matter what, I was absolutely sure we weren't going to be using the waterbed tonight.

Mike finally arrived home to a half-filled waterbed. He was thrilled by the surprise and in his usual optimistic way, told me that the end result would be well worth any inconvenience that we would put up with. Little did he know.

After 24 hours, the bed appeared to be almost filled. We were getting excited. Mike even promised Kevin that he could try it out the first night we were away from the farmhouse. Great. So now the whole neighborhood would know that we were sharing our bed with our handyman.

"Let's try it tonight, even if it's not filled," Mike whispered with that enthusiastic gleam in his eye.

"Okay," I promised, trying to look equally impetuous. After two nights of sofa sleeping, I was getting tired of being tired. "Tonight's the night no matter what."

But as it kept filling up, the waterbed began to take on a life of its own. It started to resemble a science fiction monster from the fifties, like the blob that ate Toledo. It laid on the floor like a breathing, amorphous being, heaving and sighing, trying to give birth to itself. We decided we would use our king-size sheets until I could find a set that would fit this jumbo creature.

The time came to try the bed. Although it wasn't quite filled, we were committed, or as it turns out, should have been committed. We stood at the foot of the bed trying to figure out how to get onto it. The cold damp moisture rising up from the bed caused the temperature in the bedroom to drop by at least fifteen degrees. As we giggled and whispered to each other in the dark, we could see the vapor from our breath.

"You first," Mike urged.

"Oh, no, you. This was your idea, remember?"

"Yeah, twenty years ago, it was!" With that, Mike took a giant leap onto the bulging bed.

"Yikes," he screamed, as he landed on the frigid plastic. "It's freezing!" he screamed, as he hopped from one foot to the other. The bed rolled and undulated beneath his feet. He jumped off the bed. "I'd better go get that piece of foam rubber cushion we use for camping. Otherwise, we'll freeze to death."

The last thing I wanted him to do was to go trudging through the cellar looking for foam rubber in the middle of the night, but he was insistent.

So insistent, that he went and retrieved the foam rubber and returned within minutes with the confident air of a Celtic warrior. This was definitely going to be the night, come hell or high water, literally.

He tore off the sheets which had been partially covering the bed's surface, and tossed the cushion into the middle of the bed. "Believe me," he said, "You just wouldn't have been able to stand the cold," implying *he* would have been just fine lying in his underwear on 2,000 gallons of ice water.

I looked out at the five foot by six-foot foam rubber cushion he had tossed onto the bed, which now resembled a raft floating in the middle of the ocean. "Okay, let's try it."

We stepped up onto it. Then we walked across the bouncy plastic blob, trying to steady ourselves against the current. Because the bed was not completely filled with water, there were large air pockets causing the water to swish and slosh beneath our feet. It probably needed another 150 gallons. When we reached the raft, we collapsed in a fit of laughter. "Happy birthday," I said as I threw my arms around his neck. "Let's make this an experience to remember."

The next day, we took the whole thing down. It was fun for one night, but the major problem was that we kept nudging each other off of our tiny little raft, causing each of us to nearly freeze or drown in the middle of the night. Also, Mike's Irish step-dancing kept the waves rolling so that by morning, I discovered that not only had I not gotten any sleep, but now I was seasick. Worse, it proved impossible to get out of the bed in the middle of the night without creating a tidal wave.

"Whatever you do, don't tell Kevin we're giving up on the waterbed," I said.

"I won't tell if you won't," he said, as he stuck the hose into the bed and siphoned the water to run down the gutter along the outside of the house and into the drain.

It wasn't long before Kevin caught sight of the rubber hose running down the side wall. When I answered the door, Kevin inquired with a smirk on his face, "So now Pat, how did you and the birthday boy make out last night?"

"Don't start," I said. "I couldn't take your teasing. I haven't slept all night!"

"I see," he said. "Sounds like you're braggin' a bit, Pat."

"Believe me, I'm not."

A picture was worth a thousand words, so I led him up to the bedroom where the bed was finally starting to deflate. He looked at the enormous gelatinous thing that lay across the entire bedroom floor and said, "What's this? It looks like a swimmin' pool!"

I turned to him and mustered up all of the sarcasm I could. "Now Kevin, haven't you ever seen a water bed before?"

The Bard

The best part about running an Irish Bed and Breakfast is the *breakfast* part. All Irish B & B's include "a full Irish breakfast" with their nightly rate. The traditional breakfast evolved from the high protein meals given to sustain farmers and laborers who would be out in the fields all day. It consists of two eggs, sausages, bacon, toast, and homemade breads, either brown bread or soda bread. Because of this high protein and fat enriched meal, the Irish euphemistically refer to it as the "cardiac arrest" breakfast.

Oftentimes, black pudding or white pudding or both are served. Pudding, in Ireland, is not to be confused with a creamy sweet desert. Rather, it is a type of sausage made from the internal organs of livestock which is mixed with meal and then fried in lard. It was never meant for the health conscious or faint of heart. Guests either love it or hate it, and, usually, those who love it don't have a clue as to what's in it.

In fact, it's become an unwritten rule in "The B & B Code of Ethics" not to divulge the pudding's rather unsavory ingredients until after the guests have tasted it, or better yet, after they have checked out. One guest, who was quizzing Mary as to its contents was abruptly cut off by her, who, after the guest questioned her incessantly on what was in the pudding, simply answered, "It's Irish pudding. There's black and white."

"And what's the difference between the two?" the guest persisted.

"Why, *the color*," she explained.

What is unique about our Farmhouse B & B is that breakfast is served promptly at nine o'clock in the morning. This is unlike other B & B's who provide breakfast during a three hour window, usually from 8:00 to 11:00 AM, to allow guests to come and go as they please. At the Farmhouse, we prefer that the guests meet in the dining room at the same time, to eliminate the constant interruptions which tend to curtail the flow of an interesting breakfast conversation.

Eating breakfast and sharing in the experience as a group is part of the B & B ambiance, not to be found in larger guesthouses or hotels. We have discovered that when a group of people are gathered at one table to break bread, a magical experience unfolds. Each guest becomes a colorful character providing the group with a unique experience or story of his own, not unlike a mini Canterbury Tale.

The large dining room table is set for the number of guests staying, the most being twelve persons. Irish linen napkins and tablecloth, silverware and china are always used. Fresh jams are displayed in Waterford jam jars. Orange juice and water are served in crystal glasses. After all of the guests arrive at the table, their orders are taken and coffee and tea are served, introductions are made and the conversation begins.

"Would yas like some more coffee, young ladies?" Mary asked.

"Oh, we'd love some," said one of two elderly women who sat at the end of the breakfast table. They were dressed in matching powder blue polyester pantsuits, each with a floral print blouse with a sash tied in a bow at the neck. They both had short, sprayed once-a-week salon coifed hair. One was orange-blonde, the other gray-blue.

"Your coffee is much better here than home in Baaston," the other one chimed in. "It has some body. It's hard to find good coffee in the States. It's all so diluted."

"Well, then help yerselves to all ye want." Mary placed the thermos coffee server between them.

"May I pour anybody else a cup first?" asked the blue-haired woman. "Don't let me have any more. The doctor told me my limit was two cups!" She laughed lightly.

"My name is Helen and this is my sister Katherine." She gestured to the orange-blonde haired lady beside her. "We've come all the way from Baaston," she said in a heavy Bostonian accent, "to fulfill our life-long dream of returning to the land of our grandparents."

"So this is your first time in Ireland?" Mary asked.

"Why, yes it is," Helen answered for both of them. "We're both retired schoolteachers from Boston, third generation Irish. We've been planning this trip together since we were kids. But, more importantly," she said as she looked across the table, we'd like to know your names and where you're from."

"I'm Aidan," the youngest man at the table offered. "I'm from County Donegal."

"My name is Ian," a young man next to him, volunteered. "I'm from Donegal, too."

"Are you two together?" Katherine asked.

"Well, kind of," Ian said, as he looked over at Aiden. "We're both traveling musicians."

"Oh, that's marvelous!" Helen said. "We were going to ask our hostess where there was a good place to hear Irish music tonight. Maybe you could steer us in the right direction."

"We could try," Ian replied.

"So, who are the rest of you?" Helen asked as she glanced around the table, in a teacherlike, all-inclusive tone.

A plump woman with bright pink lipstick and several strands of beads and chains hanging around her neck replied enthusiastically, "I'm Joan McKenna and this is my daughter Kaitlin." She gestured to the teenager beside her. "I'm showing my daughter the West of Ireland."

"We're from Dublin," Kaitlin added. "Have you been there? There's so much *to do* there, like pubs, music and nightlife. Out here, the most exciting thing to do is watch sheep and cows graze in the fields."

Kaitlin had a round, pretty face with an upturned nose and full, pouting lips. Her large brown eyes were framed by long, dark brown tresses. She wore a plain white tee shirt and jeans and unlike her mother, wore no makeup or jewelry save for a silver stud pierced into her left nostril.

"Ever since I got this," Kaitlin said as she pointed to her nose, "mom has decided I need to get out of the urban scene and see more of the country."

"Nice to meet you," Helen said, now speaking for the rest of the table. "We think both you and your mother have excellent taste in jewelry."

"Thank you." Kaitlin beamed.

A middle-aged man put his arm around the woman next to him and said, "I'm Danny McNamara and this is my wife Mary Ellen. This couple," he said as he looked to the couple next to them, "are Patrick and Deirdre Flannery. "All four of us are from a suburb outside of Dublin, called Howth. The four of us are here on holiday, and we've been friends for twenty years. Right?"

He looked back to Patrick and Deirdre who nodded in agreement.

"Yes we have," Patrick said. "They're the only couple we could imagine traveling with." He chuckled and slapped Danny on the back. "And, we've been traveling for a whole week and we're still friends, believe it or not!"

"That's maarvelous," Helen responded, her accent even more pronounced. "My sister and I travel well together, too, although this is the first time we've traveled outside the United States. Let me see," she said. "We've been to Niagara Falls, California and Miami, isn't that right Katherine?"

Katherine blushed. She nodded silently looking into her plate for an answer. It appeared that speaking in front of a group of strangers wasn't Katherine's forte.

Helen saved her. "Katherine's a little shy."

"Well, we don't want these people to think we're bragging and sounding like rich Americans," Katherine said softly, defending herself.

"Oh, Katherine, don't worry," Helen responded. "Look at us. Do you think anybody at this table could mistake us for being rich?"

Katherine looked back into her plate.

Helen cleared her throat. "So who can tell us where we can go to hear some good Irish music tonight, our last night in Ireland. We leave from Shannon tomorrow. We just can't leave Ireland without hearing some good old traditional tunes!" In spite of her doctor's orders, she poured her sister and herself another cup of coffee.

"What do you consider to be traditional Irish music?" Ian asked.

"You know, the kind that sounds like lyrical poetry put to music, with pipes, fiddles and flutes." Helen sighed. "I can hear the pipes callin' me now. *Oh, Danny Boy, the pipes, the pipes are callin'....*" she began to sing.

Kaitlin rolled her eyes at her mother.

"I think what my sister means is the type of music that *The Chieftains* play," Katherine added timidly.

"Ah, *The Chieftains*," Ian said. "They are indeed a legend in their own time. They're the ones responsible for putting Irish music *on the map.*"

"And don't think we musicians don't appreciate it," Aiden agreed.

Helen looked at Katherine. "We have every one of their albums don't we Kate?"

"There you go bragging again," Katherine said.

Helen ignored her comment. "We saw them live in Boston, twice. They were magnificent. The crowd went wild for them. We have a lot of Irish in Boston, as I'm sure you all know."

"Well, maybe they like them in Boston, but nobody in Ireland listens to them anymore," Kaitlin said.

"What do you mean?" Helen asked, crestfallen.

"That's old fogey stuff, no offense," she answered.

"No offense taken dear," Helen replied patiently. "But they got their start in the sixties. Do you think that makes them old fogies? Do you think the Beatles and The Rolling Stones played old fogey music?"

"Well...kind of," Kaitlin answered.

"So who do *you* think are Ireland's best musicians?" Kaitlin's mother asked, clearing her throat, indicating that if her daughter had a strong opinion she had better be able to support it with facts.

"Sinead O'Connor, of course!" Kaitlin exclaimed. "Everybody in Ireland knows that!"

"Everybody but me," Danny McNamara retorted rather sharply. "She's the one who blasphemed the Pope."

"Blasphemed?" Kaitlin asked innocently. "What's *blasphemed*?"

"Yes, young lady. Blasphemed!" Danny's face turned red and he searched the table for the coffee urn and waved to Helen to pass it to him. Helen obliged. He poured himself a cup, his hand shaking. "Blasphemed is when you publicly revile or talk profanely about somebody. She just happened to select, as her object of contempt, the head of the Catholic Church, the Holy See himself. In Medieval times, she could have been ex-communicated or even burned at the stake!" Danny's face was getting redder.

Kaitlin shrugged. "I don't know what the big deal is."

"Didn't your mother ever tell you it wasn't polite to blaspheme the Pope in front of the whole world by tearing up his picture at one of her concerts?" Danny blurted.

"Oh, *that*," Kaitlin said. "That was just her style of protest against the establishment. I don't think she meant anything personal against the Pope. Right mom?"

"The man's right, dear," her mother replied. "It wasn't polite. But as I've always taught you, everyone's entitled to their own opinion, even if it isn't the status quo."

Kaitlin looked triumphant. "You see?" She said. "Even my mother, who is *in her thirties*, agrees that Sinead O'Connor is the best singer in the world! That is, next to Barbara."

"Barbara who?" Danny asked.

"Barbara Streisand, of course," Kaitlin answered.

"Speaking of old fogies," Danny said.

"I didn't exactly say that, dear," her mother said calmly. "I just said that you have the right to have your own opinion about music."

"I have to agree," Ian said. "Sinead and Barbara may be the two finest female vocalists in the world, that's for sure. And now we have Celine."

Kaitlin glowed, thrilled that at least one of the adults at the table was agreeing with her.

Danny's face became redder. He raised his fist in the air. "Well anybody who tears up a picture of the Pope, who happens to represent everything the Holy Church stands for, shouldn't be admired!"

"Sinead did publicly apologize..." Kaitlin's mother said softly, trying to support her daughter but not willing to further raise the ire of Danny McNamara.

Danny's friend, Patrick, interjected, "There is certainly enough of a variety of Irish music to keep everybody happy, wouldn't you agree? I happen to love the Chieftains *and* Sinead O'Connor."

Danny looked at his turncoat friend as if he were reconsidering the continuation of their twenty-year relationship. He poured some milk into his coffee and stirred it furiously.

"When did you and Katherine see the Chieftains, Helen?" Patrick asked.

"Well, let me think. It was a couple of years before I retired from teaching. I guess it was over ten years ago," she replied. "How time flies! But I know they're still playing to sell-out crowds all over the States."

"Sinead O'Connor plays in concerts all over the *world*," Kaitlin insisted. "She has played in concerts where all the proceeds went to refugees and world peace. Isn't that something to be admired?" She looked at Danny, then turned to Helen. "Maybe the next time you go to a concert, you and your sister should go see her."

"Maybe we will," Helen replied.

"That's enough, now, Kaitlin," her mother said as she patted Kaitlin on the hand.

"The girl's right," Aiden said to the table, trying to break the tension. "So do you like Van Morrison, Kaitlin?"

"Who's he?" Kaitlin asked.

"Why," Aiden chuckled, "you might consider him to be a bit of an old fogey, too. But he's the one who invented a style of music new to Ireland in the 70's called *Shamrock*."

"I was born in the *eighties*." Kaitlin replied politely. "What are some of his songs?"

"*Wild Nights* and *Brown Eyed Girl* are probably two of his most popular," Aiden said. "I'm sure you've heard of one of them."

"*Brown Eyed Girl* was one of my favorite songs when I was a kid!" Kaitlin exclaimed. "My father used to sing it to me. That was his pet name for me, "brown eyed girl." He passed away two years ago. That was before I was into music." She hesitated, then changed the subject. "Are you a U2 fan? They're my favorite Rock 'n Rollers."

"I am, indeed," Aiden said. "Can't you tell by my haircut?" He raked his fingers through his bleached blonde buzz haircut.

Ian mimicked Aiden by running his fingers over his prematurely balding pate. "I'd have a buzz cut too, if I had anything to shave off" He grinned. "Aiden knows everything about every kind of Irish music."

"Is that so?" Helen asked.

"Aiden is a professional Bard," Ian answered.

"A B*aa*rd?" Helen asked. "B*aa*rd as in the medieval b*aa*rds that entertained in the courts of Europe?"

"The same," Ian said. "Go ahead and tell them, Aiden."

"In ancient Celtic society," Aiden began, "there were poets whose put their poetry to music, to entertain and educate. Playing a musical instrument resembling a lyre they sang satires and eulogized the history and traditions of the tribes and their chieftains."

"Does any of their music still exist?" Helen asked.

"Yes, thanks to bardic schools, although they existed long before musical scores were ever recorded. Bards would pass down oral compositions to their students by singing with their pupils repeating. In fact, the Celtic word *to teach* means *to sing over*. It was all taught by recitation of the oral songs and repeating it, all learned by rote. It was only in the eighth century when they were written down."

"Isn't that fascinating," Helen said. "Being a teacher, I was interested in a new method of teaching grammar by setting certain grammatical rules to music similar to the old model we all know from childhood." She sang while she gesticulated into the air. *ABCDEFG, HIJKLMNOP, QRS, TUV, tell me, tell me, what do you think of me?*

"That's the same concept!" Aiden said. "The students would study this way over a twelve year apprenticeship in a bardic school in order to learn the complicated meters and the wealth of heroic literature passed on through the centuries. Classical Greek and Roman writers refer to the bards as the most intellectual of all the classes in ancient Gaul. Bardic schools flourished in Ireland as late as the seventeenth century."

"So you yourself are a b*aa*rd?" Katherine whispered in awe.

"So to speak," Aiden said. "I have studied Celtic mythology and music for more than twelve years, so I guess you can say I've gone through the required apprenticeship."

"What do you play?" Kaitlin asked, suddenly engaged by the romance of the story.

"All the traditional Celtic instruments," Aiden said, "pipe, the fiddle and bones, the tin whistle, the flute and the bodhran. The same instruments, in fact, the old fogey Chieftains play." He smiled at Kaitlin, then winked at Helen.

"Okay," Kaitlin said. "Maybe they aren't old fogies. I'll give them a listen if Mr. McNamara agrees to give Sinead a listen."

Danny laughed. "Like Patrick said, there's enough Irish music to go around for everybody's tastes. It's a deal."

"As far as recommendations for Irish music, Helen" Aiden continued, "there are several places in Limerick that offer music. I'll write down a list if you would like, Helen."

"That would be gr*aa*nd," she beamed. "Actually, I'd like to hear *you* play. Do you think you could give us a sampling of what a bard can sing?"

"Oh, I think I might be able to arrange that," Aiden replied. "Why don't we all go into the parlor. I'll go get my instruments."

"Wonderful!" Kaitlin squealed with delight. Then she jumped up from the table. "Now I'm glad you brought me out to the country," she said as she kissed her mother lightly on her painted pink lips.

After the group adjourned into the parlor, Aiden and Ian appeared with three instruments each. Ian sat on an ottoman next to the fireplace and Aiden pulled up a footstool beside him. Everyone grew silent as they tuned up their instruments. Aiden was strumming and tuning up his guitar, while Ian blew softly into a tin whistle.

"First, I will begin with a short ballad, a Cornish poem from the seventeenth century, the type that the Ancient bards might have played." He strummed the strings slowly."

"Where are you going, fair maid," said he,
"with your pale face and your yellow hair?"

Aiden's sweet, melodic Irish tenor voice filled the parlor. He strummed and picked the lyre as if he were improvising as he spoke. Somehow the music seemed to accentuate his words. Ian sat with his tin whistle in his hands, not playing a note.

"Going to the well, sweet sir," she said,
"for strawberry leaves make maidens fair."

Ian accompanied Aiden by fingering the tin whistle lovingly. He countered Aiden's strumming with shrill, seemingly unreachable notes. Then Aiden continued his bardic ballad.

"Shall I go with you, fair maid," said he,
"with your pale face and your yellow hair?"
"Do if you wish, sweet sir," she said,
"for strawberry leaves make maidens fair."

Aiden and Ian stopped simultaneously.

The group was mesmerized. They didn't know whether to keep still or clap.

"That was just lovely," Helen gushed. "Beautiful! Now we can say we left Ireland having heard the real traditional music. Thank you so much."

"It was my pleasure," Aiden said, "as well as Ian's, I'm sure. Now we'd like to play something from the Chieftains, for Helen, Katherine, Danny and Patrick. The Chieftains played this song in 1979 in Phoenix Park, Dublin to a crowd of 1.35 million people during the visit of Pope John

Paul II to Ireland. Maybe this will make up for Sinead O'Connor's sins."
He winked at Danny.

Aiden removed the lyre from his lap, and placed it carefully on the
floor. Then he picked up the Irish fiddle which he had leaning against the
wall, stood up, and placed it under his chin. Ian also got up, still grasping
the tin whistle.

With a nod of Aiden's head, they started in unison. Aiden fiddled
furiously and Ian blew intensely into the flute. The music of the two
instruments sounded like an orchestra. The pace picked up until it
blended into a familiar Irish jig. Aiden fiddled up and down, his whole
body squirming with so much energy, it seemed to try to jump outside of
his being. Ian kept pace, bobbing up and down, trying to control the
writhing whistle. They kept it up for several minutes, until it looked like
they were both going to collapse. Suddenly they stopped.

Again, the group didn't know whether to continue their silence or
applaud.

"Fantastic," Danny bellowed. "*Gaar*geous," called Helen. "Fabulous,"
yelled Patrick.

Then Aiden and Ian both collapsed exhausted, onto the ottoman and
foot stool.

"Now, at the risk of paling in comparison to the one of *the* best female
vocalists Ireland has ever produced, I would like to attempt to sing one of
Sinead O'Connor's hit from 1990, *Nothing Compares 2 U*. Bear in mind,
she's a female and I'm a mere male. I can't hit those notes like she can."
He strummed the guitar and crooned the lyrics of the song that made
Sinead O'Connor a household name.

Nothing compaaaares to you.

Kaitlin smiled. Danny looked uncertain.

After they finished the song, everybody stood up and clapped. "Bravo!"

Aiden and Ian nodded in recognition of their little audience's appreciation.

"Thank you," Aiden said, speaking for the two of them. "Now, for our grand finale, we will sing a little ditty by Van Morrison, dedicated to Kaitlin from her father: *Brown Eyed Girl.*

Kaitlin blushed, clasped her hands over her mouth and sat back in her chair.

"Hey where did we go the days when the rains came?
Down in the hollow,
Playin' a new game,
Laughin' and a runnin' heh heh, skippin' and a jumpin',
In the misty morning fog with our hearts a thumpin' and you,
My brown eyed girl,
You're my brown-eyed girl.
Do you remember when we used to sing?
Sha la la la la la la la la la la tee da, la tee da. My brown eyed girl."

Kaitlin couldn't contain herself. She jumped up after the first stanza and cried, "Yeaaaaaaa!" as she clapped her hands furiously. She then turned to the young bards and gushed, "thank you so much. I'll never forget this!" She put her hands together and pointed them toward the ceiling. "And thank you, too, Daddy!"

Aiden and Ian stopped playing, stood up and bowed. "That reception was better than any gold record or sold out concert," Aiden said.

Kaitlin's mother grasped Kaitlin by the shoulders and kissed her on her silver studded nose. Helen placed her hand over Katherine's who dabbed her eyes with a white handkerchief. Danny glanced across the room to Patrick who smiled.

"Well, we have a gig this afternoon, so we better get rollin'," Aiden said, as he started to pick up the instruments. "You know the life of a traveling bard, always looking for a new audience to educate and to please."

Fish Kinsale

A curious thing about Ireland is its lack of a thriving fishing industry. Ireland is actually considered a fairly large island, approximately 300 miles at its longest and nearly 200 miles at its widest points with more than 3,000 miles of continuous coastline. As this makes even the most inland Irish town conveniently located within seventy miles of shore, it defies logic that the Irish aren't all stalwart seamen.

I asked our man Jimmy Riordan, down at the fish market when he was out of sea bass for the third week in a row, exactly *why* Ireland had never developed into a seafaring nation. He wiped his hands on his stained apron, put his hands on his hips and explained in his simple, no-nonsense, straight-faced way, "Mind you, it's difficult to catch fish in the ocean. First, ye hav' ta' have a boat. Next, ya' hav' ta' *find* the fish. Because of the ocean's currents, deep-sea fish avoid Ireland's cold water coast, forcing the poor fishermen to search far out into the sea. It could take 'em all day! Besides, Ireland has some of the finest *freshwater fish* in the world. Isn't it a wee bit easier to stand on the shore and fetch em' right out of the lake or the streams? Who needs a boat?"

With that, he held out a large, freshly cut chunk of salmon, with its silver skin and textured, crimson-pink flesh laying squarely in the middle of the white butcher's paper in the palm of his hand. "Just look at this beauty! This handsome devil was just snared fresh out of a stream not five hours ago."

It was hard to resist, and I decided to add Danny's fresh water salmon to our weekly menu. "Wrap it up," I told him. "You're right. Who needs a boat?" His story made some sense as to why the Irish content themselves with lake and stream fishing leaving the tranquil harbors for bobbing sailboats.

We found that one of the most captivating of these tranquil harbors is Kinsale, less than twenty miles south of Cork. Although it bills itself as a charming fishing village, little *fishing* is actually done here. Kinsale instead prides itself as knowing just what to do with the fish after it's caught. In fact, it boastfully claims to be the gourmet capital of Ireland, and with good reason. With much public relations, fanfare and the opening of several renowned cooking schools, Kinsale has established itself as the home of all Eire's gourmands.

Although Kinsale also plays host to several international sailing events a year, its vigilant city fathers have shielded it from overly-zealous developers and have preserved it as an untouched sleepy harbor town. There is no real fishing industry in Kinsale save for a handful of tiny two-man motorboats and skiffs skimming the placid waters at sunset. It is difficult to detect, at first blush, this town's historical connection to the sea, but two fortresses, a castle, and a friary still stand, splendidly attesting to its illustrious past. From as early as the fourteenth century, this delightful town was dominated by buccaneers, brigands, pirates and protectors.

Kinsale made its debut as an important revolutionary post in 1601, when Don Juan d'Aguila arrived from Spain with a large force to assist Irish chieftains, O'Donnell and O'Neill, in their efforts to oust their English rulers. At first, it seemed that the rebellion forged by this liaison between the Spanish and Irish allies would prevail. However, the British, led by Lord Mountjoy, eventually squelched the rebels. A reminder of this early Irish *near*-victory is King James Fort, south of town.

Resting on its laurels of history, beauty and charm, Kinsale could easily make it in the most discriminating travel books without the added bonus of gourmet food. French, German and other European gourmets pour into Kinsale for its annual gourmet fest, held every October.

We had made our dinner reservations at one the most famous restaurant in Kinsale, the *Vintage*. Located on Main street, *Vintage* exudes charm and authenticity, with its cozy, romantic open fire, it's 200-year-old beams from original sailing ship masts, and a chef who trained in the kitchen of none other than *The Four Seasons*. Not to mention the menu, which boasts organically grown vegetables, free-range goose, duckling, and rabbit. The wine list includes fine French and Italian varietals. The fish selection varies from hot smoked salmon steak and sole Veronique to lake Trout Almondine. These offerings demonstrate a conspicuous lack of *seafood* items on Kinsale menus.

We knew Kinsale would be crowded because of the annual gourmet fest, so we reserved our room four months in advance at *The Moors*, whose brochure was an unabashed self-appraisal of its unparalleled views of the harbor, fresh kippers for breakfast, and American king-sized beds. We weren't sure which was more important to us as we had been in Ireland long enough to know that good food was easier to get than large beds.

We arrived at dusk, as it was a very long and curving road from Limerick. The owner and receptionist, Patrick O'Grady, greeted us with a surprising admonition that he was just about to give our room away as everything was solidly booked for the fest weekend. I wondered if this wasn't an empty threat which was supposed to make us more appreciative of the view from the room that he had promised us upon booking. He begrudgingly handed us the key while reminding us he could have gotten double the amount we were paying for the room that night. He told us the room was the last one on the right, the one we had requested, with the best view of the harbor and the only one with a balcony.

"You Yanks love those balconies, even though I've never seen one of ya' use one in all the years I've been in the business. I'm afraid to tell ya' yer breakfast is at 9:00 a.m. sharp. You seem like the type of Americans always running late. I won't be havin' any of your dilly dallyin'."

I guess we were told. We dragged ourselves and our overnight bags up the stairs and to our room. We fiddled with the key for what seemed to be eternity, and I was fearful of having to bother Mr. O'Grady again, seeing as we had put him out with our late arrival. We jiggled it again and finally, the door reluctantly opened. It was incredible, surely the most enormous guestroom I had ever seen, and with the most enormous bed. We threw the bags onto the floor and glanced over to the other side of the room where a set of lace-covered French doors beckoned us to the balcony.

This was a dream room. It sometimes helped to be American, as the Irish knew we were spoiled, way too picky and expected way too much. "Just ask and you shall receive," was my motto, as the worst they could do was to say "no." So as usual, all we'd done was ask, and we got the most fantastic room in the hotel with a harbor view and balcony to boot!

Mike quipped enthusiastically, "Before we go down for our best gourmet meal in Ireland, let's have a drink out on the balcony and watch the sunset over Kinsale Harbor."

At first I hesitated, knowing that pesky Americans always asking for ice was a standard joke among innkeepers of Ireland. Our request could only add fuel to the patron's already jaded view of late Americans and their balcony fetishes. The Irish never tired of asking, "Why d'ya need drinks loaded with ice when every good Countryman knows alcohol was always better at room temperature?"

At the risk of looking like demanding Americans, I hesitantly agreed. Mike went barreling down the stairway to ask our host for a few cubes for our self-mixed Bacardi and Cokes which we carried along with us on every trip. He returned in no time with a bowl full of ice with a small orange juice glass floating in the middle of it with which to scoop the cubes out. It reminded me of that *other* lucrative business we might consider if we stayed in Ireland besides *running* a B & B, which was selling ice cube makers and ice cube buckets *to the same* B & B's.

He fixed us our drinks, and we sipped them slowly to savor the cold sweet liquid that soothed our thirsty palettes. The balcony awaited us. The sun was beginning to set. I couldn't wait to see the view. Who said Americans wouldn't actually use a balcony?

I opened the French doors with dramatic flair, and said, "Voila!"

The doors opened outwards, just missing the railing which enclosed a three-foot by three-foot ceramic tiled patio overhang that protruded from our bedroom wall out over the water. There was a solitary white plastic patio chair to one side, which we'd have to scoot around to actually get out *onto* the patio. I stepped out onto the minuscule balcony, calling into the room for Mike to join me, but there just wasn't space for the two of us to stand out there and allow for the chair.

"Let's switch," he called out to me from inside the room.

As I reentered the room through the French doors, he contorted himself past me and out onto the patio.

"Okay," as he hurdled himself happily onto the chair. "Just do what I did. Just jump out and land in my lap. I'll hold the drinks. We'll make room for both of us!"

I passed my drink out to him, scrunching myself along the side of the French door and lunged myself forward until I landed neatly in his lap. The drinks jiggled, but we scooted and shimmied until we were both nestled into the chair. Maybe this is why nobody ever used the balcony.

The harbor shimmered in pinks and blue-grays as the sun set around us. Fluttering white sails bobbed lazily over bright green-and-yellow painted sailboats. The sky was ablaze in rose light that blended into the edges of the sea. The fortress looked down at us from across the bay. It was breathtaking. We not only had the *best* view of the water, we were practically *in* the water.

What else could you ask for? A dream room with a balcony and a fabulous view of the sea, a cold drink and reservations at the best gourmet restaurant in Ireland. We savored the sunset and sipped our ice-laden cocktails. It was half way to heaven. For the first time, I began to understand the Irish logic, "who needs a boat?"

Family Tree

Researching a family tree is a cross between a giant jig saw puzzle and an Easter egg hunt. It would seem logical to start with immediate family members and go up from there, but surprisingly, quite the opposite is true. Immediate family members know as little about long lost family members as you do. So it is much more advantageous to first seek out relatives who are as far up the tree as possible, or those hanging from the most remote branches. More importantly, it is better to seek out those relatives who haven't moved around a lot and who have had quite a few children, namely, those relatives who never left Ireland.

They answered the door together. Mickey and Kathleen stood dwarfed in their doorway with matching green hand-knit wool cardigans. They looked older than their late fifties which, according to my extensive research, is what I had figured them to be.

They were diminutive in size which was quite surprising to me as they were related on the O'Callaghan side of the family, who were a brawny bunch of Midwestern six footers, the corn fed variety who were never mistaken for being petite.

Kathleen clasped her hands in excitement, "Welcome to our humble home."

She led us into their living room, which was starkly furnished and had only two pictures hanging on the walls. One was a large photograph of John F. Kennedy and the other was a smaller picture of the Pope with a hand written salutation at the bottom. I couldn't decipher just which Pope it was from my side of the room, but I assumed it was probably Pope John the XXIII, of the same era as President Kennedy. The Pope's smaller photograph reflected his secondary importance to the Irishman in the White House.

She invited us to sit down and we made ourselves at home on an afghan-draped sofa facing the fireplace. Mickey knelt next to it and placed two generous chunks of turf onto the grate. He looked like an earnest leprechaun seeking his pot of gold as he poked and prodded at the embers until a tiny flame started to flicker. Funny, there was nothing about him that resembled an O'Callaghan.

"Let me be callin' Maureen and Eileen, as I'm sure they'd be wantin' to have a look at ya," Kathleen gushed. She made a quick phone call, shouted a few orders into the receiver and ended with, "Now, don't be forgettin' the *good* whiskey." I wondered what the *bad* whiskey could possibly be.

She returned from the kitchen, beaming. "My girls are dreamin' about goin' to the States someday and I'm sure they'd be dyin' to talk to yas about it. They're on their way over. They'll just be stoppin' in for a short while for a sip of my famous Irish coffee."

I had originally contacted Mickey and Kathleen three years earlier, at the beginning of my family ancestral search. They had responded to my family tree questionnaire with such detailed information, that it had given me the encouragement to plunge into the project. The Ahern's had, in fact, given me more information than I had gleaned from all of the birth certificates, death records, and passenger lists that I had collected. We had become great pen pals since, and I'd kept them abreast of all of my family finds and puzzle pieces that were slowly coming together.

Lugging along a bulging portfolio filled with my documentation, I was eager to show them each piece of evidence that proved we were truly long lost cousins. As Kathleen scurried into the kitchen, I painstakingly laid out all of the records I had accumulated on their dining room table, carefully placing them in neat little piles according to their chronology and matter of importance.

They were like ancient, religious relics to me. As I fingered and straightened each document, I was reminded of how exciting it had been with every new discovery. Each little piece of information linked me mysteriously and inextricably to my ancient and royal roots. It was the finding of these treasures which, eventually led to my determination to return to my land of Eire.

Kathleen brought in a silver serving tray which looked rather regal in contrast to their otherwise austere surroundings. She smiled at me and proudly placed it on the coffee table. Thick slices of Irish soda bread sat nestled in a linen lined basket. I could tell it was the authentic kind, the kind my grandmother used to make, dry and crumbly with a healthy dose of caraway seeds. My grandmother's version was so crumbly, in fact, that we used to tease her that if it weren't for the quarter pound of butter we used to spread over it, we'd never get it down our throats.

I couldn't wait to show them my family research charts and photos, but just as I was about to start in on my family history dissertation, the doorbell rang. Maureen and Eileen burst in the door and greeted us warmly. They plopped themselves on the couch next to me, and Maureen quipped brightly as she grabbed my hand. "We're thrilled at the sight of ya. We've been hearin' so much about ya from Ma and Da, it's hard to believe yas are really home." I could feel my eyes start to sting as she accentuated the word "home." My grandmother always said my bladder was too close to me eyes.

They sat perched on the edge of their seats, leaning forward, eager to hear anything and everything I had to say. Feeling a bit like an overrated movie star, I decided that I had better make my presentation as theatrical and exciting as possible, so they wouldn't be disappointed. I started my story with the most impressive and most romantic document I had, that being a copy of the passenger list from the ocean liner which carried our common relative from County Cork to New York City.

A picture of our common Irish cousin floated across my mind. He was leaning against the passenger ship rail with the wind blowing through his dark hair. Next to him stood his two children and his wife who was expecting their third, sandwiched between the helpless herds of people standing on the deck. It was difficult to imagine how desperate these

famine-struck immigrants must have been, in order to get on that strange
ship with little or no promise of a future in America.

Kathleen brought out another silver tray with six glass mugs. "Would
you be fond of the Irish coffee?" she inquired. "I'll even give ya a lesson
on the old fashioned way of makin' it. It's the family recipe I'd be givin'
ya. We'll all drink it as a symbol of our little family reunion."

"It's my favorite," was my reply, "and I never did get the real technique
right before my grandmother passed away."

"Oh, it's a dyin' art for sure. God rest her soul." As she said this, she
made the sign of the cross and bowed her head in memory of my grandmother. "May she rest in peace."

She poured the hot coffee into each mug which she explained must first
be rinsed out with plain boiling water. "That's the key," she said. "Next,
you need to pour the Irish whiskey onto the back of a teaspoon which has
just been dipped into the hot coffee. This will warm up the whiskey so
that it will not change the temperature of the coffee when you add it to
the mug."

I watched with fascination as the making of a simple spiked coffee was
transformed into an elaborate ritual.

"Now for the best part, mind you, our fresh country cream," she
continued. She took a large glob she had just whipped up herself, from a
flower-patterned bowl, and slid it off the spoon and into the brown liquid.
Because the cream was fresh, and therefore had never been refrigerated, it
was close to room temperature. Instead of melting instantly, the cream sat
stiffly on the top of the coffee.

"Now, all ya need to do is to drink it down without givin' yourself a
mustache!" she exclaimed, obviously proud of her eloquent demonstration.

I sipped at the edge of the mug, carefully avoiding any cream from
touching my upper lip, feeling the warmth of the whiskey as it coated the
back of my throat. It was like the nectar of Celtic gods. Although I was
anxious to get back to discussing the family tree, Kathleen's sharing of her

secret family recipe made me realize that now I knew just who my *favorite* cousin was.

I picked the passenger list ledger sheet up off of the dining room table and unfolded it in front of them. The passenger list was a record of all of the immigrants who left Queenstown, County Cork, Ireland, for America on September 24, 1847, the last year of the Great Famine. The sheet was divided into several columns. The first column contained the names of the passengers, followed by their ages, marital status, occupations, destination points and how much money each passenger had been carrying. I pointed to Jeremiah O'Callaghan's name, which I had highlighted with a yellow magic marker.

Their eyes grew larger as I carefully explained the O'Callaghan saga.

"Jeremiah O'Callaghan was my great great grandfather. He left his four brothers and sisters back in County Kerry when he came to the States." I pointed to the column titled, *Destination*, and ran my finger down the lines until it came to *Chicago*.

"One of his sons," I continued to explain, "was James, my great grandfather. One of the brothers who stayed in Kerry was *your* great great grandfather.

"Oh, that's grand," Kathleen responded as she reached for the passenger list to see for herself. The girls peered over her shoulder to get a look.

I pointed to the occupation column and noted that Jeremiah and his wife were listed as a laborer and housewife. The next column indicated how much money each passenger possessed when they arrived in New York. It read: $5.

Kathleen's eyes began to fill up. She began to speak, trying not to let her tears fall on the ledger sheet. "The poor, dear lads," she said, "goin' off to the promised land where they were told the streets were paved with gold. Little did they know, *they* would be the ones doing all the *pavin'*."

I tried to bring them back to the history of our lineage. "So, the fact that our great-great grandfathers are brothers, that makes us third cousins twice removed."

All of a sudden their attentive eyes, that had hung on my every word, started to glaze over. Obviously, I wasn't making myself clear. As most people do who are trying to communicate in a different dialect, I tried to make them understand by talking louder and more slowly. I pointed to the chart of the family tree and attempted to recreate the story from the beginning using computer graphic pictures of each family member. They still didn't seem to be getting it. All of my research, all of the records and documentation, and they just didn't have a clue as to just how we were related. I pondered over how I should explain it again, now that their attention and interest were beginning to wane.

Kathleen suddenly interrupted the moment of silence. "Now Pat and Mike, would you be wantin' another helpin' of my Irish soda bread?"

They really didn't understand the family tree limbs and branches that made up our common family tree. I stood up and moved to the dining room table. Slowly, I started to pick up each of my neat little piles of certificates, lists, and computer spreadsheets. They didn't seem interested, and now, in fact, I wasn't sure *I* was that interested, either. Did it really matter *how* we were related? The important thing is that we *were*.

Kathleen walked over to the dining room table, glancing bewilderedly at all the pictures and computer charts. "Now, Pat and Mike. Tell us again, who the hell are ya?" She giggled.

Maureen and Eileen looked anxiously at us, wondering if we would be offended by her teasing or by her profanity.

"Never mind about these documents," I said. "Let's just say we're long-lost cousins, and leave it at that. We don't really need any more proof, do we?"

"Of course not," Kathleen said. "We *know* you're family, just look at yas! Now, how about another cuppa' my famous Irish coffee?"

I smiled at my newly discovered relatives as we sipped Kathleen's coffee together. "And you've certainly made us feel like we are, indeed, home." I held up my cup and looked around the room at Kathleen, Mickey, Eileen and Maureen. "Here's to the family reunion of the O'Callaghan Clan."

Hare Coursing

"That was Danny MacEldowney at the door," I called up to Mike, who teetered unsteadily on the top of an old ladder leaning against the hallway wall.

"What did he want?" Mike responded.

"He's wondering if you'd mind giving him a hand with a little chore over at his place. I thought he said something about needing help moving a piece of furniture."

Somehow Mike would always much rather do a chore or favor for someone else than any task which needed to get done at the farmhouse. That's why those things were usually left for Kevin. There were also other benefits for leaving the farmhouse chores to Kevin. Kevin never complained, he didn't brag about it for two weeks, and he did it right the first time. Mike, who stood six foot four and whose weight hovered around 250 pounds, eventually became known in our new neighborhood for his strength and eagerness to show it off. Therefore, requests having to do with heavy-duty lifting, pushing or pulling, were frequent. Maybe manual dexterity wasn't his strong point, but simple bull work was his specialty.

"What did you tell him?" he asked with one hand on the ladder and his other hand grasping the end of the curtain rod. He looked down at me from the top of the ladder with a screwdriver clenched between his teeth.

"I told him you'd be delighted! You'd be right over!"

"Don't you think it would be better if we let Kevin finish this?" Mike asked eagerly. "We're not getting anywhere. Besides, it sounds like I'm needed for something I'm sure will be more interesting than curtain rods."

"Wouldn't *anything* be more interesting to you?" I replied. I knew he considered having anything to do with window treatments was just too close to decorating to suit his *macho* image. "Oh, go ahead," I said. "At least you might come home with a new story or two about Danny MacEldowney. I haven't heard any good ones lately."

The neighbors always had colorful stories regarding Danny MacEldowney's gambling habits. The generally accepted notion was that Danny had his finger in anything and everything that had to do with betting or gambling, legal or otherwise. He even had his own collection of a dozen or so greyhounds.

How lucky to have yourself surrounded by a dozen dogs, I thought. All of that unconditional love. And here I was without *even one* four-legged companion. I thought about Gizmo, our adorable, black and white ten-pound Shih-Tzu, whom we had coddled and cuddled for ten years since she was a pup. I thought about her worried little face, looking anxiously at us from the arms of my teen-aged niece, as we hugged her good-bye before leaving to fly to Ireland.

We had had no choice. Ireland, because of its rabies-free history, has never allowed any pet into the country without a six-month quarantine. Because of this, rabies vaccinations were unknown in Ireland and the quarantine law was strictly enforced. Somehow, we couldn't imagine putting our little princess through the ordeal of living in a cage for a day, let alone half a year, since she had been accustomed to sleeping on our bed every night. After much consideration, we decided to leave our precious pup at home. Gizmo would be much better off in the care of our three loving nieces than serving a six-month solitary prison sentence.

Mike interrupted my thoughts as he carefully dismounted the ladder. "See you later. I shouldn't be long."

"Yeah, that's what we told poor little Gizmo," I heard myself answer.

"Are you pining over Gizmo again? Now, I thought we were all through with that. We did what we *had* to. You know she's much better off with the girls than she would be sitting in some horrible little cage." He was trying to reassure me for the umpteenth time that we had made the right decision after all.

"Yeah, but I *miss* my little *panda bear*," I whined. 'Panda bear' was the designation given by breeders to Shih-Tzus with black and white markings.

He ignored my whimpering. "Whew! This housework is hard work. I'm glad somebody else around here is good at it." He kissed me on the forehead and hurried out the door.

When Mike arrived at the MacEldowney household, three large panel trucks were lined up like a caravan in the side yard. "Murphy Moves Mountains" was painted on the side of each of the yellow trucks. Danny emerged out of his tiny, whitewashed cottage to meet Mike as he pulled up. Danny was a compact, sturdy little fellow. What he lacked in height, however, he made up with his width. He wore a cut-off tee shirt exposing his wide, muscular shoulders. His well-defined arms displayed tattoos, each blue design ingeniously positioned to enhance his biceps. Danny yelled from his doorway across the yard to Mike, but Mike could hardly hear him for the din of barking dogs coming from behind the hedge, which enclosed his back yard.

"Just be puttin' your car over there behind mine," Danny yelled more loudly over the barking when he realized Mike couldn't hear him. He gestured to the front curb. "We'll be needin' the side yard for the unloadin,'" he added cheerily. "At least we'll be havin' a dry day for it, a day that would be better spent at the track."

Mike thought perhaps he'd ask Danny for a good tip or two on making sure bets. Mike parked the car where he was directed, and walked up to the big moving vans in the side drive, to get a better look. Each truck, sat with its rear door gaping open, exposing its contents.

When Danny approached him at the first truck, Mike asked him, "What's this? Are you moving *in,* or *out?*"

Danny laughed heartily. "Believe it or not, both! All this stuff is supposed ta be goin' in there!" He pointed to his modest little bungalow. "Can you believe I *won* all of this stuff?"

"You must be one lucky guy," Mike said as he looked through the yawning doors of the vans.

"Yeah, I guess I am, but as they say, ya can't win if ya don't play. My dogs finally came through. I suppose you can hear them now." He cupped his hand over his ear pretending as if he were straining to hear them. "Ya know, greyhounds are excitable creatures, so they create quite a commotion when strangers arrive."

He escorted Mike into the house. "Would ya like a cuppa' while we wait for the other lads? They should be showin' up soon."

"How many guys are you expecting?" Mike asked, now wondering what he had gotten himself into.

"Well, I asked ten guys, if six show up I'd be happy," Danny said, "It's all in the odds. Sure, I knew I could count on a big fella' like you who likes a good day of hard manual work, but the rest, I had to bribe."

"What do you mean, *bribe*?" Mike responded, accepting a mug of black coffee.

"I just told them, if they'd be kind enough to help they could take as much of my old stuff as they could carry." He nodded to the shoddy pieces of old furniture, which stood around him. "And since I have the three vans for the whole day, the lads can use any or all of them to haul the stuff to their places."

"I see." Mike looked around the room at the worn furniture wondering who'd want it if it were given to them, even *with* free delivery.

"Now, mind you, Mike, I didn't even ask if *you* wanted any of it." Danny seemed to be apologizing. "I know you and Pat have a fine place up there at the farmhouse, fully furnished and all." And besides, how could you get any of this stuff back to America once you leave?"

"True," Mike agreed. He was relieved that he didn't need to make up an excuse for why he'd be declining Danny's offer of his threadbare furniture. They chatted easily while they waited for the others. Ya know, the Missus is out getting all of you lads something to eat for when we're all finished with the movin'."

Mike wondered if this wasn't another one of Danny's bribes. "Well, that was sure nice of her to go to that bother. You know I'm always happy to do a favor for a neighbor. You shouldn't be feeling like you have to pay me back with lunch or anything."

"Oh, the wife is happy to do it for yas. She's beside herself with happiness over her new furniture. Maybe with this stuff, purchased out of my dog winning's, she'll let up for awhile about my extracurricular hobbies." He winked at Mike.

"I think I hear two of the lads comin' just now." Danny got up from the worn imitation leather cushioned chair. "I'll be back. I have to calm the dogs down and tell the lads to park in front."

Danny left the room and returned shortly with two of the "lads" in tow. When Mike got a good look at them as they walked into the room, he decided they wouldn't be much help, since they appeared too elderly and arthritic to lift as much as an ottoman. They introduced themselves as old friends of Danny's, Eamon and Dave. Danny poured coffee into two mugs and they sat down at the table to join Mike. As they sipped their coffee, they glanced at the furniture all about them and smiled at each other.

Mike wondered if they had known exactly what kind of condition the MacEldowney furniture was in before they had volunteered to help. They continued to smile and nod at each other as they looked around the room, seeming to like what they were seeing. Maybe, Mike thought, this is why he ended up with elderly movers, the only ones that could possibly be interested in taking any of the dingy discards. Perhaps they were just humoring Danny, pretending to want some of the stuff.

At that moment, Danny's wife walked in with an armload of groceries. "How does a nice big pot of oxtail soup sound to yas? If it weren't for you lads, that furniture could be sittin' out there for the next month! With our boys gone to college and all, we just don't have the muscles around here like we used ta."

This comment made Mike feel happier that he had volunteered for what appeared to be quite an undertaking for only four men, two of which he wasn't too sure could hold their own coffee mugs, let alone a few couches. Now that Mrs. MacEldowney was preparing oxtail soup, he was sure this project would take a minimum of four hours, knowing the meat took at least that long to simmer and become tender. Never mind. Somehow this bribe, which appealed to his childhood memories of his mother's cooking, would make it all worth while. Besides, he liked helping people out, especially when it involved a good workout, and perhaps a racing tip or two.

"Why don't we get started?" Mike asked Mrs. MacEldowney as he got up from the table. "Where would you like us to begin?"

She turned to her husband and Eamon and Dave. "I suggest two of yas be takin' the old stuff out the front, while the other two of yas start bringing in the new stuff from the sides."

"Whatever you say, Mother," Danny chirped amicably to his wife. He turned to Mike. "What do ya say, Mike? How about you and myself start unloadin' the vans? The older lads can probably handle the old stuff with no prob,' there'll be less lifting for 'em. All they have to do is roll it out the front door. There aren't even any stairs to trip over. Anyway, if they *do* drop any of it, who cares? The wife would have a stroke if they dropped any of the *new* furniture!"

Mike agreed, and he and Danny went outside to the first van. It contained an entire living room suite with two large sofas and two oversized club chairs. There was also a set of end tables, a coffee table and some lamps.

Mike jumped up onto the back of the truck. "Where are the furniture dollies and the furniture pads? And where is the loading ramp? Are they all on one of the other trucks?"

Danny stared at him blankly. "Why, do ya think we'll be needin' all that?"

"It certainly would help," Mike replied slowly, realizing there probably weren't any of these items on any of the trucks.

"Well, ya see, Mike," Danny explained hesitantly, "They were goin' to have the nerve ta charge me for them as well as the hours it took for the unloadin', so I showed them! I said no to all of it."

"That must have saved you enough to buy one of the end tables," Mike said sardonically."

"Oh, more than that!" Danny replied exuberantly. "The money it saved let me buy another dog!"

"Is the dog going to help with the move?" Mike could hardly disguise sarcasm. Then he added quickly, "I guess we can manage without the dollies and the ramps. But we had better get started or you'll be charged *two* days for the trucks!"

Mike slowly eased one of the couches out over the back edge of the truck. Danny stood ready to receive it, and groaned from the weight of it coming down on him. Mike jumped down from the truck and took the other end, thinking about how sore he'd be the next three days after this move. It seemed highly unlikely that anybody else was going to show up to help.

Mike tried to relieve his irritation by making polite conversation with Danny as each one gripped either end of the couch. "Danny, did you ever tell me about your greyhounds?"

"I don't think I did, but I'll go on and on if ya let me." Danny seemed eager to share some of his dog racing information, and Mike was eager to listen. Maybe Mike *would* get some hot tips out of this....

"Well, Mike, do ya know anything about dog racin'?" Danny asked.

"All I know is that a bunch of skinny greyhounds run around a track chasing a fake rabbit." Mike responded.

"Oh, that's American style. We have that here, too. There are eighteen tracks around the country. It's getting more and more popular. It's the poor man's sport, not havin' the status of horse racin', and probably never will. It's strictly a 'man's' sport."

"So, what's the difference between your greyhounds and the others?" Mike asked.

"My dogs are raised specifically for 'hare coursing.' They are bred to run in the fields. They are much bigger than the track type," Danny explained. "They are faster, stronger and more agile than their littler, sleeker cousins, and they're a hell of a lot more aggressive."

"So how does it work?"

"The dogs are let out to chase a live hare in the fields," Danny explained.

"Which fields?"

"Any field where two greyhounds are brought to compete against each other," Danny went on. "There are all sorts of preliminary heats for the hounds which lead up to the grand prize, 20,000 Irish pounds! And, that same big prize is what I finally won last month, thanks to my ol' buddy Borstal Boy. I named him after the prison where writer and political prisoner Brendan Behan was held. That's what probably made him a winner. He's a fighter!"

Mike was so flabbergasted, he almost dropped his end of the sofa. "20,000 pounds?" He had heard Danny MacEldowney tales, but this one was a whopper. "Come on, you're kiddin' me."

"That's my Borstal Boy, the best dog a man could have. Although my wife let me keep most of the cash from the winnings, she got to buy all of her new furniture." Danny exclaimed with pride, as he looked over the assorted furniture which, lay strewn all over the side yard. "I just hope it tides her over for awhile as far as me and my gamblin.' Ya know a guy needs a hobby! Now I'm even more addicted to hare coursin' than ever…ya know, that little taste of victory just makes you hungry for more."

Mike wondered it Danny would offer him a tip. Maybe he could win a few pounds, himself.

"I've been racin' greyhounds for years. I found the track racin' bores me. Hare coursing is the only excitin' bettin' game left in Ireland. All the excitin' games like cock fightin' are banned. Ya know, they even passed laws in '93 trying to curb my fun."

"What do you mean?"

"The government passed some ridiculous rules to regulate the racin' of the greyhounds. Now we have to make sure all the dogs are muzzled and the hares 'inspected' for injury *after every* event." Danny rolled his eyes. "Fortunately, it took all the gore and bloodshed out of the sport. Unfortunately, it did take some of the fun and chance out of the races. And we gamblin' guys don't like it, or *any* government regulation, for that matter."

"How do you mean?"

"Well, unlike what most people think who are not involved in racin', the winnin' dog isn't the one who actually *catches* the hare, but the one who *turns the hare first.* Dogs are paired off to race against each other. The hare is released between the two dogs. The way it works is that while the hounds are chasin' the hare, the hare will eventually turn away from the dog that the hare thinks is gainin' on him and would eventually catch him if allowed to.

"The winnin' dog is really the one that gets the hare to run off his straight course while he's runnin' away from the dog," Danny continued. "So, the dog isn't judged by catchin' the hare, but how the hare reacts to the dog that's *on his way to catchin'* the hare. So ya see, there's a lot of chance to it. I'll let you know the next time I race Borstal Boy, and you can see for yerself," Danny offered.

"I'd sure love to see it, even if it's just to figure the whole thing out," Mike replied.

"Well, are ya ready for a break yet? I'll just be showin' ya my big prize winner." Danny led Mike to the hedges from where all the barking was coming.

But as Mike neared the gate with him, the dogs jumped and barked ferociously. Luckily, an eight-foot high chain link fence separated them from the dogs.

"Don't ya be worryin'," Danny yelled over the barking throng. "They won't bite ya'."

Funny, Mike thought, that's what all dog owners said right before dog took a bite out of your leg. Mike hesitated at the closed gate.

"No, I mean, they can't bite ya anyways, they're all muzzled," Danny explained, and he unlocked the latch and, holding the gate barely open, eased inside.

"Now, here's my pride and joy, 'Borstal Boy'." Danny slapped the dog on the back enthusiastically. "He's one fine dog, isn't he?"

Mike, having stayed outside, looked at the animal. It was unlike any dog he had ever seen before. It was, the size of a small Shetland pony. His large body had the shape of a greyhound, but that was the only similarity. He was brown, not gray. He was heavy, not sleek. His large brown eyes protruded from an oversized head, which seemed hugely out of proportion to the rest of him. His hair looked longer and courser than a regular greyhound. From the ground to the top of his arched back, he must have measured at least forty inches.

All the dogs were staring at Mike, now. Danny grabbed Borstal Boy's muzzle and dragged him over towards Mike. Danny eased open the gate, and tugged Borstal Boy out to Mike. "Now shake paws with Mike," Danny teased.

Mike reluctantly held his hand out for the introduction.

Instead of holding his paw up to greet Mike, Bristol Boy nuzzled his snout into Mike's hand.

"Now, that's what I call a *dog*!" Mike exclaimed. "A *man's kind* of dog. What a canine specimen. He's so huge, I'll bet he could carry a jockey during the harecoursing races. What did you do, breed a *real greyhound* with an *Irish Wolfhound*?"

Danny threw his head back and let out a roaring laugh. "Now, just because you're used to only seein' those scrawny, over bred and inbred American greyhounds, don't be makin' fun of my champion!"

"Oh, I'm not making fun," Mike said apologetically, "I've just never seen such a handsome, majestic dog like this one."

The dog must have known it was receiving a compliment. It wagged its tail enthusiastically and pushed its nose further into Mike's hand. Next it leaned its body against Mike's thigh.

"He's pretty strong, huh?" Danny bragged.

"He's powerful, all right, " Mike exclaimed. "I want him. How much would you take for him? Pat is really missing our dog we left at home, Gizmo. Maybe I could surprise her with this one."

"Oh, just like a Yank," Danny teased. "Always thinkin' you can buy whatever you set your sights on."

"Well, everything has a price." Mike argued.

"Everything but *this* dog," Danny countered. "After his racin' days are over, I intend on breedin' 'im. What about one of the others? They're as big or bigger than Borstal Boy! They're all affectionate, lovable dogs. The only thing is, you'd have ta keep it muzzled at all times. It might seem cruel to you, but it's better for them. Chasing and biting just comes natural to them. You wouldn't want yer dog to be bitin' anybody."

Mike surveyed the other dogs, their brown, watery eyes looking up to him from behind their leather-bound muzzles. He thought about all of the guests coming and going at the Farmhouse. Maybe it wasn't such a good idea....

The sound of whining interrupted his thoughts. He couldn't see where the source of the yelping was coming from, but it seemed to come from behind the back hedge.

"What about *that* dog?" Mike gestured over the hedge. "Why is he separated from the rest of them?"

"Well, that one isn't a greyhound. The only reason that dog was bought was to pacify my wife, after my big win." His voice rose slightly. "She kept houndin' me for a dog of her own, a *lap* dog, a small, cuddly pooch that would sit next to her by the fire or sleep next to her on the couch, things these big fellas could never do. Unfortunately, like every time ya go to surprise your wife, it doesn't work out."

"I know what you mean," Mike agreed sympathetically. He watched Danny lug Borstal Boy inside the fence again, and then followed Danny to the back of the yard towards the hedge.

"Actually, we've been tryin' to get rid of her since the day I brought her home for the Misses. You see, the wife loved the puppy, but every time the greyhounds got a load of 'er, they wanted a chunk out of her. They think of her as their next meal, so I have to keep her tied up and separated from the hounds. It's really not fair to the poor little darlin.' She's scared stiff all day long from the hounds barkin.' Come to think of it, she *does* look a bit like a rabbit.

Mike peered over the hedge and into a cramped, makeshift pen, which housed the unwanted pet. Staring back up at him was a brown-eyed, black and white fur ball. It looked amazingly like the familiar ball of fluff, Gizmo. When the puppy saw Mike, she acted as if she had found a long lost friend. She jumped up happily on her unsteady hind legs and scratched feverishly at the side of her pen. Each time she attempted to claw her way through the wire, she fell over on her side like a little clown dressed in a panda suit.

"Have you ever heard of a *Shih-Tzu?*" Danny asked, pronouncing the first word like a scatological epithet.

Mike reached into the pen and saved the squirming puppy from her futile effort to scale the three-foot high wall made of chicken wire. She couldn't have weighed more than three pounds. She squealed with glee as he picked her up and held her quivering body to his own. He lifted her up to his face so her tiny black and white panda face touched his. Her pink tongue licked the tip of his nose.

"She's yours for the takin'," Danny said eagerly. "You could *have* her, no charge."

"You're kidding!" Mike answered, giggling from the dog tickling his face with her darting tongue.

Danny added, "Consider it a 'thank you' for helpin' me with the movin'. Besides, you'd be doin' me *another* favor for takin' her off my hands and givin' her a good home. It will sure take a load off me and the wife. It will make a great surprise for your wife, too."

By the time the move was over and the oxtail soup had been eaten, Eamon and Dave left with their lot of used furniture and Mike left with the new puppy. As Danny and the Missus waved good-bye to Mike and the tiny black and white dog, Danny yelled out. "Now *that's* a real man's kind of dog. And if anybody tries to give ya a hard time, that she's too prissy for a lad your size, just tell 'em that your puppy could easily *choke* any one of their big dogs."

"How so?" Mike asked.

"When she gets caught in their throats!" Danny laughed heartily at his own joke.

Mike arrived back at the farmhouse with the puppy hidden in his jacket.

"Did you get any good stories or hot tips out of Danny MacEldowney?" I asked.

"No, but I did get something better from him," Mike said. He retrieved the squirming puppy from inside his jacket. "I'd like you to meet our new Gizmo, Gizmo II!" He held the dog's face up to mine and Gizmo II put her paw on my cheek. "You were right. We do need a dog in our lives."

Great Grandfather's Cottage

"Please, please, please, PLEEEZE!" I begged, with my hands folded together in prayer.

Mike lifted the newspaper up to completely cover his face, pretending the paper barrier would make me stop begging, or at least keep him from seeing and hearing my begging.

"Come on, you promised," I continued, resolved not to give up."

"Maybe next week-end," he murmured from behind the business section. "We drove enough this week, give me a break. We'll go next week-end."

"Oh, no. When I agreed that it was too risky for me to drive while we're here in Ireland, you promised me you'd drive me wherever and whenever I wanted. Now, for months, I've been asking you to drive to Ballyheigue to see my great grandfather's house, and you keep putting it off."

"I said we'd go next week, didn't I?" Mike responded. "Come on, I'm trying to read the paper. Besides, weren't you supposed to try and contact the new owners first to let them know we were coming? I told you I didn't want to go knock on their door and barge in on them without warning, and demand a tour of the place."

"I told you we weren't going to do that. I don't care if we see the inside. I just want to see the outside. We don't have to bother them or anything. I didn't call or write because I don't have their names. All cousin Dora told us is that a Scottish couple bought the place and fixed it up. She didn't know their names, but she said if we ask at the Kirby Pub in town who bought the Kirby house and who's living in it now, they would gladly tell us who they are and how to get to it. It doesn't have an address. The place is simply known as *The Kirby House.* That's why I haven't called ahead. I can't call directory assistance to get their phone number without a name or address."

"Ugh huh," he answered from behind the paper.

I took off my apron, folded it and placed it on the kitchen counter. "So I thought if we left now, while things are slow today, we'd get there for lunch. We could grab a quick bite to eat at the Kirby Pub, get our information and head out to see the Kirby cottage. We could be back by dinner. I promise we won't even knock on the door. I don't want to bother the new owners either. I just want to *see* it. I've been hearing about that cottage since I was a kid."

Mike lowered the newspaper down from his face. "How long do you think it will take to get there?"

"Probably no more than two hours. I'll just go get my jacket and be right down. Where's the camera?"

"In the car. I'll go find the good Michelin map. No sense taking two hours to get there, which is what usually happens when we go *mapless*."

Five minutes later, we were in the car and heading for Ballyheigue Bay on the west coast of Kerry, the town I only knew as the place where my great grandfather was born.

Mike drove, while I traced our route on the map, which was strewn across my lap.

"Limerick to Listowel to Ballyheigue," I explained. "Actually I believe the cottage itself is in Glenderry, a little north of Ballyheigue. But, we still have to stop at the pub for directions."

"How are you so certain they'll know at the pub?" Mike asked. "This isn't too organized of a plan. I'm not really crazy about setting out for a two hour drive not even knowing where we're going."

"Can't you just have a little faith that we'll find it?" I argued. "Where's your sense of adventure? Even if we don't find it, we'll get to explore another part of the country we haven't seen. The town is supposed to have a fabulous view of the ocean. That's why the Kirby Clan had a hard time parting with it, even though nobody was living in it."

"At least we can say we had lunch in the infamous Kirby Pub," he said. "Let's hope they serve good food, and not the usual pub grub."

"We haven't starved yet in all of these years, have we?"

Feeling contrite that I had gotten my way, I settled back in my seat and quietly admired the green banks and glistening waters of the River Shannon which meandered in and out of view along the N69.

Great grandfather's cottage, I thought. *Would it be the simple, charming, whitewashed bungalow I had imagined in my youth? The couple who had bought it supposedly rebuilt much of it. I wondered if they had preserved it or had torn most of it down to rebuild a more modern bungalow in its place.*

"Are you dreaming over there?" Mike asked.

"I was just thinking how nice it would be if the couple who bought the house preserved the cottage the way it had been. From what cousin Dora told us, it had been in shambles for a long time. Supposedly there were cows living in it."

"Maybe the couple hasn't even moved in yet. Didn't they just buy it not too long ago? I thought that's what Dora told us. That they were Scottish and they bought it after several years of negotiating with the Kirbys. There were so many in the Kirby Clan, nobody wanted to be responsible for selling the cottage out of the family, and to foreigners, no less."

"I'm surprised they sold it at all," I agreed. "But from what I heard, it was in such a desolate state, and since all the Kirby descendants had moved to the U.S. and therefore had lost interest in ever living in it again, it didn't make sense *not to* sell it. Supposedly, this couple tried for a very long time to acquire it. I guess they came from Scotland looking for a little summer getaway place. I can't wait to see it, but on the other hand, I'm sure I'll be terribly disappointed if it's all torn down and modernized. I have this picture in my mind since childhood of what it will be like and I don't want to ruin it."

"Then do you want me to turn around?" Mike asked, playfully.

I ignored him and pointed to the Ballyheigue sign. "Look, we're here. Now I hope there aren't hundreds of pubs to weed through."

"There it is!" Mike yelled.

"You're right. Look, it's Kirby's Lounge. They must have upgraded from a Pub!

Isn't it darling! It looks so quaint." I was getting excited about a possible brush with a long lost relative.

The neat, little lounge was painted in a light yellow with blue lettering and trim. *Kirby's Lounge* was printed in scrolled capital lettering beneath two Art Nouveau styled lamps. Beside the door hung a large wooden advertisement with two golfers drinking a draft while hauling their golf clubs. Above the golfers was the word *Guinness* in red lettering, and under it the slogan, *That's The Stuff!* Two bicycles leaned up against the wall under the sign.

When we walked in from the bright sunlight, we focused our eyes on the bar, behind which stood a young man who appeared barely old enough to drink. He was rinsing out glasses and wiping down the top of the bar. To the left of the bar were a few small tables and chairs, and behind them a decrepit dartboard hung on a red wall that had more dart holes in it than the dartboard itself. To the right of the bar a group of men huddled around an unlit fireplace, smoking and quietly talking between sips of their lagers. They were dressed in woolen caps and tweed jackets which, together with their thick Kerry accents, made us assume they were locals. They nodded to us as we passed them on our way to the bar.

Leaning against the far end of the bar were two middle-aged women dressed in jeans and sweatshirts, who also smiled at us as we came closer to the bar.

Mike whispered to me as we approached. "We'll order us something for lunch, then I'll ask about the Kirby place, so we don't look too pushy or anything."

"Hi," he said to the bartender. "Do you serve sandwiches or any other pub grub?"

"I'm afraid not. But we have a wonderful selection of chips." He pointed to a wire rack which had several small bags of potato chips and pretzels hanging from it. "Here's a smorgasbord for ya. Take your pick."

Mike obliged him by grabbing three of them from the rack. "We'll both have a couple of Diet Cokes, too, please, with ice."

"Of course," the bartender smiled. "You're Americans, aren't you?"

"Yes, we are," Mike said. "We're on the hunt for some Kirby information."

"What kind of information?" the bartender asked, warily.

"Well, for instance, can you tell us if any of the Kirbys that own this place are around?"

"Why, who wants to know?" the young man asked.

"I do," Mike said. "I'm sorry, I should have introduced myself first. You know we Americans have the habit of coming right to the point. I'm Mike O'Brien and this is my wife, Pat. We've come all the way from the U.S. to see the place where her great grandfather was born. We were told to inquire at the Kirby Pub, er, Lounge, and somebody might be able to give us some directions in order to find it."

"Well, you came to the right place," the bartender said. "I'm a Kirby myself. My name's Sean."

"Well, then, you might be related to her," Mike said excitedly, as he gestured toward me.

"Hi, cousin," I said, while I shook his hand. "So you're a Kirby, too."

Sean then shook hands with Mike. "Well, actually, my mother was a Kirby. My father was a Lean," Sean said. "But she and my Da both died when I was young, so I'm afraid I won't be too much help with the Kirby family history. What kind of information are you looking for?"

"Well, Pat's been dreaming about her great grandfather's house and wants to see it. Don't worry, we won't be intruding or anything. She just wants to see it and take a picture of it. We heard through the family that some Scottish people now own it."

"Well," the bartender said, "you can speak directly to the horse's mouth, since that dark haired lady at the end of the bar is the actual owner. Jane, she is, let me introduce yas to her." He came out from behind the bar and the three of us walked over to her. He introduced us.

She was in her forties, slight, with a light complexion contrasted to her jet-black hair, which was tied in a ponytail. She had charming laugh lines emanating from the corners of her eyes which gave her a warm affable appearance. Her companion was approximately the same age, but sandy blonde.

"Jane," Sean said. "Here are a couple of Yanks who want to take a couple of pictures of *The Kirby House*, from the outside only, mind you. It seems that Pat, here, is related to them."

"I don't mean to intrude," I added hastily. "I've been hearing about it all my life, the little Kirby cottage situated on a cliff overlooking the sea. I just wanted to take a look at it to see if it's anything like I thought it would be."

"For heaven's sake," Jane responded, "You must be one of the Kirby's." Her eyes sparkled. "I'd be delighted to give you a grand tour of the place. In fact, my husband John is coming right now to pick us up." She shoulder-nudged her friend, which she introduced as Maggie. "We pedaled our bikes all the way here for a pint never thinking it was going to be all uphill on the way back. So he's coming to our rescue with his van to pick us and the bikes up. We can all go back to the house and he can show off all the handiwork he's done on the place."

I noticed her foreign accent. I wondered what the Irish had against the Scottish.

"Well, we don't want to bother you," Mike offered.

"I insist on it," Jane countered. "My husband will be thrilled to show you around."

With that, the door opened and a tall, lanky, white-haired fellow ducked in the door.

"There's himself, now," Sean said, nodding in the direction of John who was approaching the bar.

Jane slipped off the barstool to greet him with a peck on the cheek.

"John, these are a couple of nice Yanks who want to take a few pictures of the house to bring home to their family. Pat's great grandfather was a

Kirby and was *born* in *The Kirby Cottage*. I told them you'd love to give them a tour."

"Indeed, I would," he said. "But what's the hurry? Why don't we have a round before we head back up there? I have to catch up to yas." John also had a foreign accent, but I couldn't quite make out what kind of accent it was. I thought Scots were rather short, John looked to be at least six foot three.

John walked over to the bartender and ordered a round for all of us. Mike went up next to him and made an effort to cover the tab, but John waved him away. "Don't worry, Mike, you can get the next round, when we get to America for a visit!"

We sipped our drinks while John explained how he and Jane ended up buying *The Kirby Cottage*. It was interesting that they still referred to it by that name even though they were not related to the Kirby Clan in any way.

"It all started almost twelve years ago. The house had been abandoned for at least ten years when I started to inquire about it. It was in terrible shape, but I'm a contractor myself, and with its location on the bluff and all, I knew it had lots of possibilities. But when I tried to buy it, the Kirby Clan put up a formidable front." He winked at me and then Sean who stood behind the bar listening. "Those Kirbys can be a tough bunch to negotiate with."

"Yeah, we can be," Sean agreed.

"Anyway, for two years I continued to try to buy the property and just when I thought I was getting somewhere, I found that I wasn't. You see, they didn't like the fact that we weren't family."

Weren't family, I thought. *Weren't from Ireland, you mean. The Irish were known to be clannish, not liking outsiders buying their land.*

"Anyway," John said, "Jane and I decided we would do everything we could to get it. We finally did, and it's ten years ago this week we've been in *The Kirby Cottage*."

"Ten years?" Mike asked. "We were under the impression you just bought it not too long ago."

"Oh no. We've been working on it for the past ten years and the work's only been finished a short time. You see, we did a lot of the work ourselves and it took awhile." He laughed. "At one point it looked in worse shape than it did when we got started."

"Well, let's not keep them in suspense any longer," Jane said. "They can follow us in the van. We'll be there in five minutes. I'll make some sandwiches."

"Oh, please don't bother," I protested. "We feel like we're intruding already!" "Never mind," John said. "We can't wait to show it to you. It will be nice to have a Kirby back inside of it."

The ride to the cottage was only a few minutes along Ballyheigue Bay. It was a sunny, but brisk and windy day. The expanse of rugged shoreline spread out before us and the ocean's silvery gray surface glistened in the sun.

"This area is more beautiful than I ever imagined," I said to Mike, as I gazed dreamily out the window. "I can see why they fell in love with this place and needed to buy something here. I know Scotland is beautiful, but where could they ever find a view like this?"

Suddenly the van pulled into an unpaved driveway and we followed. The van lurched to a stop, and John, Jane and their female companion, piled out, waving for us to follow.

Camera in hand, I started snapping photos of great granddaddy's cottage. It was just as I had imagined it; a rectangular, squat bungalow with two simple windows and a steeply pitched black roof. The outside walls were painted white and the two windows and door were painted bright red. On either side of the house were two diminutive, attached stone sheds whose gray texture contrasted significantly to the stark white stucco of the cottage itself. Only an unkempt patch of grass served as landscaping in the front yard. An abandoned push-type lawn mower stood in the middle of it, probably where John had left it to retrieve Jane and her friend from the pub.

John pointed to the flag of Ireland which hung over the front door and flapped furiously in the breeze. He stood in the doorway and beckoned us in, waving his hand wildly. "You'll catch a death of cold out there. The wind is cruel today."

Mike and I stepped over the threshold. Walking into this house made me feel as if I were stepping back through three generations of time. A large gathering room with a wood beamed ceiling greeted us. On the far end was an open-hearth fireplace, whose stone surround filled the entire wall. There was an antique pot hanging inside it, and several copper pots hung on the wall. There were three oversized sofas facing the fireplace. A large pine dining table with several chairs around it was at the other end of the room.

"Wow," I said, turning, taking it all in. "I can't believe I'm here."

Jane came in from the kitchen offering us each a glass of white wine. "Welcome to *The Kirby Cottage*." As we took them, she lifted the glass into the air as a toast, saying, "To the Kirbys, all of their ancestors and all of their descendants who have passed through our door."

"Cheers!" we all said in unison.

"Now, Johnny," Jane said, "why don't you start your tour, while I make a few sandwiches?"

John stood proudly in the middle of the gathering room. "So what do yas think?" he asked.

"It's just charming!" I gushed. "Thanks for inviting us in. It looks very different in here than from the outside. You'd never know it had this much room."

"Well, that was the idea," John said. "When we bought it, I vowed we would keep as much of the original house as we could. So I only built on to the back, so that the original cottage retained its character." He pointed to an old black and white framed picture standing on the fireplace mantel. "See? From the front, it looks exactly the same as it did two hundred years ago. You are standing in what was the entire cottage without the side stone sheds.

"When we bought it, the roof was caved in, and there was grass growing there right beneath your feet. There were cattle and sheep grazing in it." He started to laugh. "In fact, I'll never forget the day I had the man with the bulldozer come over to dig out the foundation for the back addition. He asked me which end did I want him to start bulldozing the whole thing down! He couldn't believe we were going to keep any of the existing buildings, but we did."

"It's wonderful that you've respected the character of the original house," I said. "The easy thing would have been to knock it all down and start over."

"Don't I know it. Although I couldn't have done that in good conscience," John said. "Everything that's new and modern, the kitchen and the two bedrooms and bath, were added onto the back where they belong. I drew up the plans myself."

With that, he led us through a doorway and into the large kitchen, which he had added, directly behind the gathering room. It had all the modern conveniences, a doublewide refrigerator with ice cube maker, a dishwasher, a microwave oven, and a garbage compactor. Jane stood over her corian countertops, slicing sandwiches and serving them on pretty, porcelain plates.

They must, indeed, be *rich Scots* after all, I thought.

"How long did it take for John to do all this?" I asked Jane, trying to include her on our tour.

"Oh, John's pretty compulsive. It didn't take him too long. The problem was that all his other jobs that he gets paid for took priority. I just told him he had to finish my dream kitchen first. I didn't care about the other rooms too much, as long as we had a place to sleep." She winked at John.

"You must be awfully proud of him," I said. "And I'm sure you had some input on this kitchen."

"He did it all," she said, "I just had to survive through it all. I am proud of him. But not necessarily for his construction skills. It's the romantic side of him that has always gotten to me. How many other men would have had the vision he had about this place and the idealism to match? Now here's your sandwich, you can take it with you on the tour. If he goes on and on too long, just yell for me and I'll come and save ya."

"Thanks," we said, as we took the plates from her.

"Come on, you Kirby kids," John said, affectionately. "Let me show you the rest of the additions we added." He led us down a hallway with two good-sized bedrooms on either side, with a large bathroom at the end of the hall. "Remember, you are always welcome to stay here. This is the guest bedroom, and *this* is the *playroom*." The playroom had an American king-sized bed with canopy and two large chests of drawers. It was hard to imagine how all of this furniture came to this remote place in Ireland.

"Now, let me show you the best part," John said.

"There can't be more," I said, incredulous.

"Well, not more additions, just more of the original house, which I think you will find more interesting than the new rooms," John explained.

"Where?" I asked.

"Come on." John ushered us out the back door. "Go ahead, you can nibble on the sandwiches while I continue."

We crossed part of the yard and followed him into one of the side sheds. He opened a rickety door that hung crookedly from its hinges, and we followed him inside. It was dark, but John knew exactly what he wanted to show us. "Here is the Kirby memorabilia I wanted to show you. These things were left here from your great grandfather's time." He reached into a storage bin and rolled out a huge metal milk container. It was four feet tall and covered with rust.

"These are original milk tins. You can have this if you want," he said excitedly.

"We'd take it if we could fit it in a suitcase," I replied.

"It looks like it's a hundred years old," Mike added.

"That's nothing. Look at this."

"What is it?" I asked.

"It grinds beets into pulp to be fed to the livestock. You turn the crank," John explained.

"It looks like a giant meat grinder," Mike said. "And what's that thing over there?"

"Why, that's a hay harvester," he replied. "And next to it is a peat cutter. It's all rusty, but you can see here where it was attached to a handle."

While examining it, I said. "To me cutting bog is the epitome of Irish life."

"Here, take it," John said, excited about my enthusiasm for his collected relics.

"It's just wonderful that you treasure these things the way you do," I said. "I mean, your not being Irish and all."

"Who told you I wasn't Irish?" John asked.

"We thought you were Scottish. Aren't you and Jane both Scottish? I thought that's what our cousin told us."

John shook his head in disbelief and let out a tremendous groan. "I knew that was it. *That's* why they gave us such a hard time about buying the place. You see, your great-uncle, the one who last lived here, he was pretty senile by the time I became interested in the place. He had been in a nursing home for several years, but it was himself I had to negotiate with over the phone. All the other Kirbys were either in the U.S., dead, or didn't care. Each time I talked to him about buying it, he didn't seem to remember who I was. He kept calling me the Scott."

"Well, isn't Jane Scottish? She has that certain accent I can't seem to put my finger on." I said.

"*Ha!* No, she's Welsh and I met her in Wales more years ago than I want to admit. But I myself am Irish. I'm an O'Leary born right here in Ballyheigue, not one mile from this house. My parents moved to Wales when I was a child. My grandfather used to be friends with your great uncle who lived here until ten years ago."

"You're kidding," I said.

"Evidently, your great uncle couldn't understand who I was and that I was, indeed, Irish. He probably heard my Welsh accent that I've picked up over the last forty years."

When he said the word more like *farty* instead of *forty* I caught a trace of his lingering Irish accent.

"Now I feel terrible knowing my relatives kept you from getting the house sooner," I said apologetically, "only because they thought you were foreign."

"They wouldn't have been Irish if they didn't." He chuckled. "You know the old saying, *me own's me own.* All I know is I've always wanted to come back to where I was born and to live among *my own.* This house has allowed me to do that. I also know that according to the people around here, the Kirby family was a wonderful group of people. Your great uncle was supposed to be the nicest man, always having people stop by whenever they wanted to hear a kind word from him. Did you know he was a great baker?"

"Why, no, I didn't."

"Well, according to what the people who knew your family say, the Kirbys were the kindest and gentlest people alive. People would come from all over to buy his bread and sit and talk for awhile. I had many conversations myself with him. He could really tell a story. The only problem was, with his Alzheimer's and all, I wasn't sure if he really knew who I was half the time."

"Thank you for saying such nice things about my uncle and my family," I said. "I'm sure if he lived to see what wonderful care you've given to the cottage, he would have sold it to you gladly, instead of making you go through everything you had to."

"It was worth it," John assured me. "I'm happy. And now, God rest his soul, I hope your great-grandda is happy too, looking down on us standing in his own modest, stone shed."

He picked up a small wooden box from the floor and took out what appeared to be an old, rusty horseshoe. "How would you like this, to take as a souvenir Pat?"

"I will always treasure this horse shoe as a symbol of your romantic resolve to restore and preserve a cottage that represents something important to both of us, our roots."

I placed the rusty horseshoe inside my jacket pocket.

"Now let me show you the Jacuzzi I put in," John said.

St. Patrick's Day

"What happened? Did you lose a bet?" Mary asked Kevin, making fun of his new buzz haircut which resembled a military baldey-sour cut. He ignored her and moped dejectedly into the parlor, finally collapsing onto the overstuffed club chair next to the fire.

"Ya look as if ya had yer ears lowered," she tried again to elicit a response.

"The haircut is the least of my problems," Kevin replied despondently. "I'm desperate, completely desperate."

"What on earth is wrong with you?" Mary asked. "I've never seen you look so glum. What is it, *Keveen*? Why did ya have ta go and start mutilatin' yerself? Next, God forbid, it will be a tattoo! It must be a woman that's got you in this sort of state. It's got to be a woman!"

"I just can't be tellin' ya," Kevin murmured, as he looked into the dancing fire that blazed in the hearth.

"Come on, Kev, maybe we can help. Even if it's just to listen," I encouraged him.

Mary continued to try to harass him out of his foul mood. "It sure must be serious if you went and cut off yer beautiful curls! What were ya thinkin' anyway? Nobody looks good with a drill sergeant's haircut."

"Oh, leave him alone, Mary. Maybe he's just not up to telling us just this minute."

I turned to Kevin. "Would a cup of tea or coffee make you feel any better? I'd offer you a beer, but you know the house rules about drinking before 6:00 p.m. Of course, I could put a shot of whiskey in the coffee, that might make you feel a tad better."

"Nothing, absolutely nothing could make me feel better. I'm tellin' yas, I'm desperate."

"We can see that." Mary said.

"I can't concentrate, I can't work, I can't even eat," Kevin replied. "I can't remember ever losing my appetite, but I have. All I can do is think about her..." his voice trailed off somewhere in the direction of the fireplace.

Mary looked at me. "Ya see, I knew it had to be a woman!"

"Well," I started to console him. "Noreen is a beautiful, captivating woman..."

"No, not her." Kevin said, then stopped abruptly when he realized he was telling us more than he wanted to.

"Well, then who? Who else has been hangin' around your neck for the last couple of years?" Mary coaxed him.

I got up to go into the kitchen. Perhaps Kevin would be more comfortable spilling his heart out to Mary than to me. I'd be better off making us all some coffee. Whiskey was good for loosening lips. Maybe Kevin would open up with a little Irish coffee under his belt.

"I'll be back with some coffees. Maybe you two could use some time alone." Kevin wouldn't realize I could hear every word he uttered from the other side of the wall in the kitchen.

"I can't be tellin' ya, Mary. You'd laugh me right out of this house. I couldn't take the humiliation."

"Very well, then." She got up. "I'll just be goin' in to help Pat."

"No, please don't go. I do need to tell somebody. You've always been someone who I could talk to. I never felt so unsure about anything."

" Keveen, whatever it is, believe me, I can assure you I won't be laughin' at ya."

"You know the Irish Eleventh Commandment, *Thou Shalt Not Kid Thyself?* Well, I've gone and broken it, and I just can't help myself."

"You're in a sorry state, all right," Mary stated flatly. "Come on, Kevin, darlin', out with it. I promise you I won't laugh."

"Well, it's got to do with a certain lady named Eileen." He whispered slowly.

"Eileen? Eileen? You don't mean the schoolteacher down at St. Columba's? You're kiddin' me now, aren't ya?"

"You promised not to laugh."

Mary threw her head back and slapped the arm of the sofa, knocking the lace doily off. "Eileen Scanlon? Marty Scanlon's daughter?"

"That would be the one," Kevin admitted hesitantly.

Mary started to laugh uncontrollably.

"You promised!" Kevin said, hurt to the core. "I knew I shouldn't have told you. But you pried it out of me. I'll just be movin' along."

"Oh, come on, Kevin. I'm sorry. I'm just shocked, that's all. You've always had the beauties hangin' all over ya. I just can't see ya with a plain school marm like Eileen Scanlon! How did ya ever hook up with her?"

"You don't think she's beautiful?" he asked incredulously.

"Well…" She hesitated. "She's no Noreen Riley! I guess she does have a wholesome country look about 'er."

"Thanks for the compliment, Mary. I knew I could count on you."

Now that Kevin had finally spilled the beans, I decided it was time for me to reappear with the coffees. "Here you are, Kevin," I said going in and pretending I'd not heard his secret admission. This will make you feel better, no matter what is ailing you."

I handed him his coffee and offered another to Mary.

Mary tried to explain. "Ya see, I was right. Kevin seems to be smitten. Smitten, no I'd call it bulldozed over, by the school teacher Eileen Scanlon, Marty Scanlon's daughter."

"Who's Marty Scanlon?" I asked. "Do I know him or her for that matter?"

Mary walked over to Kevin and patted him on his shaved head. "Marty Scanlon just happens to be the wealthiest man in the area, bar none."

"So?"

"So?" Mary mimicked my American accent. "Marty is not only the richest man in these parts, but he has only one child, a daughter, Eileen, who is the wealthiest and probably the most educated woman around."

"And?" I was trying to understand.

"Well, when the old lady Scanlon died of the cancer when Eileen was only a child, Marty sent his daughter to a fancy boarding school in

England. He was beside himself about what to do with her and how to raise her properly."

"He never remarried?" I asked.

"Not only did he not remarry, he became a broken hearted recluse, so that when poor Eileen returned all educated with her proper English accent, she was forced to stay near home and to tend to him. It's really a miserable life for the two of them. Everyone predicted that Eileen would end up an old spinster, taking care of the old man and grading papers in her spare time when she wasn't teachin' the wee ones."

"That's a shame," I responded. "But I don't understand why this is such a problem for Kevin. You'd think she'd be happy to have him come along and save her from her dreadful life of self-sacrifice."

"It's not just that," Kevin started to explain. "It's a lot of things—"

"Truly it is quite complicated," Mary interrupted.

"How so?" I pressed.

"Well, first of all, it's impossible that she would be interested in the likes of me," Kevin remorsed. "She's sophisticated, ya know, educated and prim and proper. I think she even has her Master's degree from Trinity in Dublin. Now why would anybody like that even look at somebody like me?"

"Well, for one thing, opposites attract," I started.

"No, you don't understand," Kevin protested. "She's rich, filthy rich! And what's worse is she's confident!"

"So what's wrong with that?" I decided that would be my last stupid question. I obviously wasn't helping the poor, distraught guy.

"Well, it's like this," Kevin began. "Ever since I was a kid, I kind of got by on my good looks and charm—"

"And for your modesty, no doubt!" Mary interrupted.

"No, I don't mean to be braggin' but that's the truth. People just gave things to me, were nice to me. It made it easier for me not to be too ambitious. Look, I can't take credit for any of that. I always chalked it up to being lucky or being blessed by The Almighty."

I glanced at Mary to see if she'd respond with a laugh. She didn't.

"So I dropped out of school at the age of twelve, never thinkin' education would get me anywhere better than where I was. I never had a problem with the ladies. The pretty ones liked me and I liked them. It was easy."

"But you always attracted the clinging vine types, Kevin," Mary chimed in. "The ones that didn't say much, just sat around and looked pretty while they gazed at you."

"Like Noreen?" I asked.

"Yeah, like Noreen," Kevin responded sullenly. "I guess the ones that liked me needed me and I felt like they would always stick around. Like Noreen, I never had to worry about her looking at somebody else. I really feel bad about her. She's a nice girl. Now I know, even if I don't have a snowball's chance in hell with Eileen, that I just can't continue any longer with Noreen. Yet, I'd hate to be disappointin' her by callin' the whole thing off."

"Well, would you rather be a nice guy and walk down the aisle with her never knowin' what chance you'd have had with Miss Eileen?" Mary challenged him.

"It's no use, I tried all of my charm and it didn't seem to work," Kevin argued.

"What do ya mean? What have ya tried so far?" Mary asked.

"Well, last month St. Columba's principal called me and asked if I did any paintin' at the school. I told him, sure. So I went over there and he hired me to do some touch-ups, but the place needed paintin' badly so I was there for over a week."

"And that's where ya fell for Eileen?" Mary asked.

"Literally," Kevin admitted. "I almost fell off the scaffolding when I saw her."

"Is she that beautiful?" I asked innocently. "I just can't imagine anybody prettier than Noreen Riley!"

"Well, she's not *prettier* than Noreen. Maybe more alluring, though. I don't know how to explain it. I guess you'd call it some kind of magnetism, she's sexier, attractive, *ugh*, I don't mean showy with revealin' clothes and such, but she has a certain confidence and sparkle in her eyes when she talks to ya." Kevin continued to explain, groping for words. "She's like one of those American movie stars from the forties. Beautiful, sexy *and* smart. Ya know, like Carol Lombard or Ginger Rogers."

"So she's blonde?" I couldn't help myself.

"No, I'd say she's got um…brown, yeah, medium brown hair, long and wavy around her shoulders, very natural like. And she has a beautiful figure, shaped like a mandolin, ya know, with small shoulders and waist, but a beautiful view from behind…." His voice trailed off.

"Poor Kevin," Mary said. "He's really got it bad."

"I swear I can't think straight since I've seen her last," Kevin said, now pouring it all out. "I've been over at the school, makin' up things to do. I'm runnin' out of excuses to be over there. I've painted all the walls twice. I've heard of love knocking a guy out, but I never believed for one minute it could happen to Kevin O'Boyle! I've driven by the school and 'er house a million times hopin' I'll catch a glimpse of 'er."

"You sound like a love-struck schoolboy," I said.

"Don't I know it. And the worst part is, I know she'd never give the time of day to a guy like me. Why am I doing this to myself?" He looked at his dismal countenance in the mirror over the fireplace. "And, just look what it's doin' to me *hair!*"

I knew he was saying this to try to take the melodrama out of his confession.

I looked over at Mary for the next move. "So what, if anything, can we do for him?"

"Nothing, I'm sure. The situation is hopeless." Kevin put his head down into his hands and moaned.

"Well, we know one thing, that hair is sure hopeless!" Mary said. "Do ya think it will be grown out by St. Patrick's Day?"

"St. Patrick's Day? Why St. Patrick's Day?" Kevin reluctantly pulled his head from his hands.

"Well, Pat and Mike were sayin' they wanted to have a little gatherin' to celebrate St. Paddy's Day with the neighbors. It would be the perfect excuse for you and Miss Eileen to get together."

"How do ya figure that, Miss Matchmaker?"

"Well, they could include Marty Scanlon and Miss Scanlon on their list of neighbors. Since it's for the neighbors, that would make it all right if they don't include Noreen Riley. Then you could just be stoppin' by with the excuse that you're helpin' Pat and Mike with the party."

"It would seem really logical since you practically live here," I added encouragingly.

"I don't know...." Kevin replied.

"I think it's perfect, Kevin," I added. "It would seem so natural, it wouldn't even look like a set-up. At least you would have the chance to put on all your charm, outside of the work setting and in your finest clothes, instead of those ol' denims and work boots. Of course, you'd have to grow your hair back by then."

"Well," Kevin continued, "I could at least have the opportunity to talk to her in a more relaxed way, I mean, without talkin' about painting the classrooms or the like."

"Hey, the only two who didn't need some help were Adam and Eve," Mary chided, "and that's because they were the only two around, no distractions."

"And Romeo and Juliet," I added, "and they got together at a party, too."

"Yeah, I saw that movie," Kevin agreed. "I couldn't understand a word they said."

"Maybe they didn't need words," I added hesitantly. "Chemistry counts for a lot."

"Okay." Kevin stood up. "I have to give it a try, I've got nothing to lose. If I don't, I might always regret it. I'll do my best to grow this hair in as fast as I can. Now yas won't be embarrassin' me at the party pushin' the two of us together, now, would ya? I can do my own courtin' if I'm given half a chance."

"Cross our hearts!" Mary beamed at me.

The next day Mary and I wrote out all the invitations.

"I hope we don't get blamed if this scheme doesn't work," I said to Mary over the dining room table as she licked the twenty or so envelopes.

"It'll work, all right," she answered confidently. "I never saw a woman who's resisted 'im yet. My bet's on Kevin."

Three weeks later, all of the replies were in. Every single person invited accepted our invitation including Marty Scanlon and his daughter.

*   *   *

When St. Patrick's day arrived, Mike and I spent the afternoon decorating the parlor and the kitchen, knowing that guests always ended up in the kitchen. We strung green and white ribbons and crepe paper which we failed to realize was not a good idea. They began to sag limply from wherever we hung them, hours before the party began.

"When did St. Patrick drive the snakes out of Ireland?" Mike asked.

"I believe the date is 431 BC," I said. "And we've been celebrating it ever since with festivities and libations, although here in Ireland, it's still considered more of a religious holiday. So our party will be respectful of the two traditions. Either way, the Day commemorates my patron saint who introduced Christianity, and therefore, the concept of Christian love. A perfect day for our matchmaking scheme."

Mary and I decided to make corned beef brisket with lots of potatoes and cabbage. We'd serve it buffet style so it would be casual and so people could be free to mingle while they ate.

"Mingle, that's the key word for tonight," Mike said, as he reached to tape one more picture of St. Patrick and a harp to the parlor wall. "Now you won't be getting me mixed up in this matchmaker thing," Mike warned me. "I've never been one to push anybody on someone else. Has anyone considered Miss Scanlon's feelings? Talk about putting someone on the spot. I'd hate to be in her shoes when the conniving likes of you two move in on her."

"Where's your romantic side, dear?" I asked. "Just because *we're* living happily ever after, why can't Kevin and Eileen? Remember, if it weren't for your sister, Peggy, maybe *we* wouldn't have gotten together."

"What are you talking about?"

"Don't you remember your brother's wedding?"

"Of course, I remember it," he answered.

"But do you remember how we got together that night?"

"Well, of course, I do...." He hesitated.

"I'll refresh your memory."

"No, I remember now. I asked you how you liked the champagne. You said it was your favorite drink, which I remember thinking was a fib, since you weren't even old enough to drink." He was proud that he had this vivid recollection.

"Yeah, but what you didn't know is that your dear sister had just come up to me and told me that you had a wild crush on me. She's the one who gets the credit."

"Or the blame. Come on, she never told you that," he protested.

"You want to make a bet?" I challenged him. "Call her right now if you want, I'm sure she'll remember it the same way I do."

"And here I thought it was the champagne." He wasn't about to call long distance to lose a bet.

"So if a conniving female got us together, why couldn't it happen again?" I insisted. "Besides, I can't help but think we'd be doing Eileen a favor. She probably just needs to know Kevin's mad for her like you were for me!" I teased. "As soon as I knew you were interested, you were putty in my hands," I added, as I kissed him on the cheek.

"And you think that's the whole story," he responded. "Should I tell you the *real* story?"

"I think I would like to stick to my version."

At 7:30 the doorbell rang, the first guests arriving a half-hour after the invitation announced. This was considered being polite according to the Irish who felt arriving on time or within a half an hour of the starting time of the party, made them look too eager or might appear as if they are rushing the hosts. Mary and I had taken this into consideration when we were preparing the food. By 7:45 all of the guests had arrived. We stood around and chitchatted with all of the neighbors. Since they all knew each other, we didn't have to worry about introductions or that tired old American tradition of nametags. But we didn't see Kevin anywhere.

Mary and I called everyone into the kitchen after we had placed the large platters of sliced corned beef, potatoes and cabbage with a small bowl of mustard on the kitchen table. As everyone lined up to fill their plates, we moved into the parlor.

"Have ya seen 'er yet?" Mary queried.

"I think I figured out who she was by process of elimination," I answered. "Is she the one with the blue outfit on?"

"Yes, that would be her. How did ya know?" Mary responded.

"Well, I wore blue on my first get-together with Mike. Men love the color blue. It wasn't actually a date, but when I was getting ready, I decided that if he needed any encouraging, the blue would help."

"*Shh!*" she responded. "Here they come."

At that moment, Kevin appeared at the doorway of the parlor. His beautiful black hair was neatly groomed and he wore a crisp white long sleeved shirt and black jeans. He disappeared into the kitchen to get himself a plate of food, and was looking for somewhere in the room to stand. He sauntered over to the fireplace, which had a small fire working its way into a blaze. He leaned against the mantel and started to pick at his food.

"At least his hair is grown back in." Mary said to me, between chews on her corned beef.

"It's a lovely brisket you cooked, Mary," I answered purposely, not looking over at him. "I hope Kevin and Eileen will appreciate it."

With that, Eileen walked confidently into the room. She saw Kevin posed by the fireplace. Others were filtering back into the parlor, but she casually made her way towards him. He looked up from his plate and smiled a slow, engaging smile.

Mary and I pretended to converse, but spent most of our energies trying to overhear what they were saying but they were standing at least two feet out of range.

Mike came up to us. "Are you two ladies having a good time getting to know the neighbors?" he whispered. "How are our two lovebirds doing?"

"Mike, please mouth the words and act like you're talking to Mary and me. We're trying to get a gist of the conversation between them, but they're a bit far away."

"Why don't I just go over there and hear for myself," he said.

"Don't. Leave them be," Mary protested.

Mike ignored her and strolled over to Kevin and Eileen. Kevin didn't seem to appreciate the interruption by Mike.

Mike chatted with them for a few moments, and then turned away from Kevin and addressed Eileen directly. She responded in an animated fashion. Kevin stood idly by looking down at his plate and pretending to politely listen to Mike's banter.

"God, I sure wish I knew what they were sayin'," Mary said to me as she watched them.

"I'm sure Mike is giving her his twenty question routine," I answered.

Then we witnessed something neither one of us would have ever imagined that night. Mike seemed to be acting a little too interested in Eileen, and she, in turn, was openly and brazenly *flirting with Mike!*

I looked at Mary. "I think he's doing more than the twenty question thing. Look at her. She's giggling with him!" I could feel the heat of jealousy moving up my throat into my face. "What the hell is he doing, anyway?"

At the same time, Kevin moved closer, in between Eileen and Mike. Mike smiled and put his hand affectionately on Eileen's shoulder while he patronizingly hugged Kevin. Kevin pulled himself rather abruptly from Mike's grip, and moved closer to Eileen.

"I can't believe what I am seeing," I heard myself say to Mary.

Mary said in a reassuring voice, "I can't believe what *I'm* seein'. Why, I think you're jealous, Pat. Isn't he only helping us conniving women do the job we set out to do? Can't you see he's just playin' cupid? He's challengin' Kevin to show Eileen that he's her man!"

"Oh, is that it?" I answered. "I was wondering what was going on. I never saw Mike act quite like that."

As we looked over still trying not to be too obvious, Kevin pulled Eileen over towards himself, both of them leaving Mike out of the *menage a trois*. Mike excused himself and headed back towards us.

"And you two thought you were the only matchmakers among us," he beamed as he joined us. Nice corned beef, Mary," he added coolly.

"Nice going, Mike," I congratulated him. "Whatever you did seems to have worked."

"I kept thinking about what you said about my sister Peggy at my brother's wedding and I decided not to let an opportunity for eternal happiness pass your two potential lovebirds by." He smiled broadly.

"And every St. Patrick's Day they will remember it was me who got them together. So I'll get the credit."

"Or the blame," Mary said.

Kiss The Blarney Stone

"We haven't gone anywhere in weeks!" I lamented, as I sipped my breakfast orange juice.

"I think you're stretching it a bit on that one," Mike answered. "Why do you always have to exaggerate?"

"It's the Irish in me," I exclaimed proudly. "It's in my nature to embellish, to overstate. Haven't you ever heard of the gift of gab?"

"I've not only heard *of* it, I get to *hear it* every day!"

"Very funny," I said. "Then listen to this. I want to drive down to Blarney Castle. I just *have* to kiss the Blarney Stone! It's supposed to magically bestow eloquence to whoever kisses it."

"It doesn't seem to me as if you've ever had a problem talking! Do you really want to traipse all the way down to Cork and fight the hordes of tourists just to kiss a rock?"

"Now now, you two," Mary said, as she poured us a fresh cup of coffee. "Don't start. It's too early to bicker. Let's have a calm, peaceful breakfast." She headed for the stove where the frying pan was brimming with rashers and scrambled eggs.

"We're not bickering, Mary," I said. "We're discussing. We just happen to discuss more loudly than most. How can I be calm and peaceful when my husband won't let me go to Blarney?"

"Now Michael," Mary said. "Why would ya' not be wantin' to go to kiss the Stone? It's tradition. I thought you liked tradition."

"I do, I just hate fighting crowds to get to see tradition."

"Maybe if we go during the week, it wouldn't be so bad," I offered. "I'll call down there to see when their slow days are. Wednesday night we have no guests, so Wednesday afternoon or Thursday morning would be perfect."

"Why don't you just pretend I'm the Blarney Stone and give me a little kiss?" Mike chided.

I picked up the phone to call directory assistance. After connecting me to the Blarney Castle directly, a young woman's voice rattled off the hours on a recorded tape.

"I can't believe I'm telephoning a *real* castle," I said to Mike and Mary with my hand over the receiver. "And I can't believe I'm getting an answering machine."

At the end of the taped message, the voice suggested that if I needed any more information to stay on the line. Piped music began to play. It was a flute rendition of *Oh, Danny Boy*. After the second stanza, a real live voice answered and identified herself as Miss Brennan. When I asked which day was the slowest at Blarney Castle, she giggled and said, "You're gas! Every day is a madhouse here. Why are you in such a rush anyway? Blarney's worth a whole day. It's not just the stone yer after, is it? Blarney has some of the finest shops in Ireland."

"Is Wednesday any better than the week-end?" I asked.

"I can't be promisin' you anything, but, yes, week days are usually less mobbed."

"Thanks." I hung up, not wanting to hear any more about mobs of tourists. "She said Wednesdays are better than week-ends," I said, considering whether this was a white lie. "How about it?"

"Blarney's a beautiful little town, Michael," Mary encouraged. "I think you'd enjoy it."

"Well, with the two of you ganging up on me, what can I do?" Mike answered.

"Mike knows he'll never win an argument with me after I've kissed the stone," I said.

*　　*　　*　　*　　*

Wednesday morning, we took the N20 toward Cork through the rolling lower Shannon. To entertain ourselves along the way, I read from my travel books.

"Listen to this, Mike. It's a poem about the magical Blarney Stone written by a certain Father Prout in the 1830's.

There is a stone there, That whoever Kisses, Oh! He never misses, To grow eloquent. 'Tis he may clamber, To a lady's chamber, Or become a member, Of Parliament.

"That was written by a priest?" Mike asked. "A little suggestive, isn't it?"

"That's what it says."

"Why don't you give me a little history of Blarney?" Mike asked.

"Well, it was built in 1446 by Dermot McCarthy in a typical 15th century tower house style. This style refers to small castles or fortified residences built with a tall, square house surrounded by an enclosure, or stone wall for defense. It's walls are 85 feet high and 12 feet thick at the base."

"The origin of the actual Blarney Stone and its magical ability to confer eloquence dates from Queen Elizabeth's reign. She sent her Deputy to an Irish Chieftain, Cormac MacCarthy, who was Lord of Blarney at the time to secure his allegiance to the English crown. When the Deputy encountered MacCarthy, the Chieftain flattered, sweet-talked and charmed the Deputy into thinking he was giving his allegiance, while all the time he had no intention of giving up his sovereignty."

"What happened?" Mike asked.

"When the Deputy reported back to Queen Elizabeth what the silver tongued Chieftain had done, she became exasperated and enraged and is said to have exclaimed: *Blarney! Blarney! What he says he never means!*"

"So that's the first time an Irishman said one thing with his words and did another thing altogether?" Mike asked.

"Well, if it was the first, it wasn't the last," I said.

"It says here," I continued, "that the tradition of actually kissing the Blarney Stone didn't start until the 18th Century. It was then that a Scottish family, who built the Blarney Castle Estate adjacent to the castle, claimed the stone was part of the original Stone of Scone, the ancient place where Scottish kings were always crowned. Ever since that time, visitors from all over the world have come in droves to kiss the Blarney Stone."

"Sounds like the Scots had a little bit of blarney in them, too," Mike put in.

As we pulled into the tiny town of Blarney, Mike's fear of a mob scene was realized. Tourist buses and cars jammed the road which ran beside the town square in the center of the town. Next to the green stood the castle itself. Although it was mostly destroyed, what was left of it was impressive. Like many of the Irish Medieval ruins, it was not overly restored. It looked like it could have on the day that King William III ravished it.

"I'm sorry about the crowds," I offered, as he tried to maneuver the car around the throng of people.

"Never mind," he said. "Now that I know a little about it's history, *I'm* even interested in giving the stone a hug myself."

"Maybe you'll get the gift of gab, too."

"Now don't push it, Pat. There couldn't be two of us in the same household. Somebody has to listen!"

We parked the car, and worked our way past the quaint shops that lined the street, walking to the castle entrance. A slight, middle aged man with pointed features and thinning gray hair stood at the entry, taking money and handing out tickets.

"What's the wait like to get to the stone?" I asked him

"Oh, not too bad," he answered.

I wondered if this wasn't the blarney he was giving me. "How long, do you think?" I persisted.

"Not too long," he said, as he waved me along. "Enjoy yourselves."

Why was it so hard to get a straight answer in this country? It was the Irish blarney, again.

We took our places at the end of the line. The long string of people stretched before us, across the lush, green yard. The line then meandered up a crooked, narrow stone staircase and into an interior second story landing that overlooked a courtyard. Because half of the wall was broken down, we could see the line continue for twenty more feet until it disappeared behind another wall. From where we stood, we couldn't see The Stone, itself. There must have been 100 people waiting in front of us.

"The Castle is magnificent, isn't it?" Mike asked, trying to ignore the throng. "Can you imagine living in a place like this? A king and his castle. Isn't that all a man wants?" He then quickly turned to me. "I mean, besides his woman?" He put his arm around my shoulder and kissed me lightly on the cheek

"See?" I said. "It's already bestowing its magic on you. Would you look at the size of that tower?" I replied. "I hope we don't have to climb all the way up that to get to the stone! I'd be panicked. You know my fear of heights."

"Don't worry, I'll carry you if I have to," Mike assured me. "Now that we're here, you're going to kiss that stone."

The line inched forward.

After awhile, a white haired man in his fifties, dressed in the national uniform of tweed jacket and jeans, turned around to us. "Y'er Yanks, aren't yas?" He must have heard our accents.

"Why, yes we are," Mike answered, pleased for a conversation that might make the wait seem less long.

"This is the wife, Margaret, and I'm Tim," he said. His wife nodded shyly. "Is this your first trip to the Old Sod?"

Mike explained our situation of running the Bed and Breakfast and our dream of someday buying a place in Ireland to live out our retirement years.

"That's grand," Tim said. "Where have you looked, so far?"

"Oh, we haven't actually looked yet, but we're planning on it."

"Are you thinking about any particular area?" Tim asked.

"We love the West of Ireland. It's where our roots are, but we really don't know yet."

"Well, if I were an American looking for a place to retire, I'd buy the ocean view property over in Dingle that's for sale. It even has its own castle on it!"

"A real castle?" I asked. "You're kidding."

"Where is it?" Mike asked.

"It's outside the town of Lispole, County Dingle," Tim explained. "If you ask at the post office, they'll tell you how to get there. It's a beautiful piece of property. The entire parcel is on Dingle Bay. I'm surprised that nobody has bought it yet. I understand it's only in the two's."

"You mean two million dollars?" Mike asked, incredulously.

Tim laughed. "Oh, no, no. I meant two as in $200,000 U.S.

"That can't be," Mike said, as he looked at me for confirmation. His eyes grew as large as silver dollars. "We've got to go see it."

"This must be an omen," I said to Tim and his wife. "Several of our relatives are from Dingle."

"About how far would you say that is from here, Tim?" Mike asked.

"It's at least four hours from here, but it's only less than two from where you're living now," Tim replied, enthusiastically. "Why don't the two of you take a ride out there some day to look at it?"

"Maybe we will...a real castle, in Ireland, for $200,000.... It just sounds too good to be true...." Mike's voice trailed off.

For the next hour, the four of us discussed our favorite places in Ireland and they gave us some suggestions for new day trips they thought we would enjoy. Then we outlined an itinerary for a vacation to America, if and when they ever decided to visit. It made our hour wait fly by. All the while, however, I could tell Mike's thoughts were elsewhere. We were within reach of the Stone. We could see the line come to an abrupt end where several people were standing around and laughing.

Mike could see over the heads of the people in front of us. "It looks as if you have to lie down to get to the Stone."

"What?" I was astounded.

"It looks as if each person is taking a turn on their backs," he said, as he strained his neck to get a better look.

"No!"

"That's what it looks like."

As we got closer, we heard a young man making an announcement to those in line. "Ladies and gents. When it's your turn, we ask you to have a royal seat right here." He pointed to the limestone floor in front of him. "Then, all you need to do is lean backwards and grab onto the two handrails behind you. We will push you out over the ledge, and my partner Jimmy and I will hold onto your ankles to secure you in that position while you tilt your head back to kiss the Blarney Stone."

The crowd laughed and people grinned at each other.

I, on the other hand, saw nothing to smile or laugh at. I could see that the ledge hung out over an open space about two feet wide, that revealed a two-story drop beneath it. I could feel the blood rush from my face. My stomach churned.

"I can't do that, Mike," I whined.

"Of course you can," he answered. "Look at all of those old people in front of you. They're not having any problem with it, are they?"

"I feel sick," I argued. "I might get sick to my stomach or faint." I decided to appeal to his masculinity. "Besides, I'm wearing a skirt. I can't lay on my back and bend over backwards with this crowd around!"

"We're not leaving until you kiss that stone!"

I was starting to panic. "Mike, I can't do it. I'm completely panicked, sick! I can't."

Suddenly we were two people away from the Stone.

"I'm afraid. You can't make me do it! I'll die of fright!"

"Here," Mike said. "Take my sweater and tie it around your waist. That will protect your modesty. And, if it would make you feel more comfortable, I'll lay down next to you."

While I took the sweater and wrapped it around my hips, I answered haltingly, "I'd die of embarrassment if you did that."

"How about if I held your ankles instead of those two guys? You trust me, don't you?"

"Of course, I do.... Maybe I could do it, if I knew *you* were holding me and keeping me from falling two stories." My panic started to dissipate. "Okay, let's try it."

I stepped up to the royal seat and Mike conferred with the two attendants. He gave me the thumbs up sign and I sat down on the ledge. The two young men stood on either side of me, while Mike gripped me by the ankles. I leaned back and they pulled me by my arms over to the edge and guided my hands until I grabbed the bars, the only thing that separated me from the sheer, twenty-foot drop. Reeling with vertigo, I closed my eyes and tilted my head back and smacked the stone with a kiss. I had done it!

Then Mike pulled me back toward him by my ankles. I jumped up slightly faint with glee, and grabbed him by the neck. "I did it! I've kissed the Blarney Stone!"

The crowd clapped and one of the attendants held his hands up to quiet the crowd.

"Ladies and gentlemen, let's give another round of applause for this deserving, brave man."

"He's the first husband we've ever seen, who actually *held onto* his wife's ankles!" The other attendant nodded in agreement.

Mike took his turn kissing the stone, and then stood up extending his arms in a two-fisted victory salute above his head. I wondered if he wasn't a little frightened by the experience himself. He turned to me grinning from ear to ear. When the applause died down, he took my hand and led me down the crooked, narrow castle staircase.

"Do you think the staircase in our castle in Dingle will be as steep as this one?" he asked.

"If it even has a staircase," I answered. Now that I had kissed the genuine Blarney Stone, I could easily humor his hopelessly romantic side. "When do you want to go look at it?"

"How about tomorrow?"

"Tomorrow?" I said dizzily. I felt suddenly transported, as we said our good-byes to Tim and his wife and as Mike led me away, I considered the magic of the Stone.... was it real? I surely wasn't the same. Neither was Mike. Now, he wanted to chase after some castle and what was more incredible, now I wanted to chase after it, too.

The Ring of Dingle

With no houseguests staying the night, we were able to start our search for the castle at the crack of dawn. Mike figured if we made decent time, we could get to the Ring of Dingle and find our dream castle in less than two hours. We brought coffee along in a thermal mug to keep us warm on the way.

"What's the number of the road we're looking for once we get to Tralee?" Mike asked.

I took the map out of the glove compartment, and unfolded it to the area detailing County Kerry. "It looks as if there are actually two ways of getting there. One looks like the more direct way through Inch and Anascaul, and the other way goes via the Connor Pass and through the town of Dingle itself. The second way looks a little longer, but it also promises to be more scenic." We had a long-standing pact that when sightseeing by car, we would take the most scenic way there and the fastest way home.

"Let's take the Connor Pass through Dingle," Mike said, sticking with our pact. I showed him the map. "Look at this. It looks like the Dingle peninsula is the most westerly point in Ireland."

"And aren't the Blasket Islands off the tip of it?" Mike asked. He knew his geography.

"Yes, here they are." I showed him their location on the map. "What's important about the Blasket Islands?"

"I remember reading about a native group of Gaelic speaking inhabitants who were forced to move to the mainland in the 1950's because there weren't enough people left on the island to sustain themselves."

I looked at the map and traced the thin, gray, squiggled line with my finger, which ran parallel to the Dingle coast. We knew gray lines meant challenging roads in Ireland.

"What else is over on the coast to see?" he asked, peering over my shoulder at the map. "Maybe after we close the deal on our castle, we'll still have time to do a little tour before we go home."

"Why can't we do it all? We have all day, don't we? Will you be hungry by the time we get to Dingle? It's a fishing village. Maybe we could find a good fish and chips place with fresh mussels." The Irish knew how to prepare mussels, with thick cream and a hint of garlic, not like the French version which ruined the texture of the mussels by over cooking them in a thin, watery wine broth or the Italian version which smothered the natural sweetness of the moules with a thick tomato sauce.

"Mmmm, that sounds heavenly," Mike groaned.

"After lunch, we can head for the post office in Lispole, and get the scoop on the castle."

Good game plan," Mike agreed. "I just hope nobody buys the castle while we're eating our lunch."

We traveled down the Connor Pass, the highest mountain pass in Ireland. The narrow, two lane road curved and zigzagged upward for about five miles. There was a sheer drop on the right side of the road, and I closed my eyes when we came upon a treacherous turn. Each time I mustered up the courage to uncover my eyes, a fantastic, new vista appeared before us.

"This is breathtaking!" Mike exclaimed.

"You're right about that. I've been holding my breath for the last mile!"

It wasn't long before we pulled into the small, quaint fishing village of Dingle. Brightly painted two story houses propped each other up on the left side of the road. Hand engraved wooden signs hung from their second story windowsills, distinguishing one from the other as a restaurant, a pub, or a shop. They all overlooked a working fishing port, with a long, wide concrete platform jutting out into the estuary that served as both a

pier and parking lot. Fishing boats were being loaded and unloaded by
burley young men dressed in thick down jackets, despite the mild 60-
degree temperature. They all wore knit caps pulled down over their ears.

A banner stretched some twenty feet across a ramp, which descended
from the pier to an oversized fishing trawler. It read: *Boat Rides to See
Fungie.*

"Let's park here and walk up the street to find some pub grub," Mike
said. "With all these fishing boats around, there must be some great fish
restaurants."

We parked the car and made our way up a narrow one-lane road. It
meandered upward until it forked into two more narrow, winding lanes.

"This couldn't be any more charming," I said. "It looks like an authentic
pirate cove."

"It's great how they have preserved these old buildings," he said, as he
started over to a restaurant to read its menu taped in the window. "This
could be our place. They have mussels, salmon and sea bass. What do
you think?"

"Let's give it a try."

When we walked to the doorway, we were greeted by a set of steep stairs
to a second story. So up we went to where a cheerful, dark-haired young
woman with a sprinkling of freckles across her cheeks said hello to us and
took us over to a cozy booth by the window.

"Isn't this grand?" I said to her. "All this and a view, too. Just what we
were looking for."

The hostess smiled. "How long are yas here for?"

"A year or more, we hope," Mike said, as he slid into the booth, allowing
me to have the window seat. In fact, we're house hunting at the moment."

"The housing prices around here are quite dear," she said. "There are
all kinds of building restrictions controlled by the state." She handed us
two laminated menus cut out in the shape of a pirate's hat.

The backside of the menu described Dingle as a fourteenth century historical port which eventually evolved into a pirate town, a center for

smuggling and bootlegging. Dingle had, it said, become so prosperous from buccaneering that at one time it had minted its own coins. After reading the front and backside of the menu, a young woman returned to our table and took our orders. We each had chosen the mussels. Mike ordered the traditional Irish type with cream, and I ordered the house specialty, baked mussels in Parmesan cheese.

It seemed like only minutes when she brought us two steaming bowls of the savory seafood.

"Miss," Mike asked as she set the mussels on the table, "would you happen to know about a castle that's up for sale around here?" He dipped a slice of homemade dark bread into his cream sauce. "I understand it's near Lispole, here in Dingle."

"I'm afraid I don't know a thing about a castle for sale, sir," she said. "But there is a well-known 15th century castle out on Smerwick Harbour. It's where the soldier-poet Piaras Ferriter, the last Irish chief, held out against Oliver Cromwell's army. Right near there is another point of interest, *Dun an Oir*, or Fort of Gold, where 600 Irish and Spanish soldiers were massacred after surrendering to the English in 1580."

"You know your history," I said, marveling at how the Irish locals were always knowledgeable of the historic landmarks which were in their backyards. "Is there anything else we should see?"

"Oh, you must see Fungie," she answered enthusiastically. "That's indeed a rare treat."

"I saw the sign down by the pier," I answered. "Who or what is Fungie?"

The waitress threw her head back and giggled. She then quickly covered her mouth with her hand. "Oh, beg your pardon. Mind you, I'm not laughing at you. You see, Fungie is a Dolphin, kind of our Dingle mascot. He's out in the water somewhere and the fishing crews make a little extra money by hauling tourists out into the Bay of Dingle to get a glimpse of 'im frolickin' in the water."

"I see," I replied. "Has anybody ever really seen this Fungie?"

"Well, actually, the kids are the ones who report most of the Fungie sightings. Most of the others are just out there for the joy ride, you know, those incurable romantics who are searching for something they'll never find. You can have a look yourselves, it's only five pounds a trip!"

"Sounds like fun," I said, although taking a boat trip in search of a dolphin seemed a bit frivolous with all we had to do that day.

"Of course, you are planning on taking the coastal road tour," the waitress said. Everyone who comes to Dingle takes it. There is a heritage center overlooking the Blasket Islands, and several ancient ruins to see along the way, not to mention the unparalleled views. Besides archeological remains, the Dingle coastal road has some of the most spectacular scenery in all of Ireland."

My eyes lit up at her mention of archeological remains. I turned to Mike and gushed, "Ancient ruins! Your favorites!" I fibbed, knowing full well they were, in reality, *my* favorites. "They might be worth seeing if we have any time."

"We'll make the time."

After devouring the best mussels we had ever tasted in our lives, we left the pirate restaurant and headed back to the car. Mike took out the map, and after perusing it for awhile, said, "If we drive the Dingle coastal road now, we won't be backtracking to get home."

"You mean take the coastal road *before* we check out the castle?" I asked, incredulously.

"It's been there for several centuries already," he answered. "I'm sure it's not going anywhere in the next hour or so. We can't pass up some archeological sights."

"You're the best," I said, as I hugged him.

"Remember that, when I ask you for the money for the down payment on my castle," he joked back.

We headed out of Dingle Harbor and traveled along the R559 through the rugged terrain. Sheep were grazing everywhere. They munched lazily on the green wild grasses along the slopes, on the sides of the road, and sometimes *in* the road. Several times we had to slow the car down to a crawl in order to inch around the black-faced shaggy-haired creatures. We made our way up the two-lane road until we were stopped by two teenaged boys walking behind a small herd of sheep. Two black and white border collies nudged the sheep in front of them. One of the boys looked back over his shoulder, saw us, and then yelled at the procession of sheep filing ten abreast in front of them.

At the sound of his voice, the dogs bit at the ankles of the last row of sheep and ran back and forth in a frenzy, urging the pack to hurry along by pushing their noses into their charge's hindquarters. When there wasn't an immediate response from the lethargic lambs, the dogs began to bark impatiently. The bewildered animals suddenly leaped forward, and because there was nowhere for them to go, they jumped onto the backs of those in front of them in an attempt to move ahead. This caused a chain reaction collision as sheep piled on top of each other until they were stacked three high.

Worried that we were causing the sheep unnecessary anguish, Mike stopped the car until the boys guided the herd off the road and into an enclosed pasture. The teenage shepherds then waved their arms above their heads without looking back, signaling us to proceed.

"Roll down the window, and ask if they know where the sights are," Mike suggested. "They must know everything around here, maybe they know where that castle is."

I called out to the boys. "Could you tell us where the archeological sights are?"

One of the boys, who turned to answer us, patted his border collie on the head. "Sure, just stay on the road, there are loads of them. There are marker signs. You can't miss them."

"Famous last words," Mike whispered under his breath to me.

"Thanks," I said. And then, trying to keep Mike happy, added, "Do you happen to know where there's a castle for sale around here?"

The two teenagers looked blankly at each other and then shrugged.

"You'll be seein' a lot of ruins here in Dingle, but I'm afraid you won't be seein' any castles for sale, that's for sure. At least, not any castles you Yanks would be interested in," the other lad added. "Unless you'd be lookin' for a more modest one." He gestured toward a gray, weathered, ramshackle barn with rubble for walls. "It even has air-conditionin'. I could sell it to yas for cheap." He chuckled at his own joke.

"Charming," Mike said. "But we were really looking for something with some walls and a roof." Then we both laughed at the suggestion that we were actually contemplating buying a castle. We thanked the young lads and drove on. Less than a mile up the road, we came to our first sign. Printed neatly on a black, wooden plaque were the words *Gallarus Oratory.* The sign stood next to a gravel driveway which seemed to lead to nowhere.

We pulled into the drive which widened into a makeshift car park. Not a single car was there. Next to the car park was a one-room stone cottage. We parked, and then stepped tentatively through the doorway of the cottage, which appeared completely dark inside. As we entered the cold, damp room, we found that it was empty except for a few postcard stands and a little table and a chair near the entrance. A thin, tapered candle stood on a paper plate at the edge of the table. From the chair, an old man with a weathered face peered up at us through half-moon glasses. He was reading a wilted newspaper in the dim candlelight.

I folded my arms across my chest to try to stir up some body warmth within me. It was hard to believe this fragile old man could sit there in this dark, dank place reading a newspaper with no heat or light as if he were in a snug, comfortable drawing room.

"May I help ye?" he asked with a strong accent.

"We're looking for the ruins," I said. I rubbed my hands up and down my freezing arms. I decided not to bother the man with inquiries about the castle.

"Here are a couple of brochures for ye, half a pound each, if you please. Now you can give yourselves a self-guided tour." He held out two faded brochures to us.

"Mike took the brochures from the old man. "We didn't see the ruins when we pulled in the drive. Where are they?"

"Just follow the footpath," he answered, and turned back to read his soggy tabloid.

We stepped out into the daylight and started down the path. The foot-path led from the gravel driveway and eventually turned into wild grass within a few yards. The cold, dewy grass quickly seeped through my shoes, and I felt a chill run down my spine. We followed the path until it curved into a low, stacked stone wall which enclosed a strange looking structure, its peculiar shape and odd size were reminiscent of an upturned boat.

"The Gallarus Oratory," Mike read from the brochure, "dates from between the 6th and 9th centuries, and is the best-preserved example of early Christian architecture in Ireland."

"It's so small, I can't picture people using it as a church," I said. "How big do you think it is? It can't be more than 10x15 feet!"

"It says here that it was an oratory, a small chapel, which were com-monplace in Middle Age monastic complexes."

There was one small window on one side of it and another, larger open-ing on the other side which might once have been a door. We walked inside.

"The interior of the Oratory," Mike read on, "is a perfect example of corbeled vaulting, a system whereby stones are stacked closer and closer together until they form a peak at the middle of the ceiling."

We walked around in circles in the small stone room, and as we turned our faces upward to admire the corbeled ceiling, we almost ran into each other.

Mike continued to read. "This system, invented in Neolithic times, has kept the Oratory waterproof for the last 1400 years."

"Gee, that's pretty amazing," I said. "Our farmhouse is less than 100 years old, and parts of its ceiling have been leaking since we moved in." Another shiver went through me. I clutched my arms to my body. "It may be waterproof, but it isn't damp proof," I said. "I'm freezing! Let's go on to our next site."

"Come on, we'll get you warm in the car," Mike said, as he put his arm around me to warm me up. "The next stop is another monastic sight, and after that is the Blasket Center which explains the history of the Blasket Islands."

A couple of miles up the road, we came to another signpost, inscribed, *An Riasc.*

Again, there was nobody around. We pulled the car up next to a small shed, no bigger than the size of a newspaper stand, which stood at the side of the road. A small piece of paper with a penned message was tacked onto the side of it which read: *Will be back shortly, please place entry contribution of two pounds in bowl.*

"How trusting they are," Mike said. He tossed four coins into the bowl, and opened the brochure. "It says that this monastic settlement dates from the seventh century. There are the remains of an oratory, several Early Christian crosses and an inscribed pillar stone. The pillar stone dates from the sixth century and marks the transition between pagan Ireland and Christian Ireland. Pillar stones were precursors of the High Crosses of Ireland. The High Crosses came into being between the eighth and twelfth centuries, the Golden Age of Ireland, the period when Ireland's monasteries kept language and learning alive while Europe fell into the Dark Ages."

"It's hard to imagine what it would have looked like," I said, as I looked from one stone to another trying to piece it all together. "It's even harder to imagine a dozen diligent monks slaving over their manuscripts, in such damp, tiny rooms." Another shiver went through me, which reminded me that now my shoes were totally soaked.

"Why not?" Mike asked. "It's couldn't have been much different than the conditions for the old man back at the Gallarus Oratory."

We walked over toward the pillar stone, which stood almost as tall as I was and appeared to grow gracefully from the rocky soil beneath it. It was covered with line engravings in the shapes of delicate whorls. There seemed to be an impression of a cross running through it.

"The engraved patterns on this and other pillar stones can be found throughout Ireland, England and Europe where other Celtic monasteries once thrived," Mike read. "Apparently, nobody so far has deciphered these Celtic designs, but it has been suggested that they were an early attempt at writing." I brushed my fingertips across the engravings.

Finally, we left the ruins, and as we drove along the coastal road we could see an occasional glimpse of the sea. By the time we reached Glogher Head, we had a majestic view of the Blasket Islands. They appeared as two gigantic amphibians floating serenely in the Atlantic Ocean.

"Could that be the Heritage Center?" I pointed at a low-slung, modern edifice. "It looks more like a factory of some kind, or an unfinished building."

The building looked like it could have easily covered one square city block. It's one-story, flat, horizontal lines and its lackluster cement construction made the structure look curiously out of place, nestled in the shallow valley, with the blue ocean and the islands as a backdrop.

"I have to say, that is undoubtedly the ugliest building I have ever seen," I said. Then, trying to give the architect the benefit of the doubt, I tried to analyze it, to guess what the architect was thinking when he designed the block-like building. "Perhaps the architect was attempting a primitive look mimicking the simplicity of the surrounding megaliths, or a *less is more* Bauhaus style. Maybe he was going for a Brancusi poured-concrete design. But that doesn't explain why he would place this concrete behemoth in the middle of this idyllic setting."

"Looks like a popular attraction with the tourists," Mike said sarcastically. He turned the car into the building's immense parking lot. Only a few cars were parked there.

"There's the sign. This *is* the Blasket Center, after all."

When we walked in, we noticed a large cafeteria on the left and a reception counter in front flanked by the ever-ubiquitous post card racks. Three teenagers, two young ladies and a young man, all dressed in blue smocks with name tags, stood around the counter giggling and chatting. We approached them and as I excused myself for interrupting, I noticed that they were all talking simultaneously, and curiously enough, they were all speaking Gaelic.

"Are you interested in seeing a short video show?" one of the young ladies asked. "Or would you rather walk around yourselves and read the poster boards explaining the literature, language and way of life of the Blasket Islands? We can start the film anytime you want. It's only fifteen minutes long." The cadence of her Gaelic accent made it sound as if she were singing the words.

"We'll just take a look around, first, if you don't mind," Mike said. Our pact was that we would never allow a video to *show* us what we could see for ourselves. Why choose to watch a video which *explains* the experience when you were actually there experiencing it yourself?

"Just let us know when yas want us to start up the film," the girl responded. She turned back to the others and they all started speaking in Gaelic again.

We walked past the reception counter and headed down a long windowless corridor lined with large boards with printed material in two languages, one in English, the other in Gaelic. I wondered why a cultural center, situated on the ocean shore, would have any interior spaces that were windowless. The placards displayed maps and materials which demonstrated that the Dingle peninsula was home to a large population of Irish speaking people. The boards also explained that this center was instrumental in educating tourists about the Gaeltacht, the Gaelic speaking areas of Ireland, and the Gaeltacht's importance in preserving the Irish language.

When we got to the end of the stark corridor, we came upon a small glass-enclosed room with several benches. The windows looked out upon the Blasket Islands and the rolling hillsides which sloped down to the sea. Without speaking, we sat down to take in the spectacular view. Several minutes passed. It was inspiring, almost haunting. For a moment I felt I was being magically transported back to Ireland's Golden Age.

Mike interrupted the silence. "Should we ask to see the video?"

"I don't think so," I responded.

"Agreed," he answered. We both sat silently for several more minutes and looked out at the peaceful, panoramic view. I was starting to appreciate the architect's purpose in choosing his unique design for the center.

"Well," I said, as I got up from the bench. "Are you ready to go find that castle of yours?"

Castle For Sale

We continued along the coastal road, which formed a loop back through Dingle and into Anascaul. The town consisted of no more than a gas station, a convenience store, a pub and the post office. We inquired in the post office as to the whereabouts of the castle for sale, and a short, plump, middle aged woman with bright red cropped hair responded with enthusiasm.

"Oh, you're looking for the Minard Castle," she said, excitedly. "It's right there up the road. You're in good company with the likes of Paul Neuman and Tony O'Reilly. They both bought castles in Ireland. Paul Neuman turned his into a summer camp for kids with cancer. We're all hoping another rich Yank like yourselves will buy it."

"What makes you think we're rich?" Mike asked

"Why, anybody looking to buy a castle must be," she chirped.

"Believe me, we're not," I said, "We just wanted to look at it." I had read about Paul Neuman's Hole In The Wall Gang, but I had never heard of Tony O'Reilly before. "Who's Tony O'Reilly?" I asked.

"He's the philanthropist and chairman of Heinz catsup," she explained, seemingly surprised that we had to ask. "He's Irish born, made his fortune in America, and bought himself a castle here. He never forgot his roots! You can get to the Minard castle by taking a right at the next road and following it down to the water. If you need any information about the realtor whose handling the deal, ask at the pub in town. She has all the information about it."

Mike was so grateful for this information about his dream castle that he reached into his pants pocket and pulled out a five-pound note. He handed it to the affable postal worker and thanked her for the information.

She pushed it away and acted as if she were shocked at the notion of being paid for a favor. "Don't be insultin' me," she said, rather sternly, and pushed his hand away. Then she broke out in a smile. "Save your money for the castle purchase. You'll be needin' it."

We left the post office, following her directions, but quickly found ourselves lost in a myriad of narrow lanes punctuated by small farmhouses. The roads meandered up and down and back and forth until we were convinced that we were turned around and heading away from the water. Just as it was starting to look hopeless, we stopped a young boy who was walking along the lane with a large mangy dog.

"Hey son, can you tell us how to get to Minard Castle?" Mike asked.

"The shortest way?" he responded.

Mike hesitated for a second, trying to figure out if the boy was being a smart aleck. Before Mike got a chance to answer, the lad waved in the direction in which we were heading. "Just keep right on the way you're going. You'll know when to stop when you fall into Dingle Bay."

"Thanks," Mike called back to him, as he shifted the car into gear. "Castle Minard, here we come!"

"I'm so excited, I can't stand it," I said. With that, we drove over a slight incline in the road. As we came down on the other side, the castle magically appeared before us.

"Yeow!" Mike gasped at the sight in front of our eyes. "Look!" He suddenly hit the brakes. "I want it! We have to have it!" he said.

"Spoken like a true Yank, all right," I said, trying to contain my excitement.

The castle sat majestically on a bluff overlooking the bay. Its crumbling, black walls contrasted with the shimmering blue water behind it. The water was unusually still and its glassy surface was edged by a long pebble beach which stretched out on the shore in either direction. The castle faced out across the water to the coast of the Iveragh peninsula, known to most as the Ring of Kerry. Surrounding the castle were acres of rolling pastures.

"I wonder how much acreage is included in the price," Mike said, wistfully as he gazed out our windshield at the magnificent sight. "I'll bet there's got to be a hundred acres of empty land around it." His voice rose. "This is fantastic, beyond my wildest dreams!"

He drove the car up to Minard Castle. We scrambled out of the car and raced each other up the grassy hill leading up to it. Once we scaled the slope, we stopped, breathless. We looked up at what was left of three standing walls. One of the walls had several crumbling openings which we assumed had once been windows. The fourth wall was completely demolished. There was nothing left that resembled a roof.

"Well, it certainly has potential," Mike said, trying to sound optimistic.

"I wonder how you could heat such a monstrosity," I said. Then I stopped. I didn't want to say anything that would dampen his exuberance.

"I'm sure that all can be worked out," Mike answered. He was enraptured. "Now, my princess, let me carry you into the castle I've always promised you." With that, he picked me up and carried me in his arms across a make-believe threshold. He set me down in what we assumed to be the foyer. We both looked up at the open sky.

"We can keep the remaining walls exactly as they are," Mike said, his head spinning with images of architectural plans. "It's lucky the place is so open. That will make it easier to create a two-story foyer right there where you are standing. We'll put a grand staircase in it, so you can sashay down it to greet me every night when I come home." He gestured toward the blue sky which hovered above us. "That is, after we get a roof on the whole darned thing. I think it would be great if we could preserve as much of the original structure as we can. We want to keep the castle's architectural integrity."

"I'm sure it could be wonderful," I said doubting what I was saying. "Of course, it would take quite a long time to restore...."

"However long, it will be well worth it," Mike said determined. If it ends up taking several years of restoration, we could build a small cottage to live in on the grounds and pay for the mortgage by charging people to take a look at the castle and its restoration. Now, we'd better hurry up and find the real estate agent at the pub, before somebody buys our dream castle out from under us!"

We quickly ran back to the car. Mike threw the car into gear and, in his excitement, made a sharp U-turn in the middle of the narrow lane nearly causing the car to capsize.

"Try to settle down," I said, as calmly as I could. "You know the old adage that if it looks too good to be true, it probably is. Anyway, how in the world do you think we're going to be able to buy it, anyway?"

"When did money ever stop us before? It's my dream castle! If we can figure out a way, we'll buy it! Maybe we could get a group of investors...."

He sped down the lane and back into town. When we walked into the pub, there were two elderly men casually sitting at the bar talking to a middle-aged woman behind it. She had a bit of dignity in her manner, maybe it was her arrow straight posture and neatly coifed blonde hair pulled up off of her slender white neck and wound up in a sophisticated twist.

"Hello!" Mike said eagerly to her, approaching the bar. "We heard at the post office that you had all the information about Minard castle."

"I do," the woman answered simply.

Mike was so anxious, he was about to burst. "Well? Let's have it."

The bartender gestured for us to take a seat at the bar. "Maybe you two should take a load off your feet first. What's your hurry?"

We sat down and without asking us what we wanted, she poured us two Irish whiskeys straight up. "Now before yas get yerselves all worked up, let me tell you a little bit about Minard Castle," she said. The two patrons leaned forward on their stools to hear what she was about to say.

"The Minard Castle," she started, " was built in the early 16th century and was the stronghold of the Knights of Kerry until Cromwellian troops destroyed it in 1650."

"We know all about its history," Mike interrupted her. "That's why we're interested in it. We'd love to be the ones to buy it and rebuild it to spite Oliver Cromwell himself. The castle *is* for sale, isn't it?" He was getting more anxious.

"Yes, the Minard Castle is, indeed, for sale," she answered quickly, "but unless you're a millionaire, I'm afraid you're not going to be able to purchase it.

"Why not?" Mike asked. "I thought they were only asking in the $200,000 dollar range."

She wiped the top of the bar with a white towel while she continued to explain. "The conservationists have made it impossible for an ordinary individual like yourself to buy it. The laws which have been enacted to preserve the historical monuments in Ireland contain strict regulations whereby the property cannot be changed, altered or enhanced unless it is restored to its original state." She said it, as if she had explained this many times before. "You saw it, didn't you? Do you have any idea how much money it would take to rebuild that castle?"

"I have no idea, but I'd love to find out," Mike said, refusing to be discouraged. "Where there's a will, there's a way."

"Now, remember," she continued, "you'd have to restore it to its original shape, before the Cromwell troops ravaged it. And no other structures can go on that property, either."

"You mean we couldn't build a small house or anything else on the land around it?" Mike's voice cracked.

"Heavens, no," she explained. "There'd be hundreds of condos on the land, if that were allowed. It's priceless waterfront property. And, I can tell you for a fact, the last potential buyer who looked into it and decided against it happened to be a multimillionaire."

"What happened?" Mike asked, his face starting to fall.

"Why, he wound up throwing the towel in on the whole deal." She tossed the bar towel on the liquor cabinet behind her for emphasis.

"You mean even he couldn't afford it?"

She nodded. "I'm afraid so. It was too bad. He was a nice fella and he was totally taken with the castle. He would have restored it with love. But finally, after months of checking into it, and several estimates from engineers and architects, he learned that even he couldn't afford to rebuild Minard Castle."

Mike looked down into his empty glass. "Maybe we should have stayed in Dingle and searched for Fungie, instead of chasing castles," he said deflated.

I silently rubbed his shoulder with my hand, trying to revive him back to his usual cheerful disposition. He seemed inconsolable.

"Tell me this," he said to the bartender. "Just how many incurable romantics like us have come in here asking about that castle, anyway?"

"Well, *more* and *less* than you'd think," she responded, glibly.

Typical. They just couldn't give you a straight answer. But, somehow, the ambivalent response seemed to mollify Mike's bitter disappointment.

The two elderly patrons, who had listened in on our entire conversation, looked self-consciously at their drink glasses which were also as empty as Mike's. Suddenly, one of them spoke up, looking down the bar to Mike. "Come on Yank," he said. "This round's on me! Let's have a drink to all of the incurable romantics of the world. And never forget, you're lucky to be counted among us!"

Us, I thought. *The magical, inclusive pronoun.* It seemed that it was more than Mike who was disappointed we weren't going to be able to grasp the castle of our dreams.

The bartender then poured us another round, and we all lifted our glasses to castles in the air.

Gaelic Revival

"Watch this," Kevin said, then winked at Mike who was sitting on the sofa beside him. "Mary, dear, would ya be a darlin' and bring Mike and me a couple of lagers? The game is just about to start." He kicked his shoes off and put his feet up on the overstuffed ottoman that separated the two of them from the television.

"What's wrong with the two good pins God gave ya?" Mary yelled back from the kitchen. "What are ya, paralyzed altogether?"

"Oh, come on, Mary, wait on us a bit," Kevin pleaded. "Mike and I are just too comfy sittin' here to get up, and we don't want to miss anything."

"You do know how to get a rise out of her," Mike whispered to Kevin.

Kevin whispered back. "She'll bring them, don't worry. She just needs a little nudge."

Mary bustled into the room with two opened beers in her one hand and two clean glasses in the other. "I'll get the first one for yas, but don't expect me to be bringing them all afternoon. I'm not yer slave, mind you. If it weren't for Miss Eileen coming over to join us, I wouldn't be so nice. Don't forget to use the coasters, there on the sideboard. When is Eileen gettin' here? You'll not be orderin' her around to get your lagers, I'll bet."

"You're surely a darlin' to me," Kevin cooed as he took the beers from her. He handed one of them and a glass to Mike, who now had his feet crossed and resting on top of the ottoman. "Don't worry, I'll be the one waitin' on everyone when she gets here. That would be any time now. She said she'd stop by after her tutoring session."

"That woman never stops. What is she doing tutoring on her day off?" Mary asked.

Kevin beamed with pride. "She loves to teach. Today she's tutoring an adult class in Gaelic."

"Didn't they have enough years of Gaelic in school?" Mary asked. "What would they want with learnin' the Gaelic now?"

"They want to speak it, use it in their everyday conversation," Kevin explained. "They've all had it in school, sure enough, but now they want to use it, speak it. The class is mostly conversation. Eileen's an excellent teacher. I'm sure she'll have them talkin' Irish as soon as possible."

A commercial interrupted the game and Mike took the remote control and tried to find something on another channel. There were only two others. He clicked to the next channel. A beautiful brunette was standing in front of a map of Ireland. She pointed to several gray rain clouds that were positioned on different areas of the map. She spoke in Gaelic.

Mike quipped, "Well, I don't know any Gaelic, but it's not difficult to understand that she's saying we're in for some more showers for the next couple of days. It's got to be the easiest job in Ireland, being a weather forecaster. *Rain, light rain, chance of rain, and drizzle.* That's all they ever say, every day. Geez, even I could be a meteorologist in Ireland!"

"First you'd have to learn the Gaelic yourself," Mary said.

"That couldn't be too hard," Mike answered. "All I'd have to learn would be four expressions: *rain, showers, mist and drizzle.* Hey, Kev, do you think Eileen could teach me four words in Gaelic?"

"You'll not be takin' any tutoring lessons from my Eileen," Kevin said bluntly.

"Why?" Mike asked.

"I just wouldn't have it, that's all," Kevin said.

"Why?" Mary asked. "Mike's a smart guy, he'd probably pick up the Gaelic in no time flat."

"I wouldn't want her to be findin' out just how smart he is," Kevin said.

"Keveen! You're not tellin' us your jealous of Mike, now are ya?" Mary exclaimed.

"Well, no," Kevin stammered. "I just don't like the idea of it, that's all."

Mike tried to change the subject. "Now, Kevin and Mary, can either one of you understand what this young lady is saying to us in Gaelic?"

"Well," Mary explained, "like you said, Mike, she's tryin' to tell us there's rain in the forecast."

"Ha!" Mike said. "See what I mean? Maybe I do know some Gaelic, after all."

Mike patted Kevin on the knee. "Ya see, Kev, I won't be needing those lessons, anyway. Don't you be worrying about Eileen."

"I *am* starting to worry about her. She should have been here by now. I knew I should have picked her up myself." Kevin got up off the sofa to look out the window.

Mike clicked the remote control to the next channel. This time a beautiful blue-eyed blonde gazed out from the picture tube, reciting the latest news items in Gaelic.

"I can't believe this country," Mike said. "You only have three stations, and two of them are in Gaelic! I don't get it. I didn't think most Irish spoke or understood Gaelic. Why is that?"

"Well," Mary explained, "there are only two official Irish channels, channel RTE and Raidio na Gaeltachta. This situation has been hotly debated for years. Now, out of the two, one is entirely in Gaelic. The other has a combination of Gaelic chat shows, game shows, and other locally produced shows. The other channel, Sky television, is the one you're watching now. That broadcasts mostly sports, so we only have three. If you get a fancy satellite dish, you can get four more British stations, but we don't have that."

"But why do they broadcast in Gaelic, if nobody speaks it or understands a word of it?" Mike asked.

"Ya see, Mike," Mary said, "a quarter of the population do consider themselves Irish-speaking. We all took Gaelic in school, where it's mandatory. When the Irish Free State was established, in 1922, Gaelic was designated the national language. All government legislation is written in English but Irish Gaelic is required for entry into the National University."

"So you can understand everything that woman is saying?" Mike asked, gesturing to the news reporter.

"Well, she is speakin' a bit fast," Kevin answered for Mary.

"See?" Mike persisted in his argument. "Neither of you can understand what she is saying. You've both said you've taken Gaelic in school and you both understand as little as I do. I don't get it."

"Maybe Eileen can explain it to ya," Mary said. "I think that's her comin' now."

Mary jumped up to let Eileen in and Mike clicked the remote control back to the game.

"Now Kev, forget the Gaelic language for a minute," Mike said. "Can you explain Gaelic football to me? That, I'm sure, I can figure out."

"I'll try," Kevin responded, as he got up from the couch to greet Eileen who followed Mary into the parlor. "You look lovely, dear," Kevin gushed. "And not a minute too soon, as we need a Gaelic scholar to teach the Irish to Mike over here."

Eileen came into the parlor, looking radiant.

"Hello, Mike," Eileen said, as she held out her hand. She had the grace of a princess.

When Mike took her hand, he didn't know whether to kiss or shake it. With Kevin's new jealous attitude, he decided it would be best if he just shook her hand.

Mike said, upon releasing her hand, "Kevin and Mary have been trying to explain to me why the Irish have mostly Gaelic programs on television, even though it isn't spoken or understood by most of them."

Eileen daintily removed her gloves and took a place on the sofa next to Kevin.

"Oh, it doesn't take a Gaelic scholar to figure that out," she said. "My Kevin knows a bit of Gaelic." She patted him on his arm.

Kevin gazed at his precious Eileen as he put his arm around her shoulder. "Now, darlin', I was just bragging about what a great teacher you were, so now will ya give Mike the answers to all of his questions about the Gaelic?"

"Well, Michael," she said demurely. "Surely, you have heard the expression, *a people without a language is a people without a heart.*"

"I have," Mike replied.

"The Irish have been trying to reclaim their true language, the one that our Celtic ancestors brought to Ireland in the fourth millennium before Christ." Her voice was so sweet and gentle, so melodious, that Mike almost lost what she was saying while listening to her lyrical words.

"That would be Gaelic?" he asked.

"That would be Gaelic," Eileen repeated. "The same pure Gaelic that survived essentially untouched by any other language until the sixteenth century. Up until then, virtually the entire population spoke Irish except for a few areas within the Pale, the English controlled parts around Dublin."

"I didn't know that." Mike sat spellbound by Eileen's manner and precise diction.

"What happened?"

"The Plantation system of planting Scots and English on Irish soil. Then Cromwell's invasion in 1649 and the anti-Catholic penal laws of the early 18th century. These three things led to the imposition of English as the primary language in Ireland. Once the Great Famine caused the mass migration of Gaelic-speaking people, our country was left with less than a quarter of its people speaking their native tongue."

"So with all of this teaching of Gaelic, the numbers haven't changed in the last century?" Mike asked. "That's incredible! Why is that, Eileen?"

"It's very complicated, Michael. You see, there have been a number of attempts to revive Gaelic over the past two hundred years. And, if it weren't for these attempts, Gaelic may have never survived at all. Probably the most important visionary idea was the preservation of the Gaeltacht."

"We read about that in Dingle," Mike said.

"The Gaeltacht is the collective term for the Irish speaking communities on the western seaboard which include parts of counties Donegal, Mayo, Galway and Kerry."

"They're all not too far from here, "Mike said.

"Yes," Eileen responded. "But, there are also small enclaves of Gaelic speakers in Counties Cork, Meath and Waterford. Although the 83,500 people who live there also speak English, Irish is the language they speak in their everyday lives. The government believes that by preserving the Gaeltacht, it will preserve and extend the use of the Irish language. The hope is that eventually, Ireland will become a truly bilingual nation with Gaelic, our original native tongue, being one of those two languages."

"Eileen's very passionate about the subject of Gaelic and bilingualism." Kevin beamed at her.

"She makes me want to take some lessons in Gaelic, myself," Mike said.

Kevin glared at Mike.

Eileen noticed his scowl and tilted her head toward Kevin. "Would you have a problem with that, my darling?"

"Of course not," Kevin said as he shifted uncomfortably on the sofa. "He'll just have to sign up for your adult class"

"That would be wonderful, Kevin," Mike said. "I can be her star pupil! Why don't you take the class with me?"

"I hated every hour of conjugating Gaelic verbs when I was a kid, " Kevin whined.

"But did you ever have such a pretty teacher as Eileen?"

"If I did, I probably wouldn't have learned very much." Kevin kissed Eileen again on the cheek. "It's a wonder any of those kids can pay attention in class with the likes of lovely Eileen lookin' down at them from the front of her classroom. If I were one of those young lads, I'd be volunteerin' to clean the chalkboards every night."

"You were probably always the charmer, Kevin, a real teacher's pet," Eileen said.

She patted him again on the arm. "I know I would have given you straight A's."

"Is anybody really interested in this game?" Mike interrupted. "I thought you were going to teach me something about Gaelic football, Kevin."

"Turn the volume up, Mike," Kevin said. "Now, here are the basics. Each team has 15 players. To score, the ball has to be kicked into the net and counted for three points. If the ball is kicked over the crossbar and between the posts, that counts as one point. The rules are pretty simple, really. A player can catch the ball and pass it with either foot or fist, but cannot actually throw the ball. The ball can also be carried for four steps without being bounced. The trick is to move the ball without bouncing it more than once off the ground before playing it off the foot or fist. Got that?"

"Sounds incredibly complicated," Mike answered, "but I'm sure I'll get the gist of it. It's a little like rugby."

"There's a lot of agility required, Mike. Each player must have the ability to perform long kicks, high jumps and solo runs. It's the epitome of individual sport and team work."

"It's only popular here in Ireland, isn't it?" Mike asked.

"Very popular. For the All-Ireland finals, up to 65,000 people will crowd Croke Park in Dublin. They go absolutely wild."

"When is it?"

"It's in September. It's the culmination of all of the inter-county knock-out championships. There's still fierce rivalry between the counties! In fact, in the early 19th century, Gaelic football was discouraged and often prohibited by landlords and priests. They were afraid of all the nationalism it was creating, and they were right. Gaelic football, begun in 1527, has always stood for the preservation of Irish sport. Now that I think of it, in a way it's a lot like the preservation of Gaelic, right Eileen?" Kevin seemed pleased at himself for his enlightened observation.

"'Tis true enough, Kevin," Eileen agreed. "The Gaelic Athletics Association was created to maintain Gaelic sports from being overtaken by foreign sports like soccer and rugby. Even Irish communities in countries such as Australia, Canada and the U.S. strongly support Gaelic games. They see it as a connection to their home country."

"I see," Mike said. "Now that I understand the football, how about a little Gaelic lesson, Eileen?"

Kevin stared at Mike.

"All right, then, Michael," she began. "Repeat after me. *Dia duit*."

"*Dia duit*," Mike repeated. "What does that mean?"

"Literally, it means, *God be with you*, but the Irish speakers say that instead of *Hello*.

"Okay. Now I'll say *Hello* back. *Dia duit*."

"No. The proper response to *Hello* in Gaelic is *Dia's Muire Duit*. That literally means *God and Mary be with you*, but the Irish say that in return when somebody says Hello."

"Two ways of saying *Hello*?" Mike asked.

"Actually, there's a third. It's *Dia daoibh*. That's when you are greeting several people at a time."

"*Dia daoibh*," Mike responded. "This is more complicated than Gaelic football."

"So like I said," Kevin interrupted. "You'll just have to sign up for her class. She doesn't do private tutoring."

At that moment, a thunderous cheer rose up from the crowd. Green and yellow flags fluttered in the air. People jumped up and down, screaming and clapping each other on the backs.

"What happened? I missed it," Mike said.

"Limerick just scored!" Kevin yelled excitedly. He jumped up from the sofa. "We've got them now."

The player who scored trotted triumphantly down the playing field. The crowd roared again. Flags fluttered everywhere.

"What's the score?" Mike asked, eagerly.

"It's Limerick 2l, Galway 20," Kevin shouted. I really think we've got 'em now. All we have to do is hold 'em. There's only a few minutes left."

"Oh, God, I can't even look!" Eileen said, as she covered her eyes.

"Neither can I," Mary said. "Tell us when it's over." She covered her eyes too.

"Time's running out. The crowd's rushing the field. Heh! Heh! Heh! Limerick's won!" Now Kevin was jumping up and down, slapping Mike on the back.

"I didn't even see the play," Mike said, disappointed. "I sure flunked my first lesson in Gaelic Football." He turned to Eileen. "I hope I can do better at my Gaelic lessons."

Eileen smiled back at Mike. "*Ta failte romhat.* That means *You're welcome.*"

Kevin was now glaring at Mike again. "Eileen, tell Mike how to say *Good-bye* in *Gaelic*," he said as he stood up abruptly, almost knocking their beers off the coffee table. "I think it's time for me to be gettin' us all a few more lagers. Mike, would you like to escort me into the kitchen?"

"Sure," Mike answered, as he followed Kevin's lead.

"Looks like your legs aren't paralyzed now, Kevin," Mary called after him. "Will ya be a darlin' and bring in one for me?"

Kevin ignored her comment and the two of them sauntered to the kitchen. When they got there, Kevin turned angrily to Mike. "What the hell are you doing?"

"What do you mean?"

"I thought I told you no lessons!"

"Kevin, what is with you?"

"Mike, I don't feel comfortable with your taking tutoring lessons from Eileen. If you're serious about learning Gaelic, you'll just have to take the adult class like everyone else. None of this one-on-one tutoring."

"Why Kevin," Mike answered. "You're serious about this. I'm beginning to think you really *are* jealous!"

"I could be, but not unless you give me reason to be," he replied. "I just won't be havin' any of it. Not private lessons! It's bad enough I have to put up with her teaching all week and three hours of adult lessons on Saturday. That's time taken away from us, time we could be spending together, without you adding to the teaching load."

"Okay, Kevin," Mike replied. "Take it easy. I won't be taking any precious time away from the two of you."

"Thanks, Mike."

Mike couldn't resist egging him on further still. "I won't take any lessons from Eileen if you say *please*, better yet, *please* in Gaelic?"

"I guess I could do that," Kevin said, happily. "*Le do thoil.*"

"*Tá failte romhat.*" Mike answered, with a thick Irish accent. "You're right, Eileen is some teacher."

Kevin cracked a slight smile. "No hard feelin's?"

"No hard feelin's," Mike repeated. "Now, let's get back to the ball game."

The Feis

The telephone rang. Mike made an attempt to reach the phone by contorting behind the tiny reception hall desk, which had been pushed against the stairway wall in order for Mary to do her weekly housecleaning. As if on cue, when he answered the phone, Mary turned on the vacuum cleaner in the parlor. He pressed the receiver up to his good ear and cupped the palm of his hand over the other.

"Hello! The Farmhouse," he yelled over the din. He paused for a response.

I automatically walked toward the desk and grabbed the guest ledger. He waved me away and mouthed the words, "I can handle this one!"

"Yes, yes, this is the Castleconnell Farmhouse," he shouted into the receiver. "You'll have to excuse me, I can hardly hear you. We're doing a little housekeeping. It seems to impress the customers when they call for reservations." He paused for another reply.

"Well, let me see…" He grabbed the ledger from my hand and flicked his hand in my direction as if to wave me away.

I stood there. I had always zealously guarded my reservation-making role and I wasn't about to give it up now.

"Let's see, the twentieth and twenty-first. The third week-end, the week-end after next," he yelled. He scanned the ledger. "How many people in your party? Oh, I see." He paused again to listen.

I waved frantically and mouthed over the roar of the vacuum. "We had a large group cancellation for that week-end. Tell them they can come!"

Mike shifted the phone receiver from his good ear to his bad ear. "I'm sorry but we're fully booked that week-end. We have a wedding party reserved."

I waved my hands frantically in front of his face to get his attention. "We have five rooms available," I whispered. "The wedding party canceled!"

He ignored me.

"I'm really sorry," he continued staring directly at me and shouting a little more loudly into the telephone. "I'm sure you saw on the brochure where it suggests the farmhouse *is unsuitable for pets and small children.*" He waited for a response.

"How many?" I asked, pulling the ledger away from him and looking at the five rooms scratched out for the third week in June.

"Five women with five children," he repeated what the caller had told him, then looked over at me to see if I understood his turning them down. "Maybe you can try the Rectory. It's a nice hotel and I know they have accommodations for families. It's not far from here."

I looked at the ledger again. It was hard to imagine how we could fill the five empty rooms in the next two weeks. I hated to think we would be forced to charge the wedding party for the rooms they hadn't used. If they had only canceled sooner, but then again, the bride didn't know she was canceling any sooner, either. Poor thing.

Mary turned off the vacuum cleaner.

"So you've tried them and they're booked, too?" Mike asked into the receiver then raised his eyebrows at me in supplication.

"How many children and what are their ages?" I whispered.

Mike took his palm from his ear and talked cautiously into the receiver, "How many children did you say there were in your party?"

There was another pause.

"Five?" he asked.

"Ask what their ages are," I urged optimistically.

"Listen, let me hand you over to our reservationist," Mike said. "Maybe she can help you." He handed the phone over to me and wiped his hands as if he were relieved to be free of the decision of accepting or rejecting the children.

I took the phone.

"Hello. My name is Pat. May I help you?"

The woman sounded a bit hysterical at this point. She introduced herself and told me how she and four other mothers were stranded with their five daughters. There was an annual Irish step dancing competition in Limerick, and did I know, by the way, that Limerick happened to have one of the oldest and best Irish step dancing schools in Ireland. They had called all the hotels and guesthouses in Limerick but they had waited too long and now they were in dire need of a place to stay. It was only for two nights.

Her plea was hard to resist, yet I mustered up my courage to sound like a police interrogator. "Do you mind telling me the ages of the girls? You see, our policy is, which I didn't make by the way, that we don't encourage pets or small children."

"Well, the two *oldest* girls are twelve," she said, "and you'll see, they're very mature for their ages. They're champion level dancers." She seemed to think this bit of information would convince me to take them. She was obviously proud of the girls, but I didn't know what championship level meant. I assumed she thought I was a soft touch and wouldn't refuse them in the end.

"And what about the others?" I continued to grill her. I always thought the farmhouse policy was a bit strict, but we promised we'd go by the rules.

"The other three are seven, nine and ten," she said. "They are very well behaved children, you'll see." The woman was definitely convincing.

"Seven, nine and ten," I repeated slowly, trying to decide if these ages fit into the category of *small children*. I was tempted to ask how tall they were.

"Listen," the woman said. "It's all my fault. I should have made these reservations long ago and everything is booked. We'll keep the girls locked in their rooms if we have to! They'll be terribly disappointed if they miss their chance to compete."

How could I say *no* to this imploring mother? Besides, I wanted to find out what championship dancing was all about.

"You can stop worrying," I said. "I don't want to be the one blamed for their not being able to compete. What did you say your name was?"

"It's Fionna Flaherty and God bless you!" the woman gushed. "What is the address for me to send you the check for the rooms?"

"That won't be necessary," I said. " I have a feeling we don't have to worry about the ten of you not showing up." I winked at Mike and hung up the phone.

Mike said, "I don't know if you remember correctly, but that's exactly what you said to the bride when she booked *her* party of ten. And look what happened to them."

"That poor bride," I said, ignoring his sarcasm.

"What about the *poor groom*?" he responded. "So how many kiddies will we be having?"

"Only three," I lied. "The other two are teenagers. They're step dancers." I started to sound like the proud mother I had just hung up from.

I placed two large neat X's over the twentieth and twenty-first in the ledger. "It seems there's a big Irish step dancing competition in Limerick," I proclaimed. "And these girls are going to be the winners."

With that, Mary entered the foyer pushing the unplugged vacuum cleaner. "That's the *feis,* pronounced *fesh*. It's held every year." She plugged the vacuum cleaner in and turned it on."

"What's a feis?" I yelled to her over the din.

*   *   *   *   *

Two weeks later, my question would be answered. At 8:00 a.m. sharp, three cars pulled into the driveway crammed with women, children, suit bags, luggage and makeup bags. They looked as if they were prepared for a Hollywood stage production. The mothers climbed out of the cars and helped the girls scramble out of the back seats. Wearing matching black sweat suits with *Pat Roche Academy* emblazoned on their backs over a gold and green embroidered harp, they stood eagerly in the driveway waiting for their mothers to take charge. Each girl's long hair was carefully wrapped up around large hair rollers with a white crocheted hair net keeping it all in place. They each clutched a large make-up bag under their arms.

The youngest girl, came directly up to me, shook my hand, introduced herself and thanked me for allowing them to stay at the farmhouse.

I now felt ashamed that I had ever questioned their ages. This must have been the seven-year-old. "We're delighted to have you with us, have you ever stayed in a farmhouse before?"

"Oh, yes I have!" she beamed. "I live in a farmhouse up in Donegal." She looked around at the other girls. "In fact we're all from there."

"That must have been a long ride," I said.

"Not too bad," she responded.

"So *you* two must be the champions," I said, as I walked over to the two oldest girls.

"We are," they responded in unison, grinning at each other. "I'm Peggy Flaherty and this is my best friend Bernadette Burke. Thanks for having us."

Now I felt they were purposely trying to rub in the fact I might not have given them shelter for two nights.

One of the mothers walked up to us. "These two are best friends and best competitors, too. I'm Fionna Flaherty, the one you talked to on the phone."

"You and your champion girls are welcome here. Let me show you to your rooms young ladies, so you can make yourselves comfortable." I led them into the foyer and up the stairs. "We'll be serving breakfast in the dining room at nine o'clock. You'll be needing a big Irish breakfast for energy for your competition. What time does it start?"

"We have to be there promptly at 11:30, the competition itself starts at noon and runs until 7:00 or 8:00 in the evening," Peggy Flaherty chirped.

The girls each dragged an individual wheeled suitcase behind them as they climbed the stairs. They also had garment bags slung over their shoulders. It seemed like a lot of gear for two days and nights. An hour later, we could hear the girls giggling as they filtered into the dining room for breakfast. They had apparently discovered Gizmo.

"She's darling," the one girl exclaimed. "What's her name?"

"Gizmo," I responded. "She's still only a puppy."

"Oh, now we know why you don't allow pets," Marilyn McCabe said.

"Well, no," I said. "Actually, she's not supposed to be here either."

The girls laughed as Gizmo chased around the dining room table legs. Having taken out their hair rollers and removed their hair nets, their shiny, banana curl ringlets bounced and swung merrily about their shoulders as they continued the dog chase.

Mrs. Flaherty called to the girls. "Now come on, girls, let's all be seated, so you'll have plenty of time to put your costumes on before we leave!"

They all took their chairs immediately.

After they helped themselves to a generous portion of ham, eggs and toast, Mrs. Flaherty introduced the rest of the mothers and daughters to Mike and me. "You've already met my daughter, Peggy," she said.

"Could you tell us a bit about the feis?" I asked the group.

Mrs. Flaherty took the lead. "I think Peggy and Bernadette, our two championship contenders, could give you a little history of the feis. Bernadette?"

Bernadette began, "*Feis* is the Irish word for *festival*. Irish step dancing has its roots in Gallic times. The first Irish dances were recorded in the mid-1500's: the Rinnce Fada or Fading, where two lines with partners faced each other, the Irish Hey, a round or figure dance, the Trenchmore, which is similar to a free form country dancing and of course, the jig, and we all know what that is!" She looked around the table and all the girls giggled.

"Those dances evolved over the centuries to become today's standards of Irish step dancing: the reel, the hornpipe, set dancing and the jig. It is important that Irish step dancers perform intricate steps while keeping their upper bodies straight. It is the only ethnic dance that depends solely on natural balance without the use of arms.

"Did you know that until the Penal Laws were repealed, traditional Irish step dancers could only pass their skills in secret schools called *hedge* schools, since the children had to perform behind the hedges. However, once the laws were repealed, dance teachers or Dance Masters, as they were called, began to travel around the country, staying for weeks at a time in each town, teaching children the art of Irish step dancing in their kitchens. Dance Masters eventually created the first schools of dancing. The best known are from Counties Kerry, Cork and Limerick."

Bernadette's mother beamed at her daughter's eloquent explanation. She said, "And that's why we're here today. Limerick has the largest Feis in the country."

"That's fascinating," I said. "And just what happens at a typical Feis?"

"There are five competitive levels," Bernadette's mother continued. "Beginner, novice, open, preliminary championship and championship. My daughter and Peggy Flaherty are competing at the championship level." She grinned proudly.

"And may the best young woman win," Mrs. Flaherty cheered, as she held up her glass of orange juice.

"Best of luck to all you young ladies, and mothers," I responded.

Mrs. Flaherty ordered the girls to get a move on. She clapped her hands and the girls politely excused themselves and hurried out of the room and up the stairs.

"You know," Mrs. Flaherty said, "This is a very important competition for our two daughters. We've been traipsing around the country, from competition to competition for the past five years to get to this championship!"

Mrs. Burke responded, "And every minute of those five years has been a joy."

Mrs. Flaherty rolled her eyes. "I'll agree it's been a joy when my Peggy wins!"

"She has a very good chance," Mrs. Burke responded.

"What do you mean *very good chance?*" Mrs. Flaherty said, a little strongly.

"Of course, she's going to win! Everybody who knows anything about Irish step dancing knows my daughter's the best competitor in Ireland in her age group and at her level."

"What about *my* Bernadette?" Mrs. Burke's voice rose in annoyance.

"Well...Let's face it, she hasn't exactly performed the level of complicated steps my Peggy has."

"She will tonight!" Mrs. Burke responded. "You know your Peggy has been tutoring Bernadette with her new program for the past four months. There's no reason why Bernadette can't perform as well as Peggy."

Mrs. Flaherty carefully folded her napkin and placed it on her plate. "We'll just have to see about that!"

Peggy entered the room and interrupted the two mothers. "Pat, have you seen the girls costumes, yet? Mrs. Burke worked on most of them." She looked over at a smiling Mrs. Burke. "They're brilliant. No matter what the outcome of today's feis, we will definitely have the most beautiful dresses on the stage!"

Mrs. Flaherty sighed, then smiled in agreement. "That they will, Peggy," Mrs. Flaherty said. "Mrs. Burke's handwork is more detailed than any of the other costumes, there's no question."

"Oh, here come our little darlin's now!" Mrs. Flaherty said, as the girls slowly filed into the dining room.

The costumes were indeed brilliant. Each garment was a unique design, cut from dazzling shades of garnet, royal blue, kelly green and orange velvet. A triangular shawl was draped over each girl's shoulder forming a V in the back of each dress. These shawls were covered with decorative silver and gold embroidery, and Celtic interlacing patterns were embroidered onto the brightly colored fabric of the bodices and skirts.

The material of the costumes fell in stiff folds below their waists, flaring out just above their knees so that there was little movement in the garments when the girls walked. Contrasted to their sumptuous frocks, the girls wore simple white cotton sleeve-socks pulled up over their calves and black leather shoes with silver square buckles at the arches. Velvet headbands that matched the color of their dresses held the masses of long curly ringlets off of their faces. With their arms straight at their sides, and their heads held high, the girls automatically formed a single line and stood poised with one foot in front of the other as if they were ready to perform.

"Well, if you dance as well as you look," I said, "you will all be winners! Do you think you could do a little jig for us before you leave?"

"Oh, surely they'll scratch your beautiful wooden floors with their hard shoes." Mrs. Burke protested. "Don't ya know, the heels are made of fiberglass!"

"That's why we have linoleum in the kitchen," I said.

The girls beamed at their mothers and, still in line formation, followed each other into the kitchen. We adults followed them in.

Peggy spoke from the end of the line. "We will now be performing a set dance to the music, *The Three Sea Captains*, choreographed by our talented instructor, who also happens to be my mother, Mrs. Flaherty."

The girls leaned forward, extended one pointed foot in front of the other, and started an energetic tapping, alternating with apparent ease between each step. They moved in perfect unison, their upper body and arms perfectly straight contrasted to their bouncing curls and frenzied feet. They moved across the kitchen floor and then back to their original position, the only music being the clicks and trebles of their heels. All of a sudden they stopped.

We all clapped enthusiastically.

"More! More!" I heard myself shout.

The girls bowed in unison. Peggy and Bernadette looked at each other.

"Should we show them the new number I taught you?" Peggy asked Bernadette. "We can do it together."

"Sure," Bernadette said. "It will be good practice in front of our most critical judges." She winked at Mrs. Flaherty and her mother.

The younger girls moved off to the corner of the kitchen to watch their older virtuosos. This time the two girls clasped each other's hand, stepped forward, leaned forward and started to tap. They seemed to be dancing double time compared to the number they had just finished. One girl would slip under the arm of the other reel style and end up dancing back in unison with her partner. They released each other's hand and criss-crossed the kitchen as if they were floating on air. They repeated this move backwards and ended up back where they had begun. They grasped each other's hand again and kicked their legs up over their heads. They tapped rigorously, then crossed their feet at the ankle and rocked back and forth. They both stopped suddenly, hardly out of breath. They seemed to be happy with the show of their athletic prowess.

We all clapped and cheered. I noticed a tear in Mrs. Burke's eye.

Peggy and Bernadette took a long, championship bow.

Mrs. Flaherty walked over to the girls and put her arms around their shoulders. "May I present my two best students, both forever champions in my eyes!" she blubbered.

Mrs. Burke went up to the three of them and tried futilely to embrace them all at the same time. "Like I said before, may the best girl win!" she exclaimed.

Tears were now rolling down Mrs. Flaherty's cheeks. She shrugged her shoulders and embraced Mrs. Burke in a heartfelt bear hug. "Now, I guess my Peggy is in for a little more competition than I thought!"

"Now, now, Mrs. Flaherty," Mrs. Burke said as she released herself and patted Mrs. Flaherty on the shoulder. "They're both equally talented, and thanks to your Peggy's tutoring, Bernadette may have a fair chance. Maybe we can both learn something from them, just as they have learned from your brilliant teaching."

"But sadly, there can only be one winner," Mrs.Flaherty said.

Mrs. Burke responded by rubbing her hand up and down Mrs. Flaherty's arm. It seemed to comfort her.

"You're right, Mrs. Burke," Mrs. Flaherty said, as she whispered into her ear. "I know winning isn't everything but I also know both of our girls will always be winners in my book."

The two of them gazed at their offspring as all the girls formed a single line and filed out of the kitchen.

I thought of how many lessons had been learned and how many Irish step-dancing championships had been won in the kitchens of Ireland. I considered visiting the Limerick feis myself. I also considered amending the farmhouse rules regarding children.

My Wild Irish Rose Garden

A plastic flower marker labeled "Rosa Gallica" peered up at me from next to what was most probably a budding weed. Anyone who first lays eyes on the Emerald Isle from the air hovering over Shannon Airport is struck by the lush, ever-changing checkerboard of green: a vision vast, pastoral and verdant. It would seem that anyone could grow anything, anywhere, anytime in Irish soil.

Perhaps that's what each invading group of Celts, Saxons and Vikings believed as they gleefully drew their crossbows to overtake the next bit of green turf. Their faith in the fertility of the soil must have been greatly assured when they eventually reached the Burren, in western Ireland, the rocky pre-glacial moonscape where exotic flowers bloom through layers of flinty rock deposited centuries ago. The whole country is one green thumb!

The mistaken notion that anything can grow in Ireland has caused otherwise reluctant horticulturists to fall to their knees with spade in hand in hopes of producing a blue ribbon garden. I regarded the plastic flower marker, which mockingly reminded me with its miniature picture, of what the flower should look like in full bloom.

Had I become the eccentric optimist that I had heard all gardeners must be? Or was I truly in denial that my budding flower was indeed a thriving weed? For one second, I felt like throwing my garden tools down in despair and heading for the sanctuary of my reading chair next to the fireplace. It would be much easier to read about the glorious gardens of Ireland by the warmth of a peat fire and not even get my fingers dirty.

Reaching into my gardening pail, I unenthusiastically pulled out my pink gardening gloves which were purchased last fall to match the predominant color of my prospective garden. The gloves were damp and caked with dirt. I uncurled the fingers and recalled all of the work I had put into this little patch of dirt only seven months ago.

After having dutifully researched all flowers that would produce a color scheme of pink, fuchsia and purple blue, I had settled on a variation of Monet's garden in Giverney, France. It wasn't a really original idea, but I was convinced that with the ideal conditions of high humidity and alternate sunshine, it would be easy to create. My mail order of slightly more than three hundred plantings, cuttings and bulbs arrived directly from Holland in late September. Even the postman commented on my hopeful attitude as he lugged the brightly colored bags onto the porch. "You'll be havin' lots o' work ahead of ye, hopefully, with some reward," he said, and hurried along on his bicycle.

Ripping open the bags, I dumped their contents out onto the soil.

It had taken the better part of two weeks to dig up old grass, sod, weeds, leaves and twigs to prepare the planting beds. My idea was to arrange the plantings in a crescent shape so that when the flowers came up it would resemble a flowered arm embracing the side of the yard.

I dropped the cuttings and bulbs into neat, shallow furrows according to the plan that I had painstakingly drawn up, which would guarantee me full color all spring and summer long. No sooner had I planted the first dozen bulbs than I started getting what was to become a long list of unsolicited suggestions, comments, and constructive criticism from well meaning neighbors. These helpful hints ranged from warnings about planting the bulbs too close and too deep, to under watering and over watering. Each well-intentioned gardener was convinced that his method was the one and only way in which to achieve success.

One of the most original suggestions came from Johnny Ryan, the barber from the adjacent village. He was a big, burly man who could have been a spokesperson for testosterone and was renowned for his prize-winning roses and free advice. As I knelt over my flowerbed, I noticed his car pulling into the drive. He stepped out of the car and ponderously shuffled along the walkway.

Johnny Ryan was a man of few words. Well aware of the fact that my garden could benefit from his expertise, I extended my soiled hand and thanked him, probably a little too enthusiastically, for taking the time to stop by. He grunted in acknowledgment and turned a critical eye towards the rows waiting to be filled.

In eager anticipation, I awaited his appraisal of my work thus far. He poked the soil with the toe of his shoe. Then he picked up a handful of earth. He sifted the dirt through his fingers and smelled it. After brushing the dirt from his hands, he stood silently for what seemed to be an eternity. He then crossed his arms and pronounced his diagnosis with the confidence of a blue ribbon winner, saying, "All you need is a little hair!"

"Hair?" Did I mishear him? Was he commenting on the texture of the soil? What on earth was he talking about? Was he chiding me? Seeing my puzzled expression, Johnny Ryan proceeded to explain that human hair is a great source of protein and one of the secrets of perfect roses. "One should place a handful of hair clippings into the hole before planting each bulb. If you do this, you will have the most beautiful rose gardens in all of County Limerick."

This is the advice I get from the Blue Ribbon Winner of Ireland? I marveled at this new information. How could I have not known this? How could I have missed this vital piece of information in all of the garden books and journals that I had dutifully digested? I was torn between skepticism and delight. Could it really be that easy to produce an award-winning specimen? After all, he had done it, so why couldn't I? My Irish side warned me that he was just telling me this to throw me off. Perhaps he considered my fancy Holland varieties a personal threat.

"Now my dear man," I asked with true skepticism, "just where would I be getting enough hair to do the necessary fertilizing for these fine specimens?"

The man of few words and cryptic advice replied confidently, "Just stop by my barber shop on my slow days, Mondays or Wednesdays. I'll have

plenty of clippings to fertilize your entire garden, and then some. I'll look
forward to finally having some keen competition at the next flower show!"

It was ironic that most gardening advice came from those who knew
the least. Mickey Flaherty, whose mud patch at the front of his house was
the shame of the neighborhood, liked to stop by every time I was out
doing some weeding. After awhile, I started to pretend that I didn't notice
him coming down the drive. He was starting to become a bit of a nui-
sance. He had this annoying way of letting you know what you should be
doing without actually coming out and sounding like a total know-it-all.

He would say things like, "Mary Riley always does it this way" or "I
told Pat Finnegan not to plant too early, he did it anyway and look what
happened." I tried many ways of responding to these statements without
biting at his bait, but he had an uncanny way of manipulating the conversation so that in the end, he was telling you exactly what to do and how
to do it.

Very often, I came close to challenging him by saying, "I'll just have to
try it that way, Micky, as soon as your garden looks as good as mine." But
the guy was so pathetic and seemed to care so much about my success even
in light of his own failure, that I decided to let him live vicariously
through me and let it go at that.

Oftentimes, I had to gauge my gardening times so that I would avoid
constant interruptions. After checking to see if the coast was clear, I
would quickly run out to do a quick weeding and clipping. If I were
lucky, I could get in a good half-hour of work with as few as two or three
visits from neighbors. It was becoming increasingly evident that gardeners were the experts of chitchat, and were never in danger of being without company.

I enjoyed the neighborly camaraderie, but the most difficult part was
trying to get rid of people once you engaged them in conversation. They
just never got the hint when it was time to leave and time for me to get
back to work. Many times I resorted to pretending the phone was ringing, or claiming I needed to use the rest room. This would give me the

opportunity to excuse myself and flee into the house. Now I knew why people took up greenhouse gardening. Crowd control was so much easier when you were indoors.

Eileen McMahon, a serious gardener, would always offer her services, but it always seemed whenever she came over to help, it often ended up being more work for me. One beautiful sunlit day she stopped by to tell me that Shaunesey's nursery had a half price perennial sale going on. For added incentive, she told me she could use a lift over there anyway, as she needed a bit of potting soil.

Two hours later, we returned with one perennial planting apiece and ten bags of potting soil. Since Eileen had a bad back, I did most of the lugging of the bags myself. My reward was usually something wonderful in the way of Irish soda bread or date nut bread, something I wouldn't take the time to make myself. The problem was that all of the hours I lost catering to Eileen's excursions, I could have started a small bakery business!

Having mulled over all of the precious time, labor and effort I spent trying to get my garden going last fall, I was now determined to plow onward. All of my work just couldn't have been in vain. As I pulled my pink gloves up to cover my wrists, I thanked God I didn't have to rely on farming for a living.

Now it was May, and the little bit of green that poked through the brown twigs and dead leaves didn't look too promising. What had I done wrong? Maybe I had planted too early. Maybe I had planted too deep. Luckily, I had kept all of the plastic markers in place to remind me of what I had planted and where. I thought I had followed all of the planting directions meticulously. I had even taken all of my neighbors' advice, at least most of it.

"Rosa Gallica" stared blankly up at me. Halfheartedly, I scratched at the ground with my hand rake. It was unbelievable how much debris and thistle had accumulated over the winter. Being careful not to disturb anything that might be growing underneath, I picked around until all the dead was cleared away.

Suddenly, I saw three tiny lime-green shoots piercing the ground's surface. I continued raking until five more shoots appeared. My anguish turned to joy as I raked, pulled, poked and dug around the dead to reveal all kinds of shiny new sprouts sticking their cheerful green faces into the damp air.

A magical, maternal feeling swept over me as I saw my little offspring struggling to sprout. I felt truly touched and rewarded by their determination to thrive and flourish in spite of all my horticultural shortcomings. Carefully, I straightened all of the white plastic flower markers with new optimism. Maybe I would be giving Johnny Ryan a run for his money at the next rose competition, after all.

The Quiet Man

John Wayne is probably considered by the Irish to be *as* important a celebrity as St. Patrick, maybe *more*. And to American tourists, the sight where his most famous Oscar winning movie, "The Quiet Man," was filmed is one of the most popular tourist destinations in Ireland. Recognizing Ireland's ability to offer built-in sets such as ruined castles, ancient stone walls and original thatched roof cottages, filmmaker John Ford selected West Ireland over Hollywood as the backdrop for his legendary love story in 1952.

An Irish American, played by Wayne returns to his father's homeland in search of his identity and instead finds a fiery and rebellious redhead, Maureen O'Hara, whom he subsequently courts and marries. The Quiet Man introduced the magic of Ireland to millions and placed Ireland permanently on American tourists' itineraries. Luckily, Cong and Connemara, where the movie was originally filmed, are a short ride from Shannon.

And so, many American film buffs searching for the Hollywood fantasy, will fly to Shannon Airport, tour the tiny village in search of the romance portrayed in the movie and visit little else in the whole of Ireland. They return home with poster sized pictures of John Wayne and Maureen O'Hara and are content. So it became a rather peculiar phenomenon that many Americans would travel all the way to the Emerald Isle for something, well, *really* American. What about the Blarney Stone? The Book of Kells? Prehistoric ring forts?

And, in fact, bemused at ourselves, that's *exactly why* we chose County Galway as our destination for the weekend. We were starting to feel that empty, yearning, aching feeling that occurs when you have been separated for too long from friends, family and all of those familiar things that you know and love, namely home.

One night at dinner we played a game as we watched the third day of drizzle beat against the dining room window. It was called "Try To Outdo This, What do You Miss the Most?"

The dueling match usually went something like this.

"Television," he'd say.

"No, cheap books," I'd say.

"Okay. What about Jays Potato Chips?"

"No, you know we'd rather have a Thirty One Flavors."

"Okay, Monday Night Football. For me, that is the *singular* thing I miss the most."

"All right, I give up. I can't beat you on that one."

We were definitely homesick. We needed, no, we *craved* something American, some connection with the good ol' U.S. of A. We wanted to satisfy our hunger-for-home pangs, yet we wanted something that would have some meaningful historical significance between home and Ireland.

And so, the search for something American started with a visit to County Galway. We had read where a brand new Heritage Center had just been built at Teernakill in Maam Valley. It was stone's throw away from the original cottage, now ruined, where John Wayne's character made his home and where he and Mary Kate would spend their tumultuous wedding night. As far as Heritage Centers went, it was supposed to be worthwhile, as it was new and catered to Americans.

We arrived at the Heritage Center just as three tourist buses pulled up.

As we stood in a line with at least one hundred other curious Americans, a misty rain started to fall.

"I knew we should have brought that umbrella," Mike said flatly. He always used the term "we" when he was trying to blame me for something. "Never mind," he said. "It's not going to be that bad of a wait. Maybe they sell umbrellas inside."

Two hours later I wondered just what they did have inside besides umbrellas. It seemed as if each tourist took at least an hour before we saw them come out the other side.

"This might not be worth the wait," I said, still feeling responsible for the absent umbrella.

"Oh, come on. We're here. We're not leaving without a photograph of John Wayne for my mother. You know he was her favorite of all time!"

The unusually cheerful group chatted and waited patiently. The line inched forward. It looked like we were only five people away from the entry.

"At least the Irish don't try to fool you with those Disneyland type lines where they zig zag and turn back on themselves so that you think you're almost to the ride when really you're another hour away," Mike said.

A burley, balding man who was passively taking tickets, suddenly yelled out in a barely audible monotone. "Only two more people and then we break for lunch."

Mike didn't waste a second. He reached into his pocket, walked directly to the ticket taker and shook his hand vigorously. This was the old maitre'd trick I had seen so often when our dinner reservations became lost and we were left standing helpless in a fancy restaurant with important clients. As Mike slipped him the folded pound notes he looked straight into the man's eyes and assured him that there *must* be some mistake.

Just like all the other maitre'd's, the man didn't even bother to check out just how much he could be bought for. I guess he figured if this guy has enough guts to bribe him into getting in, it must have been enough. The man lifted the rope and let my prince and me into the packed cottage.

The ground floor was an exact replica of the interior set, at least the way I remembered it from the dozen or so times I had seen the film. It was complete with painstakingly reproduced furniture, costumes and props. Now this was history. I grimaced at our touristy thrill of seeing the infamous honeymoon bed, which like in the movie, was collapsed in the corner of the mocked up bedroom.

"You've got to take a picture of me pointing to the collapsed bed," I said.

Mike blushed.

"Come, on. For your mother. She'll love it."

Mike slipped the pocket camera out of his jacket and took a quick shot. "Okay, that's enough. You're embarrassing me."

"My reason for living," I replied. "Come on, let's see if this gets any better upstairs."

When we reached the top of the stairs, it was apparent that this was indeed a Heritage Center, after all. Rows and rows of trinkets hung from an endless number of stainless steel rounders. Key chains abounded: key chains with Irish surnames, key chains with three leafed clovers, key chains with pieces of authentic prehistoric rock carved into Celtic crosses. Well, at least we could find something to send to our dog sitters. They loved kitschy key chains.

Two aisles contained the ever-popular woolen goods. Capes, skirts, mufflers and caps displayed and sorted according to size. Now I knew what was taking the tourist bus group so long. They were trying everything on in the place. White haired ladies helped each other pull on sweaters, scarves and skirts. They were pulling things off the shelves as if they were giving them away. When they had successfully found their treasured souvenir in their size, they moved slowly to a check out line which was longer than the one we waited in to get in!

I still hadn't seen any Quiet Man memorabilia and found this to be particularly peculiar. I couldn't believe Hollywood was missing out on the chance to reap all of the royalty possibilities. I saw Mike flagging me down from the other side of the store. "Over here," he yelled excitedly.

I shoved my way through the crowd feeling like a fresh water salmon swimming upstream. These people just did not want to budge. Of course, I was starting to feel the same way, as I figured it took us two hours to get in, we were at least entitled to stay two hours now that we were inside. I inched my way through the crowd. Mike was holding up two items that I couldn't make out from where I was.

"Hurry, there's only two of these left."

I pushed more determinedly through the last aisle. I finally popped out a couple feet from where Mike stood holding his prizes above his head in fear that someone might grab them out of his hands.

"Good job," I congratulated him. "What are they?"

"They're pictures of the whole Quiet Man cast. Look, there's John Wayne in the middle!"

"Thank God you grabbed *two* of them. One for your mother and one for our Mary. We always referred to her as *our Mary* to differentiate her from all of the Marys that we knew, which were plenty.

"Our Mary?" he repeated. "Why does she get one?"

"Oh, I promised I'd bring her back a photo of John Wayne. She's crazy about him. Don't worry. Your mother can have the other one."

"What about *me*?" he asked with an uncharacteristic whine.

"You're kidding."

"No, I mean it, I want one, too. I was the one that bullied my way over here and grabbed the last two left."

"In that case, I'll just tell our Mary they didn't have any."

"How can you do that if I have mine framed and hung on the wall?" he insisted.

"I guess you'll have to give her your mother's, then."

"Never mind." He stated blankly although a little crestfallen. "I really don't need a photo of John Wayne now do I?"

"No, " I smiled broadly. "Not when you can look at the *real* Quiet Man every day." I pointed up to the reflective mirror which, stood alongside the woolen cap rack. He looked up at himself. "Thanks." He blushed. "It wouldn't be very gentlemanly of me to deprive *two* women whom I care about. John Wayne wouldn't do that. What would I be doing with an old souvenir photograph, anyway? I'll just get myself a key chain instead." He selected a key chain with a picture of John Wayne from the trinket stand, and led me to the check out counter line.

I looked down at the Quiet Man photos in my hand. "You will always be *my* John Wayne," I said.

The Connemara Pony

Straddling his candy-apple-red Harley Davidson 450, Kevin pulled onto the gravel parking lot and came to an abrupt halt. He revved his engine to alert Mike, who was washing the mud off the black walls of *The Purple Bomber,* the name we had affectionately given to our plum colored, four-cylinder O'Brien family sedan. Absorbed in the intensity of his labor, Mike did not notice Kevin's arrival, and continued to splash and rinse off the last of the suds from his weekly routine.

Kevin balanced the bulky bike between his legs and revved up the engine a second time. This time he put it in full throttle, yelling above the din.

"Hey, Mike, what have ya got planned for today?"

"Oh, hi, Kev." Mike said as he tossed the sponge into a bucket beside the car and walked over to greet him. "What's up?"

"I was wonderin' if the misses would mind if ya took a little ride with me today? Think ya could be up for a little horse tradin'?"

"*Hoss tradin?*" Mike asked, with an affected cowboy drawl. He liked to use accents in an effort to be funny. Then he rubbed his back and hobbled over to the bike mimicking an old bowlegged cowhand. "*Where ya headin', partner, into the West?*"

"That's the idea," Kevin said. "I'm planning on tradin' my hog for a wedding present for Eileen. I want to get her a Connemara pony."

"You're kidding." Mike backed up to admire the motorcycle's shiny chrome trim. He gently ran his hand along the smooth, silvery metal of the handlebars. "She's a real beauty. Why would you ever think of getting rid of it? "

The bike returned the compliment by flashing Mike a reflection of himself off of its oversized chrome exhaust pipes.

"You're really selling it? Why?" Mike asked, as he regarded himself in the sleek chrome mirror affixed to the handle bar. "You just don't see a bike like this very often. I bet she has a lot of power."

"Well, you know women.... I promised Eileen I'd get rid of it once we got married. She's afraid it's too dangerous. She thinks I might end up killing myself. She doesn't like the idea of my makin' her a young widow." He looked down at the bike and added quickly, "You don't think I sound *whipped* or anything, for doin' as she wants, now, do ya, Michael?"

Mike threw his head back in laughter. "Now, Kevin, if you're mature enough to get married, you're mature enough to realize that doing what she wants will only make your life easier. Think of it this way, you're not acting *whipped,* you're being smart, practical, pragmatic. You can live a lot longer without this bike than you can with the wrath of a wife."

Kevin smiled his broad smile. "So ya don't think it's wimpy or anything. I don't mind gettin' married, and givin' up most of my freedoms, Eileen's worth it. But I don't want to end up like one of those guys who is brow beaten and nagged to death." He hesitated. "Although, Eileen isn't the type to ask too much from ya."

"Well, if three's a crowd, and the Harley is the third wheel, sounds like you'll have to get rid of it. Besides, a woman always wants you to get rid of the things that represent your life before she came into it, you know, your life as a single guy. I'd say the bike might qualify as that. I just can't picture you *and Eileen* riding around on it. She doesn't seem like the biker type."

"It's the truth, all right," Kevin said. "She really hates the sight of it. I never understood, until now, why that was. My plan is to sell it and buy Eileen a pony. I already have someone interested in the bike, and I can get a pretty good price from him, too. He's single."

"Poor guy..." Mike said.

"Yeah, now I'll be feelin' sorry for all of those guys, too. The ones that don't have a chance of findin' anybody as wonderful as Eileen...Pat, too," he quickly added, trying to show he was now entering the exclusive club of married men who pat themselves on the back for their good fortune.

"So why the Pony?"

"Oh, Eileen's always wanted one since she was a kid. So for her twelfth birthday, she asked for a Connemara pony. She tried to convince her old man that they could simply put the pony in the second stall of their two-car garage, since they only had one car and weren't using it anyway. She would groom and care for her little pony in the garage, saving her Da the expensive boarding costs."

"What happened?"

"I guess her Da' wasn't convinced. She didn't get her pony. The way she remembers it, the Connemara pony was the only birthday gift she asked for and didn't receive. She said it was her first realization that perhaps she wouldn't always get what she wanted. Of course, now that it's up to me, she will always get what she wants. The present of the pony will be symbolic of that. I'll give up the motorcycle, which, I have to admit I'm very fond of, in order to give her that pony she never got for her twelfth birthday…her Connemara Pony."

"Great idea, Kev. Wives love gifts. I've heard of Connemara ponies. They're famous…aren't they?"

"They are, indeed," Kevin said. "The Connemara pony is the only native pony breed of Ireland. It's an ancient breed, and has run free in the mountains of Ireland's West Coast since prehistoric times."

"So now, where are we going to go to buy this pony, The National Stud?"

"No, the National Stud is only for thoroughbred breeding. We'll be goin' to pony country. There's an annual horse tradin' show in a town called *Ballinasloe*. It's not too far."

"Sounds terrific. When do we go?"

"If you don't have much to do, I thought we'd go today," Kevin said and then added wistfully. "It's funny you suggested The National Stud, though, as my Da worked there for many years."

Kevin dismounted the Harley and sauntered over to The Purple Bomber to examine Mike's car wash. "You don't really want to wash this thing anyway. Maybe if ya let it get dirty enough, people won't notice it's color." Kevin laughed. "Now Mike, what possessed ya to buy a car this color? He opened the driver's side door. What do ya know? The inside's purple, too." He sniffed the air of the car's interior. "Is it my imagination, or does it smell like a plum in here?"

"Go ahead and laugh," Mike said, "but it won't be long before you'll be driving a practical family sedan to hold all those little Kevin's and Eileen's that will be coming along soon enough."

"Never." Kevin said.

"You never thought you'd be getting married, either. I'd like to see you try and fit a whole family on the back of a motorcycle or a pony, for that matter." Mike closed the driver's door. "So your dad worked at The National Stud?"

"Most of his life."

"What did he do there?"

"Well, in his later years, he gave tours of The Stud. Before that he did just about every job there was on the farm. For instance, the first job he had was keeping the astrological charts of each of the thoroughbred foals."

"Astrological charts?" Mike asked. "What do the stars and planets have to do with breeding racehorses?"

"Well, accordin' to the eccentric colonel William Walker who founded The Stud, astrology had *everything* to do with how the horses were bred. The colonel believed that the moon and stars could enhance a horse's chances on the racetrack. My Da would study the astrological charts of each foal born in the stud, and if it was favorable, the foal would be kept. If not, it would be sold. In fact, astrology was considered so important at The Stud, the stallions were housed in 'lantern boxes.' These were stables which contained skylights, so that the horses could be touched by sunlight or moonbeams."

"It sounds like someone was touched by moonbeams," Mike said.

"You're not a believer in astrology, Mike?"

"Well, let's say I *believe it*, but I'm just not sure I believe *in* it."

"Horse trainers have always used a lot of unorthodox methods. For instance, Da used to feed a bottle of Guinness per day to Arkle, who became one of the greatest steeplechasers in history. Today, you can see his skeleton which is on display at The National Stud museum."

"His skeleton?"

"Yeah. He had to be put down after he broke a bone, so I guess the museum decided it might as well keep all of his bones for posterity."

"That's pretty weird, isn't it?" Mike asked.

"If you saw it, you'd really think it's weird, but he was one of the greatest thoroughbreds in history. My father was in charge of him."

"For awhile, he brought the mares out to the stallions. The stallions are kept in one-acre mini-pastures, surrounded by fences, in order to keep them from killin' each other when the mares were brought out. It seems stallions don't like the idea of sharin'. My Da was kept pretty busy, as most of the stallions were expected to cover 50 mares per season. Sometimes the price of stud service for one mare for one time could reach $1,000 American dollars, and that's without guaranteed results."

"What do you mean, no guarantee?" Mike asked.

"I mean, if the mare didn't become pregnant, The Stud still charged for the services of the stallion."

"Really?" Mike asked.

"Oh yes," Kevin said. "The stud service was, and still is, a real production. First, soft music was piped into the mares' stalls to relax them. After that, a so-called 'teaser horse' was introduced to each mare to get her 'into the mood', so to speak, before she was taken to the stallions. The use of the 'teaser' insured that the mare was not only ready but eager to receive the stallion. That way, few stallions were rejected. It kept everybody happy."

"Sounds like one hell of a matchmaking operation," Mike said.

"For a few of his years there, he kept vigil over the foaling mares, who generally only foal during the night. His job was to quietly watch over the mares who prefer to be alone during birthing. He would track their progress and alert the vet as to any unusual difficulties during their deliveries. Sometimes The National Stud would have five to ten mares foal on the same night."

"Almost like an assembly line," Mike said.

"Thoroughbreds, being the fastest horses in the world, have become the most valuable. Breeding has become big business in Ireland. The Irish have always loved their horses, ever since that first Celtic warrior harnessed a fiery steed to his chariot and charged into battle."

"The Stud has provided breeding services all over the world, second only to America and France. Speaking of France, did you know Napoleon's famous steed, *Marengo*, is said to have come from Ireland? You can probably tell, I've grown up around horses and loving them almost as much as my Da did. That's how I got the idea about giving Eileen the Connemara pony she always wanted for our wedding present. It's symbolic for me, as well as for her."

"So where is the trading fair we are going to?" Mike asked.

"To Ballinasloe, County Galway, the site of the oldest horse fair in the history of Ireland. Come on, hop on the ol' Harley." Kevin gestured to the padded vinyl seat behind him. "We'll take the hog on one of its last jaunts. We'll pretend we are like Peter Fonda and his sidekick in *Easy Rider*, taking our last ride into the West.

"Okay, partner," Mike said. Then he hesitated. "I better ask 'the wife'. As a future husband, this might be the best lesson you want to learn. If you ask, she'll always say 'yes.' If you don't ask first, no matter what it is, she won't approve and it won't be worth doing."

"I'll put that in my notes. Go on and ask her. Tell Pat it's for Eileen, for her wedding present. She'll love that. If she sounds like she's leanin' against your goin', just tell her it's all her fault we even got together in the first place."

"I'll be right back."

Mike burst into the kitchen. "Kevin asked me to take a ride with him over to Galway."

"What for?"

"Well," he hesitated, "its, kind of a surprise."

"For me?'

"Well, no. It's Kevin's surprise for Eileen for their wedding. I told him you wouldn't mind."

"So why did you ask?" I said.

"It's my first lesson in how to train Kevin to be a good husband."

"He has a good teacher." I kissed him on the cheek. "Have a good time."

Mike slammed the side door behind him, and hopped on the back of Kevin's candy-apple-red motorcycle, leaving his car-washing task 'til later.

"Let's round up that pony," Mike said, with his goofy, deliberate, cowboy drawl.

Kevin revved up the motor and skidded the Harley out of the drive with total abandon. The gravel kicked up from the motorcycle's tires and bounced off The Purple Bomber.

Mike and Kevin sped silently through the rolling hills of County Galway. They adhered to the unwritten rules of motorcycle riding by two men; which means refraining from talking to each other while the man riding behind the driver clings to the biker's belt so that the passenger doesn't have to put his arms around the driver. As the Harley sped down the road, Mike held on to Kevin's belt, and they never spoke a word.

Horse tradin', Mike thought. He knew something about the tradition of Irish horse racing: the Irish Grand National, the Irish Derby, and the Dublin Horse show. He also knew that the Irish bet 90 million Irish pounds a year on horse racing.

But horse trading, *this I know nothing about.*

*   *   *   *   *

As the Easy Riders road into county Galway, Mike noticed a marked difference in the terrain. Unlike many areas in the West of Ireland, with their characteristic low, stone-piled Cromwell walls carving the land into a lattice work of uneven squares, the Galway countryside was covered by a network of green hedges. Wild fuchsia grew into thick, twenty-foot walls flanking either side of the road. The profusion of purple and red flowers formed a kind of topiary tunnel through which Kevin, with Mike clinging to his belt, barreled on through.

After an hour of hard riding, Kevin slowed the Harley down to a gallop on the hilly outskirts of Ballinasloe. Cars, trucks, vans and horse trailers were parked anywhere and everywhere. Throngs of people filled the streets, which were set around a large green. The elegant tower of St. John's Church, sat on high ground at the edge of the green, providing a picturesque backdrop to the fair.

Kevin slowed the bike down to a crawl, searching for a place to park. He called over his right shoulder to Mike. "Although there are two fairs in Connemara itself which sell their famous ponies, this is the largest and oldest horse tradin' fair in all of Ireland. Today, Sunday, opens the fair which lasts an entire week."

As they drove further into the green, it became more and more congested. Kevin squeezed the motorcycle through two large groups of people, who moved over to accommodate him. Spotting a narrow opening between two horse trailers, Kevin turned the bike sharply into it, creating his own parking place.

"I'm amazed," Mike said as he got off the bike.

"And, it's been goin' on since ancient times." Kevin got off the bike and brushed the dust from his jeans. "It became famous in the 1700's when all the major European powers came to Ballinasloe to buy cavalry horses. Supposedly, 6,000 horses changed hands on a single day when France and Russia were at the height of their power. Even today, the number is close to 4,000 per day."

Kevin led Mike in through the crowds of people. They meandered between several smaller groups, who stood in a semi-circular fashion gaping at a horse presented before them by a handler. The horse handler was usually a tweed capped, middle-aged male, who held each horse by a leather strap tethered to his horse's bridle.

"Notice, there aren't any thoroughbreds here," Kevin said. "They're sold up in Kill, County Kildare. These are all non-thoroughbreds. Now all we have to do is wade through all this horseflesh, and find us the Connemara beauties."

Mike squinted as he scanned the enormous crowd. He pretended to search for the Connemara ponies, although he knew full well he couldn't tell the difference between a Shetland pony and a Shetland sheepdog.

"I think I see them over there," Kevin called, "over by the Draft Horse."

Mike wondered if *Draft* had anything to do with Kevin's Da feeding his horses Guinness beer. "Oh," he said, trying to keep up with Kevin's quickening pace.

Kevin came to an abrupt halt near a large group of spectators which included many young children. "Connemara ponies, at one time were used as a general purpose animal. Today, they're more valued as a children's riding pony. That's why all the kids are standing around here."

"They're adorable!" Mike gushed. He found himself impulsively pushing through the children to get a better look. A mother, holding the hand of her little girl, glared at Mike for nudging her as he pushed past them.

"Sorry," Mike said. "Aren't they beautiful?" he asked the little girl and her mother, in an effort to make amends for his rudeness.

"That's the one I want," the little girl replied. "The little white one, with the brown ponytail!" She regarded the size of Mike, looked back to the horse and said, "You could probably pick that pony up, if you wanted to, couldn't you?"

The mother's glare melted into a reluctant grin. "I don't think the owner would appreciate people picking up his ponies without first asking permission," the mother explained.

"Then I'll go ask him," she said. She let go of her mother's hand and ran in between two of the ponies to get to the owner. "May that man pick up that little white pony? He's my favorite pony in the whole fair."

The horse owner scratched the back of his head, which caused his curly, graying hair to stand on end. "How's that, lass?"

Mike, who had followed her over to him, answered for the little girl. "She wants to see if I can pick him up."

"Well," said the owner, "I don't know about that, but I'm sure you could pick her up and set her on my pony. Would you like that, little lass?"

The little girl jumped up and down. "Yes, yes," she squealed. The she looked over at her mother and hesitated. "That is if my mommy will give me permission."

"Don't be botherin' these poor men, dear," the mother said, as she took her daughter's hand again.

"Mommy, can't I have a ride? If I can't *have* the pony I picked out, can't I at least *sit* on it? Can I, Mommy?"

Without waiting for her mother's reply, Mike whisked the girl off her feet and sat her down on the pony's back.

The little girl's faced beamed with delight. "Thanks, mommy. And thank you very much, sirs," she added demurely.

At that moment, Kevin walked up and placed himself directly between Mike and the owner.

"I'll give you four hundred Irish pounds for that pony," Kevin stated flatly.

"Go on!" the owner replied, in a no-nonsense, brusque tone. "That's the prettiest one of the bunch, even this little lass could tell *that*! I wouldn't take a shilling less than six hundred pounds, and even that would be givin' it to ya!"

The owner then spit into his own hand and slapped it into Kevin's. "Six hundred pounds and she's all yours."

The girl sat happily, watching the two men dicker over the price of the pony.

Kevin looked at his hand in disbelief, and turned around as if he were starting to walk away. This attracted some of the onlookers who pressed around the owner, the pony, the little girl…and Kevin, who didn't get too far.

Suddenly, a slender, older man who resembled a priest, with white bushy hair and eyebrows, timidly ambled into the fray. "Perhaps you could be usin' a negotiator, over here," he said, extending his open palm to greet them. He was the first one to offer a hand without previously anointing it with saliva. "Now, ya fellas both want to make a deal, so why don't we work out something that both of yas will be happy with."

This suggestion caused the owner to completely spin around and walk away, yelling loudly to the watchful crowd, "I won't be needin' a 'tangler' to help me with this deal. This little pony will sell herself."

He walked over and looked Kevin up and down. "This young fella here, must think I'm some kinda arse or something. He offers me four hundred pounds for the loveliest pony that has ever come outta Connemara. Will ya look at this fine animal?" He gestured dramatically to the little girl perched on the pony and then looked pleadingly at the audience. "Don't yas agree that this charming little pony, with a pedigree as long as me arm is worth at least six hundred pounds?"

The crowd all responded at the same time, cheering "*Yea.*"

"Ya see?" the owner said. "The crowd agrees with me!"

In response, a heckler cried out from the crowd, "Is the little girl included in that price?"

The crowd roared.

The owner didn't miss a beat. "No, I'm afraid she's not included. Nobody can have her, as she's comin' back to Ballinasloe to marry me some day! What do ya think of that, young lady?" He took her porcelain hand which had been clutching the pony's mane, and kissed the back of it.

The little girl pulled her hand sheepishly away from his. Then she looked directly at her mother and asked loud enough for all to hear, "Mommy, isn't he a little old for me?"

The crowd roared again.

The owner chuckled along with the rest of them, then yelled to the crowd. "For that charming comment from this very lovely and truthful lady, I'll knock fifty pounds off the price." He bowed to Kevin and then to the crowd. "I'll take 550 pounds, take it or leave it. You look like an intelligent lad, what's your name, anyway?"

Kevin stood his ground. He kept his arms folded across his chest, keeping his spitting hand tucked under his arm. "Kevin O'Boyle," he said, firmly, "and my offer still stands at 400 pounds."

The 'tangler' jumped in, unable to contain himself any longer. "Gentlemen, gentlemen. Now we must find our way to a resolution. Young man, you haven't budged off your mark. I suggest you make a small compromise, and maybe we can see a happy ending to this, after all."

Before Kevin had a chance to make his final counteroffer, the owner walked willfully up to Kevin, threw his arms around him in a bear hug, and lifted Kevin off his feet. "Keveen O'Boyle! Now I know ya, the same Keveen who used to visit us at The National Stud. Your dad and me pitched hay to the horses when we were lads ourselves."

The owner then released Kevin from the hug, and stood back to admire Kevin. "Yer the image of your Da, by God."

"You must be Mickey Cahill," Kevin responded.

"Mickey Cahill, it is, Keveen."

"You're the one…" Kevin said, "who sold the Stud foals with my Da."

"I am."

"You were a tough negotiator then, maybe tougher, now I'd guess. "I was planning on splitting the difference with ya', but instead, I'll give ya the 550 pounds for your pony in memory of my Da. Besides, I'm buying it for a wedding present for my bride to be, and I know she would love it."

"And my 'luck money' will be your wedding present, since this little lady has refused me. He looked at the little girl still perched on her pony. Then he lifted her off the pony and set her on the ground. Let's make it 500 even." He spit into his hand and clasped Kevin's open palm.

The 'tangler' shrugged his shoulders at the crowd, who started to clap and applaud, a bit confused by the quick end to the negotiations. They almost appeared to be disappointed. This had the beginnings of one of the most memorable horse trades of the season.

"Eileen will be thrilled!" Mike said.

Kevin scooped up some dirt and clasped it on the backside of the pony, which according to fair tradition marked the signing of the deal. Mickey Cahill walked on over to Kevin and the pony.

"God rest your Da's soul," Mickey said. "I'm glad to know the pony will be in good hands as I'm sure you're as fine a horse handler as he ever was. And..." he winked at Kevin, "this pony has the best astrological chart of any horse I've ever seen!"

"Thanks, Mickey." Kevin shook his hand. "I can't wait to see the delight on my bride-to-be's face." Kevin looked at Mike. "Mike, you brought me luck. Maybe tomorrow you and I can start lookin' for a nice practical family sedan. Hopefully, one that isn't purple!"

The Huntmaster

Four Jack Russell Terrier puppies chased the car up the long driveway and we slowed down in fear that we'd run one of them over. I wondered if the brown and white spotted pups were a staged reception, for the host and hostess were well aware of our three p.m. arrival time.

As the idea of actually committing to buying a Bed and Breakfast in Ireland became more attractive to us, we decided to " try out" various Inns that were advertised in the "Irish Blue Book." This " Blue Book" was the Michelin Guide of Irish B&B's. An establishment could only advertise in it if the inn were clearly a step above the rest of the hundreds of bed and breakfasts strewn over Ireland. Qualifications for the Blue Book included special features or unique settings, such as a thirty-acre view of the Irish Sea, a 200-year-old history, or a bedroom where Brian Boru had once slept.

This particular Blue Book recommendation was selected by us for its location in Ireland's horse country, The Curragh in County Kildare. The country house was reportedly designed by an early Nineteenth Century architect, who built it as a hunting lodge. Three renowned race courses (The Curragh, Punchestown and Naas) were nearby. The National Stud Farm was within a stone's throw away, so we thought we could easily get a flavor for the Irish horsy set as well as their elevated tastes. As we entered the circular driveway, we counted thirteen chimneys on the grandiose Tudor style mansion, and felt assured that this would meet all of the Blue Book's claims.

We stopped the car and the puppies scratched at the driver's door. Mike opened the passenger's side and they eagerly spilled into the car, sloppy tongues lapping at our appreciative faces. We were won over. If this weren't staged, it was certainly great PR. I'd have to put this down in our marketing strategy notes for our B&B. Even if should decide that we didn't like anything else about this place, we were now certainly prejudiced in its favor. We finally managed to collect the squirming pups and placed them down on the gravel driveway. A rustle behind the bushes distracted them, and they scurried into the garden nipping at each other's ears along the way.

We walked up the irregular stone steps to the main entrance, and rang the bell. Nobody answered. We tried again, at least four different times, waiting politely between each ring for what seemed to be ten minutes. Very odd…as we had phoned ahead. Two wrought iron chairs flanked the heavy wooden door. We might as well make ourselves at home while we waited. We sat down.

As we relaxed in the chairs considering what to do next, I contemplated what a field day a lawsuit-crazed American lawyer could have at this place with four unleashed attack dogs and stairs not built to code. This thought suddenly vanished as the mother of the pups came trotting up to us with the four following behind her. She flipped over on her back and pumped her front paws to signal that she wanted a belly rub. As we gently stroked her stomach in unison, we surveyed the grounds and thanked God we were in a country where lawyers were considered luxuries, not necessities.

The mansion had an aura of elegant, old-world charm. The Blue Book had described it as a fifty-acre country house, which had catered to Huntsmen for one hundred years until its demise in the 1970's. One could definitely see this as a backdrop for a pack of hounds chasing a fox across the thicket in the near distance. You could almost hear the sound of the horn signaling the start of the Hunt, with nervous thoroughbreds mounted by distinguished men in red coats.

This dreamy vision was abruptly disturbed by someone trying to open the bulky wooden door.

And there smiled a cheerful, freckled-faced woman with auburn hair pulled back in a disheveled bun, who introduced herself as Margaret. She wiped her hands on her flowered apron and apologized profusely for keeping us waiting. At first I thought she was the housekeeper by the way she was dressed, but her accent was clearly educated Irish.

She seemed genuinely happy to see us, as she then introduced us to the "bitch and four pups." Ignoring my shocked, blinking eyes, which reacted automatically to the use of the "b-word" in mixed company, she went on to describe at great length how each pup could be distinguished from the other. She pointed out how their markings and personalities could be used to remember their names—ancient, Celtic names of Dierdre, Bridget, Dara and Eamon.

These names seemed so significant to her, I started to pay attention. It seemed as if their names were just as important as the Irish family names and crests engraved on several walnut plaques which hung on the wall behind her. She explained that these were her ancestral family names and crests. I asked why our surname, O'Brien, wasn't among them.

Margaret modestly reminded me that *the* O'Brien was the historical Earl of Thomond. He had built the famous fifteenth century Bunratty Castle in Limerick. *The* O'Brien, she stressed, was an *actual* Earl, and therefore clearly too far above Margaret's station to adorn her wall. I blushed at her flattery and my stupidity and wondered if I had insulted her somehow at the possibility of our being related. The only O'Brien relative I had known of from Limerick was forced to leave the county after he was arrested for borrowing a horse that apparently didn't belong to him. From this point forward, Margaret referred to us as *the* O'Briens, and I wondered if there wasn't the slightest bit of sarcasm in this new titular reference.

Mike and I usually refrain from bringing in the bags until we have seen the room, but having seen their impressive list of Family Crests, and having reserved the best room at $200 per night with dinner, we weren't particularly worried. Mike retrieved our bags, and then Margaret beckoned me to follow her.

She led me into the drawing room. An elegantly dressed elderly man stood poised with pipe in hand. His yellow striped ascot and royal blue satin smoking jacket gave him an air of sophisticated aristocracy.

This refined man gestured for us to sit down on a sumptuous sofa next to the wood-burning fireplace. Above the fireplace hung a large, gilded-framed portrait of a man in full riding regalia. I recognized the man in the portrait to be the man who stood in front of us, in his younger days. We had met the Huntmaster. At first, I thought he was Margaret's father, as he was a good twenty years her senior. His silvery-white hair was streaked with the yellow stain of age. He looked rather frail but in spite of this, took his job as official greeter rather seriously. When he extended his hand, a worn dress shirt cuff slipped out from under his jacket sleeve. He had a strong and somewhat affected British accent, each syllable deliberately and carefully pronounced.

He gripped my hand warmly, made the necessary introductions and asked us again to take a seat on the down-filled chintz sofa, which was invitingly positioned next to the roaring fire. Perhaps this picture-perfect blaze had been the reason they had taken so long to answer the door; after all, there were no gas starters in the thirteen fireplaces in this house. Margaret brought tumblers and two types of sherry. Never having tried the strong, sweet liquor before, I slowly raised the glass for a toast, trying to not look too unsophisticated.

My husband recognized my discomfort at making a toast, and quickly interceded. "To the huntmaster in the portrait," he said. We lifted our glasses. Margaret beamed at her gentleman. The patron, whom we now knew as Richard, actually Sir Richard, as we were gently reminded, immediately adjusted his ascot and pulled his shoulders back.

His simple "Merci beaucoup," in exaggerated French, acknowledged that he was indeed the same man in the portrait and was eager to tell us of his glorious days as Master of the Hunt.

I often chide my husband by calling him the twenty-question man. Having always been in sales, his technique has always consisted of keeping the customer as the center of attention, by asking them a stream of questions about themselves. And he was right. It always seemed that the best way to get people to engage in polite conversation was to get them to talk about their favorite subject, themselves. After all, people usually would rather talk about themselves than just about anything else. Mike had made a pretty good living using this philosophy.

Mr. twenty-question man proceeded to ask our aristocratic host every question he could think of about hunting which were innumerable, as he knew nothing about it. Sir Richard patiently explained the different roles of the hunters, including that of huntmaster, which, of course, was *the* most important position.

He explained how the hounds were not like other domestic dogs and were boarded on the premises and raised exclusively for the hunt. He bragged about his prize horses, winning jumpers who were bred at the world-renowned National Stud Farm. But times had changed. There were laws being proposed to outlaw hunts that used live foxes. He sadly admitted that the only dogs left, on the estate, were the four puppies and their mother who were saved from the local Humane Society.

He illustrated each of his narratives with photos from worn leather albums that were stacked handily next to the fireplace. Each photo bore testimony to an age of landed gentry and nobility, who, in their leisure, had chased fox for sport. It seemed a pity that this gentle man lived in an era where foxhunting was only a romantic anachronism at best.

Margaret rushed in and out refilling our Sherry glasses, and soon we didn't care if we ever got to our room. Sir Richard told his stories with such alacrity and enthusiasm that we listened to them throughout dinner and well into the early evening. After desert, Margaret insisted that we join them for after dinner cocktails in the library. We were such a great audience for Sir Richard.

We thankfully accepted, and Mike was happy to have the additional time to learn more about hunting. He asked about bridles, crops and saddles. Next, he grilled Sir Richard on riding techniques, teamwork and etiquette. Sir Richard answered each question with infinitesimal detail and relish until Mike got to what we were all hoping was one of his last questions.

"So, how do you actually get the fox in the box?"

Sir Richard looked puzzled, as if he thought he had misunderstood. "What do you mean, *get the fox in the box?*"

Mike replied, "You know, how do you get the fox to go *into* the box before you let him loose to begin the chase."

Sir Richard looked astonished, then threw his head back and laughed until his whole body shook. He tried to compose himself, but the effort to stop his laughter made him almost choke on his Sherry.

"My dear man," he explained. Where did you get the notion that you had to let a fox loose in order to begin the chase? The whole chase is about *finding* and *catching* a fox which runs wild in the forest. My God, they're all over the place!" Sir Richard giggled again, and sipped his drink. "I guess you can take the boy out of the city, but you can't take the city out of the boy!"

The laughter and the Sherry began to loosen Sir Richard's tongue. His heretofore impeccable and eloquent accent started to unravel. As he waxed eloquently about the days of old, I noticed his grammatical usage began to slip. He no longer sounded like an English gentleman, but rather like an American stage actor with a studied British accent.

Mike was just getting around to his last question, the mainstay of the salesman's twenty-question technique. "So, just where are you from originally?"

The aristocratic Huntmaster leaned forward and spoke in a slow, halting whisper. "Well, you might be able to detect a faint trace of my American accent," he said. "*Actually,*" he said with a slight Sherry induced slur combined with a deliberate London accent, "originally, I'm from the Eastern Seaboard...." he hesitated...."Why, New Jersey, to be exact."

"You're kidding," Mike said. "You could have fooled me. You sure don't sound like you're from anywhere near *Joisey*. I'm very familiar with New Jersey, as I used to fly into its airport for business several times a month."

"Well, then," Sir Richard said. "Maybe you're familiar with ABC Plumbing."

Mike hesitated. "It does sound rather familiar—"

"Oh, it's been out of the family for years, you're probably too young to know of it." Sir Richard reached into his silk smoking jacket pocket for his pipe. "I sold a lot of plumbing fixtures in the sixty's. When I had the opportunity in the seventy's, I took the company public. Then I took the cash and came to Ireland to live out my dream as a country gentleman."

And, indeed, Sir Richard the elegant country squire had created a convincing dream from which we wished we hadn't been awakened. We thanked Sir Richard and Margaret for a charmed evening and retired to our room. Richard untied his ascot and sank back into his chair. He then sipped on his Sherry, lit his pipe and gazed up at the portrait of The Huntmaster above the fireplace mantel.

The Wedding

"Are yas stayin' in Ireland much longer?" Mary asked as she cleared off what was left of the morning's breakfast.

A middle-aged couple, who sat next to each other, responded in unison while folding their napkins and placing them on the table. "Yes." "No." Then they looked at each other, puzzled.

"Well, which is it?" Mary asked. "It never ceases to amaze me how many of the married folk we have stay with us, can't seem to agree on anything. Although you two have probably been together for many years you have completely opposite responses to the same simple question. How long have yas been together, anyway?"

The couple again replied in unison, "Nineteen years. Twenty years." They looked defiantly at each other. The husband spoke first. "We've been together twenty years, but married nineteen."

Mary persisted. "Now which is it?" she asked. "Yes, you are staying on in Ireland for awhile, or no, you're not." Mary shook her head. "I swear I don't know how people stay married. Either you are or you're not."

The couple looked hesitantly at one another. They were embarrassed. The wife decided not to answer this time, but instead returned the question with another question to her husband. "Why did you say 'no?' We have another whole week."

"I guess you're right," he said. "I feel like the first one went by so fast that it won't be long 'til we're back in the States like we never left."

"You're right," she answered. "It won't be long." She smiled at him and patted his hand.

"Marriage!" Mary exclaimed as she picked the remainder of the napkins off of the table. "I'll never understand it!"

The husband chuckled. "Well, when they come up with a better alternative, would you let us know?" He took his wife by the elbow and gently guided her out of her chair.

Mary wondered if she had offended them. "Hope you two lovebirds have a nice day. Twenty years…now that's pretty amazing. Are you traveling far today to your next Bed and Breakfast?"

The couple looked at each other and hesitated. "Yes. No." they said at the same time. Then they giggled at themselves, but didn't change their answers.

Mary sighed loudly. "Have a nice trip," she said, shaking her head again.

"Oh, we will," they called back over their shoulders as they headed back up to their room.

"Marriage," Mary said as she walked into the kitchen. "Go figure."

With that the side doorbell rang. Mary opened it to let Eileen in.

"Well, speak of the devil," Mary said. "You're just the one I need to explain marriage to me."

"Me?" Eileen asked. "At least don't ask until after tomorrow. That is, if I survive tomorrow."

"I'm sure everything will be perfect," Mary reassured her. "You'll make the prettiest bride anybody's ever seen. How are the plans? Everything all set?"

"Yes. We finished making up the table arrangements this morning. We put you, Pat and Mike at the good table with all of the fun people."

"That's grand," Mary responded.

"Actually things are quite under control, except maybe for Kevin."

"Don't tell me he's got a case of the cold feet!" Mary chided.

"Oh, no. Nothing like that. He's his usual cool self, except we haven't heard from his best friend from his home town who was supposed to call last night and was supposed to show up here at the farmhouse today. You haven't heard from a Pete Doyle today, have you by any chance?"

"I haven't." Mary said. "Let me check the book." Mary walked into the foyer and looked down at the record book perched on the phone stand.

"We don't even have his name down for a reservation. Are you sure he was going to stay with us?"

"Yes," Mary said. "I'm positive. Now, Kevin will really be fit to be tied. Pete was supposed to be his best man. We better get an alternate. We mustn't let it get down to the wire. I'll have Kevin try to contact him again. He's been trying all week. It seems Pete has been on the road."

"Maybe Mike O'Brien would fill in for him," Mary offered.

"We might have to ask him," Eileen said.

"I'm sure he'd be delighted." Mary looked up at the kitchen clock. "You're running out of time. I'll call you the minute I hear from your man Pete Doyle."

"In the meantime, I'll ask Mike if he'd mind being a stand-in," Eileen said, as she headed for the door. "Let me know if you hear anything. Maybe Pete's planning on surprising us by just showing up at the church tomorrow."

*   *   *   *   *

An elderly priest with thinning white hair stood on the altar so that he was facing Kevin and Eileen and the entire congregation. He was dressed in a gold vestment with gold and silver embroidered trim. He turned to Kevin. "Kevin, do you take this woman to be your lawful wedded wife, to have and to hold from this day forward until death do you part?"

"I do," Kevin said.

Mike handed the simple gold wedding band to Kevin.

Kevin took the ring and placed it on Eileen's delicate finger.

The priest boomed. "I now pronounce you man and wife. You may kiss the bride!"

Kevin grabbed Eileen and planted an uncharacteristically passionate kiss on Eileen's lips.

She withdrew from him, slightly embarrassed, her face beaming. She put her arm in his and he led her down the aisle.

Everyone in the little gray church clapped and cheered.

When the bride and groom reached the church doors, they clasped hands and ducked under a shower of rice pelting down upon them tossed by an enthusiastic group of children waiting outside on the church stairs. They shrieked with glee as Kevin and Eileen raised their hands above their heads in a futile effort to shield themselves from the onslaught of rice.

Soon the entire church had emptied itself onto the front steps, and each person found himself vying for the attentions of the new bride and groom, each wanting to be the first to congratulate them on their marriage. Eventually a reception line formed from Kevin and Eileen all the way down to the curb where Kevin's car, decorated with streamers and signs, waited for them.

Mike and I stood at the end of the line. After we finally reached the bride and groom and the four of us exchanged kisses and hugs, Mike whispered into Kevin's ear. "Do you want me to move all of these people along? They'll stand out here all day if you let them."

Kevin looked around at the throng of people. "Thanks, Mike," he said. "Do you think you could make an announcement for everybody to start moving along to the reception hall?"

"Just let your best man take care of it," Mike said. "That's my job, isn't it?"

Mike stood at the top of the church stairs and made the announcement.

People politely listened but didn't move from their places.

"We better make a move toward the reception hall," Mike said, "or they never will." With that, Mike took me by the arm and we led the newly-weds to their awaiting car.

Next, Mike helped Eileen and Kevin get into the back seat and then proceeded to escort me into the front passenger side. Then Mike turned on the ignition and revved up the motor. The dramatic gesture caused all of the wedding guests to rush the car and wave excitedly into the back seat, calling for the newlyweds to kiss. As the crowd watched Kevin kissed his bride. Then the car with its hand painted *just married* sign pulled out slowly from the curb.

"Are you two all right back there?" Mike asked as he peered into the rearview mirror.

"Couldn't be better," Eileen replied.

"It looks like a rowdy crowd," Mike said. "The reception should be a real blast."

"And Eileen put us at the fun table," I added. "Right, Eileen?"

The newlyweds were too engrossed in each other to respond.

*   *   *   *   *

We joined Mary at the back of the reception hall where 200 name cards were displayed with each person assigned to a numbered table.

"Looks like we're all at table number six," Mary called to us as she found our name cards. "There must be ten people to a table."

Soft violin music was playing as we entered the enormous ballroom. The orchestra members wore black tuxedos. They played from a small stage at the far end of the hall, which was decorated, with silver balloons and white crepe paper. On each table, a cascade of fresh fuschia-colored roses stood on slim pedestal vases which served as centerpieces. In the middle of each spray of flowers was a black and white plastic table number. We spotted table number six and made our way over to it.

Two couples were already seated when we reached our table and another couple joined us as we sat down. After all of us had taken our seats, Mike started the introductions, introducing himself as best man, me, the wife of the best man and Mary, as one of Kevin's old girlfriends. A couple who appeared to be in their sixties, introduced themselves as relatives of Eileen's. The husband had a thick crop of white hair and his wife, whom he introduced as his better half, was a redhead with smiling, shining eyes. The other two couples, who appeared to be in their thirties and forties were friends and relatives on Kevin's side.

Mike explained his role as best man by default. The one couple explained that they were surprised at the sudden disappearance of Pete

Doyle because they did, indeed, actually know the mysterious Pete Doyle quite well. "Maybe he'll show up later," one of them said. "Pete always was a little spacey. Nice, mind you, but spacey."

The servers started to bring around the salads, and the conversation moved easily from couple to couple. As we passed the salad dressing around the table, each couple began to tell the story of how they had met and fallen in love. The youngest couple beamed at each other as they explained in meticulous detail how, when and why they discovered each other.

"It was definitely love at first sight," he said.

"It was?" his wife asked.

"Of course it was. At least it was for me," he said.

"That's impossible!" she argued. "How can it be love at first sight, when you had been living with me for two years?"

"A prenuptial apartment?" Mike asked.

"Oh, no, nothing like that,'" the young woman answered. "I'm very old-fashioned. You see, we were in college together and a common friend of ours asked us to share an apartment off campus with her. We were all in the nursing program together."

"Oh?" Mary chimed in. "That must have been quite a cozy arrangement."

"No, it was nothing like that," the young man explained. "You see, we were all friends. At least that's what Kaitlin thought. She always had guys coming round trying to take her out, but she was crazy about a fella named Jack. I kind of hung around and played big brother, patiently waiting."

"For two years?" Mike asked.

"One night," he explained. "Kaitlin came home, brokenhearted. In fact, I'd say she was devastated. It seemed Jack wanted to break up with her. She couldn't take the rejection. She needed a shoulder to cry on."

"What did you do?" Mary asked.

"Nothing. She wanted to cry on my shoulder all night and I let her." He grinned at his young wife. "Two months later she was Mrs. O'Hara. You see, lads, patience does pay off. We've been married eight years next week."

"Congratulations," the elderly gentleman said, then winked at everybody at the table. "Did you know there are only *two* questions that are always answered by *a number of years?*"

"How's that?" the young man replied.

"*How long is your prison sentence?* and *How long have you been married?* Both are always answered by the number of years. Ha!"

The whole table roared.

"And how long have you been serving time?" Mike asked.

"Thirty years to life!" He shot back.

After the laughter died down again, Mary asked the self-appointed comedian, "So how did you meet your charming little bride?"

"Please, I'm eating!" he shoveled a forkful of greens into his mouth.

His wife looked over at him, rolled her eyes and giggled. This was the table's signal that it was okay to laugh at his wife's expense.

"I'll tell it," his wife said. "We met at the local roller skating rink. Jimmy wasn't fat then. He was gorgeous and quite a skater. All the ladies were after him."

"Oh, go on!" he interrupted her.

"You wanted to eat, so I'll just have to tell it," she continued. "My parents wouldn't allow me to go to the skating rink when all the older boys would skate on Tuesday nights. So I would look through the window and watch Jivin' Jimmy showing off for all the girls who would swoon all over him when he skated backwards."

"Now stop, would ya?" he protested. "You make it sound like I was a show off!"

"Well, you didn't mind all the attention you were getting in that white v-neck sweater you used to wear," she teased.

"So what happened?" Mary asked, as the servers began collecting our salad plates and serving the main course.

"After several weeks of peering at him through the window, I finally couldn't stand it any more. I sneaked into the rink, and although I was a pretty good skater myself, I pretended that I couldn't skate. He eventually

came up to me and offered to give me a few lessons." She winked. "He
turned out to be a very good skating instructor."

"Yeah, I chased her, chased her and chased her around that rink until
she finally *caught me*." The husband grinned. "Then she bought her own
white v-neck and we've been pairs skating ever since."

It was hard to imagine these sixty-year-olds in matching sweaters skimming gracefully across the roller rink in each other's arms.

Our stories were interrupted when one of the members of the band
asked that the best man come up and make a short speech. Mike accom-
modated him by walking up to the podium, clearing his throat, and starting an eloquent address about Kevin and Eileen being the epitome of a
happily married couple, and how we all wished we could turn the clocks
back to the first day of our marriages.

Next, Kevin and Eileen got up and thanked Mike for being the best
man. They each addressed the crowd, thanking them for coming and sharing their special day. Kevin ended his speech by reminding anybody who
knew the whereabouts of one Pete Doyle to please contact him. He was
sorry he hadn't made it but happy he hadn't waited to get married until
Pete showed up.

At the end of the evening one of the couples suggested we all go into
an adjoining bar for a nightcap to wrap up the evening's fun. We all agreed
and adjourned into the cozy tavern. Smoke swirled throughout the bar
and we pulled up some stools to form a circle at the end of the bar.

Mike ordered a round and the bartender set the drinks on the wooden
ledge of the bar. "Here's to all of us who are serving time," Mike toasted,
"and to all those just starting their life sentence."

With that, a handsome young man in jeans and a tee shirt approached
our group and yelled to one of the couples. "Hey, Sean and Peggy Shea!
Long time no see! Funny to run into you! We're going to have one hell of
a time at Kevin's wedding next week, huh?"

We all looked at each other in disbelief.

"You must be the long lost Pete Doyle," Mike said, as he got up to shake his hand. "I hate to tell you pal, but you're a day late and a dollar short. We all just now came from Kevin's wedding. Have you been here all night?"

"Yeah. Why? Kevin's wedding is next Saturday, isn't it?"

Mike removed his dinner jacket and threw it around Pete's shoulders. "If you hurry up, Pete, you just might be able to make an appearance as best man, after all. Go see if Kevin and Eileen are still in there!"

Pete scratched his head as he moved slowly away from us and toward the reception hall door. "I'll see if I can catch up to them." He hesitated, and turned towards us. "I feel like a jerk. Do you think they'll be mad at me?"

"Yes. No," we all answered simultaneously.

The Skellig Experience

"It was a wonderful wedding," Eileen said to her new husband of one day as the two of them climbed into Kevin's car.

"I didn't realize we had so many friends," Kevin said. "And all of them said exactly the same thing. You were the most beautiful bride they had ever seen. And I couldn't agree with them more."

"Thanks, dear." Eileen said dreamily as she rested her head on Kevin's shoulder.

"I'm so tired, though. Maybe we could consider postponing the honeymoon and go later this month. Haven't we had enough commotion the last few weeks? We could just relax and hang around the house."

"No way," Kevin answered. "They'll be plenty of time for just hanging around the house. We agreed the night we were engaged that we would go to Skellig Michael for our honeymoon and that's exactly what we're going to do. Besides, postponed honeymoons never get taken."

"You're right," Eileen said.

"Why don't you relax, put your seat back and take a little nap? You'll feel better after a little sleep. Maybe I shouldn't have kept you up all night." He winked at Eileen.

"I'm not complaining, mind you," Eileen teased back. She adjusted her car seat to a reclining position. "Promise to wake me if you see anything exciting on the way. I don't want to miss anything."

"I promise."

Eileen nestled into her seat, pulling her sweater up around her shoulders. She thought of the night of their engagement, just two short months earlier. She thought of how nervous Kevin had been acting, the first time she had ever seen him lose his otherwise cool composure. And he had seemed quieter than usual, distracted, and she had to drag the slightest of conversation out of him. At one point in the evening, she assumed he was-n't having a very good time, so she suggested that they call it an early evening. That's when he really became unglued and apologized for his weird behavior. Then he pulled a little black velvet box from his pocket.

"I've been rehearsing this for weeks, Eileen, but I'm afraid the words might get in the way. So I'll just blurt it out. I love you and want to spend my life with you. There, I said it, and here's the ring I picked out for you." He handed her the box, and added quickly, "The jeweler said you could exchange it for something else, if you didn't like the setting, or didn't say yes to my wedding proposal."

"Now, Kevin, you know I wouldn't think of returning a gift from you!"

"It's not a gift," Kevin said, haltingly. "It's supposed to be an engagement ring," Eileen giggled, as she opened the little velvet box. She removed the ring from the box and admired it. "It's absolutely stunning, Kevin!"

"Not half as stunning as you are. Will ya say yes to being my wife, then, Eileen?"

"Happily," she blinked to keep her tears from flowing.

"Give us a hug," Kevin said. Then Kevin took the ring from her and placed it on her finger. "And I won't be havin' any of these long engage-ments. I don't believe in them. We should be able get a wedding together in a few weeks, can't we?"

"Sure, I suppose so," Eileen said as she admired the diamond. "Whatever you want, dear."

"I could get used to hearing that," Kevin grinned, relief flushing over his face. He heaved a huge sigh. "I don't know why that was so hard. I really didn't think you'd turn me down."

"That's what I like about you, Kevin," Eileen teased, "your modesty."

"And I know where we can go for our honeymoon," Kevin said. "In fact, I believe I decided when I was twelve years old. Skellig Michael."

"Skellig Michael?" Eileen asked. Isn't that the romantic island off of Kerry where a monastic settlement was established?"

"It is romantic, indeed," Kevin replied wistfully.

"And you decided on our honeymoon at the tender age of twelve?"

"I did. You see, at that time, the priests at school were appealing to the manhood of all the pre-teens, trying to cajole us into joining a religious order or entering a cloistered monastic order. They used Skellig Michael as the ultimate example of how harsh and rigid the monastic life could be; a remote, solitary place to offer yourself up to God in prayer and solitude. Although the monks left the island in the 13th century because of its desolate location and brutal living conditions, it was considered, by the priests, at least, to be the most macho of monastic orders to join. I have to admit, at first, the macho idea appealed to me. The priests took us on a field trip to see the island, hoping it's magical allure would entice some of us into the priesthood."

"You weren't convinced?" Eileen asked.

"First of all, I never did actually get onto the island itself. I guess it was too expensive for the school to pay for a busload of kids to be shipped over to the island. Instead, we were only allowed to look at it from the seashore."

"So what was it like?" Eileen asked.

"It was a magical experience, one I'll never forget. I fell in love with Skellig Michael and the sight of it has haunted me ever since. It's jagged, twin peaks jutting fiercely out of the sea seemed so forbidding and mysterious. It was like an elusive, unrealized dream. That's when I vowed I'd some day come back to it, to actually walk on the island, up the stairs, and to the abandoned monastic ruins. It's a very powerful and mystical place that draws you to it. So my dream since then was to return with my wife on our honeymoon to have her share in its mysterious charm."

"I can't wait to see it," Eileen exclaimed. "You make it sound so magical. But not magical enough to make you join the monastery?"

"When I learned the harsh reality of a handful of monks eking out a living in austere conditions, I knew then, I wasn't that macho, at least not macho enough to be a monk or a priest. In the end, although I was seduced by the Skellig experience, I realized I wasn't monastery material, after all."

"Lucky for me," Eileen teased.

Kevin grinned at her. "So, in my stubborn way, I showed the priests. In order to keep the good fathers from pushing the priesthood on me for the next few years, I quit school the day after we got back from our little field trip."

"You showed them!" Eileen teased.

Kevin put his arm around Eileen's shoulder. "So I want to fulfill my dream of taking my wife to Skellig Michael on our honeymoon. I can't think of a more isolated, idyllic place. It's so wild, romantic. I can't wait to share it with you."

"I've always wanted to see it," Eileen said. "Let's plan on going the day after the wedding."

Now, two months later, that day had come. Kevin and Eileen had arranged to stay a few nights in the resort town of Waterville from where they could take a boat over to Skellig Michael. There was also the Skellig Experience Center which they planned to visit, even though Kevin had done quite a bit of background research himself. He was eager to show off for his new bride.

They arrived at The Smuggler, a 100-year old, whitewashed hotel in Waterville where they had reserved the honeymoon suite. The hotel was situated in the heart of the town with a panoramic view overlooking Ballinskelligs Bay. After checking in and bringing their luggage up to their room, they enjoyed dinner at a table with a water view in the Inn's charming restaurant. After dinner they took a stroll along the boardwalk and watched children playing fetch with their dogs on the water's edge.

The following morning, they drove to Valentia Island, where the Skellig Experience Center was located.

"I don't know what they can tell us that I haven't researched already," Kevin said, as they paid for their entry tickets to the Center.

"Then you can be my private tour guide," Eileen responded as she took the receipt from the ticket attendant.

They walked into the exhibit hall where large billboards displayed pictures of the Skellig Islands. Kevin read from one of the posters. *The Skellig Islands are a group of small rocky islets which lie approximately nine miles off the southwest coast of the Iveragh Peninsula. Of all the islands, Skellig Michael is the most renowned for being the place where St. Fionan founded his monastic settlement in the 9th century. Skellig Michael was continuously occupied by monks until the 13th century. Skellig Michael is the largest of the islands, and its lighthouse, stands 164 feet above the sea and can be reached by climbing the some 670 steps hewn from rock over 1,000 years ago.*

"Are ya up for a climb like that?" Kevin asked.

"I've got my hiking boots on and I'm ready," Eileen said.

"Did ya know there's a lighthouse on top of Skellig Michael? The story is that the lighthouse keeper lost two children who fell to their deaths from a rocky precipice. He finally had to quit after the second child's death out of remorse and shame."

"That's terrible!" Eileen said.

"They don't explain here that an airplane crashed into Michael during World War II."

"That's amazing."

"Besides the monastic ruins," Kevin explained, "another thing that Skellig Michael was noted for was that often, young couples in love would paddle their boats over to the island when Ireland forbade marriage during Lent. The island was still on the ancient Celtic calendar which allowed the eager couples to go ahead and take their vows on Skellig Michael."

"How romantic!" Eileen gushed.

A young attendant in a blue smock with a white nametag pinned to it called out, "The slide show will begin in five minutes. We are also taking tickets for the Skellig cruise which may or may not leave in the next half hour."

Kevin turned to Eileen. "What's that supposed to mean?'

Eileen walked up to the attendant. "Miss, what did you mean *may or may not leave in half an hour?*"

"It's a windy day, Miss. The water's a bit choppy, so we're not sure if the regularly scheduled four o'clock cruise will go after all," she answered. "You can always try back tomorrow."

Kevin replied, "I've been waiting twenty years for this. I'd hate to wait another day."

Several people filed into the projection room. Kevin and Eileen followed them. Wooden benches were positioned in tiered rows in order to accommodate large crowds. A narrator came on, welcoming the tourists to the Skelligs and then three slides were projected onto the wall at one time. As the presentation continued, the slides alternated automatically illustrating each point. The narration described the importance of monasticism in sixth and seventh century Ireland. Ireland's natural physical attributes proved ideal for the monastic cult of voluntary exile and isolation, which had its origins in early Christian Egypt.

A slide of Skellig Michael flashed on the screen, with its group of beehive cells and two oratories terraced into the side of a rock five hundred feet above sea level. Alongside the monastic ruins stood a tiny graveyard, the only remaining remnant of human habitation. Each monastery was self-contained and controlled by its own abbot. The monks bartered for food and spent many long days praying and copying manuscripts in their *scriptoria*. Eventually, these monasteries spread throughout the British Isles and into Europe where several separate monastic orders were founded. By the early eighth century, the missionary movement Christianized much of Europe.

The lights went on, and Kevin and Eileen left the projection room.

"I'm so excited," Eileen said. "Let's see if we can get on that cruise."

They walked up to the same attendant they had talked to before.

"Miss, could you tell us what the status is with that cruise?" Kevin asked. "Is it going?"

"There are only two other people who want to go," she said, apologetically, "and it's still pretty choppy out there, according to the captain." She gestured to a large man with a windbreaker standing at the souvenir counter.

Kevin walked over to him. "Well, captain, are ya up for takin' us to Skellig Michael for the *real* Skellig experience? We don't think the slide show could replace seeing the real thing."

The captain scratched his chin and shook his head. "Looks doubtful, for today, anyways. Sorry."

Kevin couldn't take no for an answer, especially now that he had Eileen excited about going to the island, too.

Without thinking, Kevin said to the Captain. "I'll pay you double for both of us and for the other two who want to go." He pushed a wad of bills at the Captain.

"Now lad, hang on to your money," the Captain said. "I'll go, surely, if you can take the bumpy ride."

"We're up for it if you are." Kevin answered.

"Well, come on then," the Captain said as he pushed Kevin's money away. "I'll get the other couple." He walked away from them and into the exhibition hall.

A few minutes later, he returned. "It seems the other couple have decided against it."

"That's okay," Eileen said. "We can come back tomorrow. I don't think the Skelligs are going anywhere soon."

The Captain chuckled. "I'll still take yas if yas want to go that badly."

Kevin beamed. "That would be grand of ya, Captain. We'd really appreciate it. I've been waiting a long time to finally get to Skellig Michael."

"Mind you," the Captain said, "its a three hour trip. It's an hour boat ride out there and we give yas an hour to climb and tour the monastic settlement, then it's an hour boat trip back."

"We can't wait!" Eileen said.

"Follow me," the Captain said, as he led them out of the Center and out to his blue van. The wind was blowing fiercely, and Eileen pulled her scarf up over her head to keep her hair from flying.

They got into the van and headed down toward the water.

"My husband is a Skellig aficionado," Eileen bragged to the Captain.

"Is that so?" the Captain answered. "So you know all about the magical seduction of the place?"

"We do," Kevin replied for Eileen and himself. "Why do you think we'd make you take us over there on a day like this?"

When they arrived at the pier, a blast of air came off the sea, and they had a difficult time bracing themselves against the wind while walking toward the boat which would take them to Skellig Michael.

A brown stained fishing boat, called a curragh, with an oversized motor attached to its back, was tethered to the pier by a thick rope. The boat bobbed up and down and occasionally banged into the dock from the rough waves which were pounding against the pier.

"It does look a bit rough," Kevin said tentatively.

"I'm still up for it if you are," Eileen assured him. "I think we can handle it."

The Captain got on board first and held out his hand to Eileen who carefully stepped off the dock and into the boat, followed by Kevin who was guiding her from behind. The Captain passed two life jackets to them and put one on himself. He pulled the starter on the engine several times until it finally kicked over and began to hum. The Captain then unhooked the rope from the metal mooring, and the boat careened into the open sea.

The water was rough. Huge swells collided into one another while smaller waves built up their momentum, eventually crashing against the side of the boat. Instead of skimming across the water, the boat bounced violently up and down making slow headway against the strong undulating currents. The boat pushed onward until they saw an island appear in the near distance.

"There's Little Skellig!" Kevin pointed out the window. "That's the island which is inhabited by tens of thousands of seabirds. Gannets and puffins are the two particular species which are attracted to this island."

"Listen to them," Eileen cupped her ear as she called over the din. "They're screeching and screaming," Eileen said. "It sounds as if they're calling out to us."

As they drew closer to Little Skellig, the waves became more ferocious and the boat bounced wildly causing it to take in some water.

"Don't be alarmed," the Captain said, matter-of-factly. "I'll just pitch some of this water back into the sea where it belongs." He calmly retrieved a small bucket and began to scoop water from the bottom of the boat and threw it over board.

"Maybe I should be doing that while you're navigating," Kevin said, as he leaned over to take the bucket from the Captain. "You do the driving, I'll do the bailing."

The boat began to shiver violently. Eileen's face began to turn white. She was starting to worry. "Kevin, do you think we could go a little slower or stop at Little Skellig?"

Kevin looked at Eileen's face. "Are you all right? I think we should consider turning back at this point. Would you be too disappointed?"

"I was afraid *you'd* be disappointed," Eileen responded. "No! I'm not ready to turn back. We're almost there."

"What do you think?" Kevin called to the Captain, over the din of the crashing waves and screeching birds.

"It's not too much further," the Captain hollered back. "We can make it if you can put up with the turbulence."

"Okay!" Kevin responded. "You keep steering and I'll keep bailing."

The sturdy little curragh swung from side to side letting more water in with each pitch. In an attempt to lessen the water coming in over the sides, the Captain managed to maneuver the tiny craft directly into the waves, which caused more bouncing. The boat continued to forge onward.

Eileen pulled her scarf over her face to shield herself from the spray of water, which was by now constantly slamming against the boat. Her stomach felt queasy, and she pulled herself to the side of the boat in the event that she might indeed become seasick.

When Kevin stopped bailing water he realized her condition. He called up to her, "Maybe it's time we turned around. You don't look too well."

"I'll be all right," she protested.

The Captain cried out, "Look, there it is coming into sight now, Skellig Michael." He pointed ahead of them.

Kevin helped Eileen stand up to get a glimpse of the island.

"It is a vision," Eileen said tentatively and then collapsed onto her seat. "Yeah," Kevin said. "I don't know how those monks ever survived. Are you all right, dear? Can you make it until we get there? I'm sorry I put you through this. I know we're both dying to see it, but we don't want to die *getting* to see it."

Eileen smiled. "I think I can make it."

The Captain grinned at the two of them. "You're not the first to come under the spell of Skellig Michael. The island's charm is legendary. When the island casts its spell upon you, it draws you to it, sort of hypnotizes you."

"It's magic is hard to resist," Eileen managed to say. "My husband has been dreaming about coming here since he was twelve."

The Captain turned the boat sharply. "It's so choppy," he said. "I might not be able to dock the boat, but I can get close enough for you both to jump out onto the rock."

"Are ya ready?" Kevin turned to Eileen.

"Sure!" Eileen answered weakly.

"Come on, give me your hand," Kevin said, as he stretched out his arm to guide her. "I'll jump first, so you'll have something soft to fall on! Ha!" Kevin jumped out of the boat and landed on a wide step, the first of several hundred steps clinging to the side of the rock which led to the top.

With the help of the Captain, Eileen flung herself from the curragh and onto the step where Kevin grabbed a hold of her. "We made it!" he cried.

"It is like a fantasy," Eileen smiled at him. "It's even more romantic than you said. It makes me feel as if we're the only people in the world."

She looked up at the irregular set of stone stairs that zigzagged up the shear side of the cliff.

Kevin pulled her tighter towards him. "You know, Eileen, you make me the happiest man on Skellig Michael." He chuckled, "Never mind that I am the *only* man on Skellig Island!"

Eileen laughed. "I'm thrilled you finally got to share your dream island with me."

"It is a captivating place. But, now that we've actually made it," Kevin said, "I'm more concerned about you. You still look pretty sick. I've put you through a lot getting here. I'd feel better if we got you back to shore as soon as possible." He waved over to the Captain.

"I do feel a little weak to be climbing 670 stairs," Eileen admitted. "Why don't you go on up yourself and have a look. I'll wait down here for you."

"No way," Kevin said. "Getting here with you was my dream, and now we have done it. I don't need to climb all those stairs to prove it. Right now, all I'm worried about is the most important thing to me, my wife. Let me get you back to the hotel where you can get some rest after this roller coaster ride."

Eileen smiled. "This is the most romantic roller coaster ride I've ever taken."

Suddenly the wind subsided and the water became calm. The Captain pulled the curragh up to the pier. "Do you two need a bit more time to look around the island?" he asked.

Kevin and Eileen moved toward the boat. "We have all the time in the world in front of us," Kevin said, as he helped Eileen step into the bobbing craft. They sat down next to each other and Eileen rested her head on Kevin's shoulder.

Book of Kells

We were running out of time. There was still a long list of things we wanted to see and do before we left Ireland, and now we were having a hard time figuring out how we would get it all in. The trick was to some-how squeeze twenty sights into two days of weekend sightseeing around Dublin. Mike called out to the kitchen from the parlor, for me to "aye" or "nay" each item on the list.

"Need I ask?" he started. "You had it on the top of the list a year ago. The Book of Kells."

"A big 'aye'," I said. "I won't go to the airport if I don't get to see it."

"Here's a hard one. The National Museum," he continued.

"Ditto. We can't leave Ireland without stopping there," I replied. "In fact, I think they're right near each other, so we could probably see the Book of Kells and The National Museum in a couple of hours."

"Did you forget that we are supposed to be paring this list down, not adding on?" he asked.

"Yes, I remember, but those two are top priority, we can't take them off."

"Okay. What about Malahide? You have a question mark by that one."

"Oh, don't take that off! I thought we'd do that Saturday evening and stay the night. It's supposed to be a great nightspot with terrific restaurants and pubs. I think we should have dinner there, and then spend the evening checking out the pubs. It will be our last big night on the town. We'll eat and drink everything we can that is typically Irish, our kind of 'Last Hurrah'. Now, what's on that list that we have a chance of eliminating?"

Mike scanned the paper silently, then responded. "Nothing I can figure."

"Are you sure?"

"Here, take a look." He entered the kitchen, handing me the list.

I looked long and hard at the list of ten items. "You're right," I agreed. "The only thing I can see to take off the list is The Post Office. We've seen that already."

Mike replied quickly, "Oh, no you don't. My favorite landmark is there, Cuchulain. He is Ireland's most famous warrior."

"Well, it isn't too far from Trinity College. I guess we could squeeze it in."

"No 'I guesses' on that one," he replied. "That will take two minutes. We don't even have to go in! We'll just wave to him as we drive by."

"Okay." I agreed. "What about the prison, the Kilmainham Gaol? Do we really need to see a jail on our last day?"

Mike reacted a little too strongly. "You told me six months ago that the prison would be our next sight-seeing trip. That was six months ago. You know I really want to see that."

I didn't say anything.

He offered an olive branch. "Look, why don't we start at the Post Office, drive by and wave. Then I'll drop you off at Trinity to see The Book of Kells. I'll go out to the prison and you can walk over to the museum and spend the whole afternoon there. You'll have plenty of time to see all your favorite works of art, and I'll get to see the two things I want to see."

It sounded like a good idea, a practical, "Mike" kind of idea. By splitting up, we could both get to see what we wanted. But it was so unromantic.

"You mean, we wouldn't be together on our last day in Dublin?" I cooed.

I looked at the list. Let's see. I read item number five. The Literary Pub Crawl. I really wanted to do that, but we'd be pubbing and crawling in Malahide later that evening. I crossed it off. Good. Now we were getting somewhere. I continued to the next entry.

"Guinness Hop Store." I really wanted to see the world-renowned 200-year-old brewery. Well, there's no way we'll have time, I realized. We'd just have to have a Guinness on tap in Malahide at one of the quaint pubs. I scratched it off.

The next entry looked up blandly, defying its reputation. "The Temple Bar Area." I really had wanted to see that. That's where the best impromptu entertainment and Irish pub music could be found. What had originated as one of Dublin's most famous traditional pubs had, through gentrification of the surrounding neighborhood, become an "area." It is supposedly the hottest scene in Dublin. I crossed it off.

I came down to the last four items on the list: St. Patrick's Church, Christ Church Cathedral, The National Gallery, and the Daniel O'Connell monument. All of a sudden, my Irish got the best of me. Why would I, go see two Anglo-Norman churches or an art museum with no Celtic art? I'd rather spend the afternoon at Trinity looking at Celtic manuscripts and late Bronze Age gold jewelry at the National Museum. I crossed the first three items off and hesitated at the Daniel O'Connell statue. He'd be only half a block down from The Post Office.... I left Daniel on the list.

So much art and history so little time. It would be a perfect last day in ol' Eire. If we split up, Mike and I could each see what we wanted and still gaze at each other over a candlelight dinner in Malahide, with Irish dancing and pub music afterward. I decided to make reservations at a cozy Georgian guesthouse on its outskirts.

*   *   *   *   *

We drove to Dublin in a little less than three hours, and proceeded to look for a parking spot. I noticed how parochial, how small, Dublin felt for a major capital city. We made our way easily to the city center since it was a Saturday morning. We tried to find street parking just for the challenge of it and then finally settled on the parking garage two blocks from Trinity. Mike had decided he couldn't pass up The Book of Kells either. So, our new game plan was that both of us would go to Trinity to see The Book of Kells and afterwards he would drive out to Kilmainham Prison while I visited the National Museum. We would meet at 4:00 at the Daniel O'Connell memorial across the street from the General Post Office.

Let Mike enjoy his old prison. Men found pleasures in the weirdest of things. Prisons, Celtic warriors. I, on the other hand, would have three full hours to absorb Celtic gold interlacing patterns.

Leaving the din of the street, we walked through the 300 foot-wide Palladian facade and into the courtyard of Trinity College. Although it was founded in 1592 by Queen Elizabeth I, its remaining architecture is predominantly seventeenth century Georgian. It was here that we would view the world's most richly decorated medieval manuscripts, The Book of Kells, scrolled sometime in the early ninth century, Ireland's "Golden Age."

A group was gathering just inside the courtyard. Since I was becoming increasingly reluctant to follow an organized tour, we headed towards the rear of the courtyard. Small signs posted on great oak trees pointed us in the direction of the new exhibit area where the Book of Kells was displayed. I reminisced about the only time I had seen The Book, which was in my junior year of college. Our student group was hushed by a severe uniformed guard as we were ushered into the magnificent Old Library.

The Library, which was built in 1732 was reminiscent of a grand, Romanesque church, with its barrel vaulted ceiling and a spectacular, 210 foot long nave, known as *The Long Room*. Thousands of antiquarian texts and busts of famous Trinity graduates lined its walls. Also displayed was an ancient harp, which was supposed to have accompanied the Irish giant, Brian Boru, into battle against the Vikings. Indeed, it was the oldest surviving harp in Ireland. It was here in this sacrosanct atmosphere, that I had first viewed The Book of Kells.

But The Book of Kells was no longer displayed in this magnificent and awe-inspiring room, but rather, in a modernized section of the college redesigned to accommodate the hordes of tourists who often reached several thousand a day. As we walked past the 19th century Campanile, I stopped to eavesdrop on one of the many guides who offered their versions of what was important about Trinity College. The guide was speaking in a Dublin accent to a group of attentive Chinese students.

"Trinity College," he began, "was built on the site of an Augustinian monastery. Among its many famous students, have been several known writers like Edmund Burke, Oliver Goldsmith and Samuel Beckett. Samuel Beckett, the Nobel prizewinner, entered Trinity in 1923 where he placed first in his modern literature class. Unfortunately, as many writers did, Beckett moved to France in the early 1930's. Many of his major works such as *Waiting for Godot,* were first written in French and later translated into English."

I wondered if these Chinese students read *Godot* in French, English or Chinese. It would seem that it must lose something in the translation. It might be an interesting Master's Degree project for an earnest student to read all three versions and analyze the differences.

Mike nudged my arm to move me along.

"Do you think we have a chance of getting in?" he asked, as we turned the corner of the quad and moved along to the Kells exhibit area.

"Can you believe this crowd?" I said. I thought of his precious prison. "It's going to be at least an hour wait. Why don't you go along to Kilmainham and leave me here. I know you hate lines."

"Well, I'm here now and now I intend to see it," he said.

"At least we get to wait outside in this beautiful and historical court-yard," I responded. I looked around the green quad at the students loung-ing and reading on the grass. "Did you know that women were not admitted to Trinity until 1903? And that was only Protestant women."

"No, I didn't," he responded, trying to listen and read his guidebook at the same time. "It says here that Trinity alumni include Robert Emmet, Jonathan Swift, J.M. Synge, Thomas Moore, George Bernard Shaw and Oscar Wilde. That's quite an impressive bunch. Funny, I thought that guide back there reminded me of a dandified Oscar Wilde with his affected *Dubliner* accent."

A large group of perhaps one hundred students got in line behind us.

"Just let me know when you want to cut bait," I whispered gently into Mike's ear, but he continued to read from the guidebook to himself.

We moved slowly up in line another twenty feet, and made our way into what appeared to be a small bookstore.

I looked around at the shelves of books, each shelf clearly marked *Irish Authors, Celtic Manuscripts, Modern Irish Playwrights, Irish History, Irish Humor.* Even though it wasn't the Long Room, I felt like I had died and gone to heaven, being there.

"Mike, do you mind if I have a look while we're waiting anyway?"

"Sure, have a ball. If you find me a Brendan Behan book or a Roddy Doyle, I might just save your place in line."

"It's a deal." I headed over to the Celtic Manuscript section. On the display shelves before me were dozens of books dedicated entirely to Celtic illuminated manuscripts. They ranged from soft cover pocket-sized to coffee table-sized picture books. Before I could pull a big coffee table book from the shelf, I knew I was going to buy it. I perched the book in the crook of my elbow, trying to balance it and turn to the beautiful multicolor reproductions of manuscripts I had never heard of. The only problem was now I had to contend with the problem of lugging this ten-pound book with me through the National Museum.

As I perused the room to see where the Irish humorists were, I noticed a beautiful leather bound book perched separately on an intricately carved wooden bookstand, which stood waist high in the corner of the bookstore. I clutched my picture book and walked over to see why it deserved such a special display. The book was an identical-size reproduction of one of the four gospels comprising the original Book of Kells. A little sign in medieval script identified it as the Book of Matthew. The pages were yellow and textured as if they were real sheepskin.

It was opened to a page I vaguely recognized as one of the well-known Celtic manuscripts. Hand written on a white card beneath it was its description: *The four volume illuminated manuscript had been laboriously handwritten in Latin by monks in the early ninth century, and was discovered in the monastery in Kells, in County Meath, Ireland. The scribes who copied the texts had embellished their calligraphy with intricate interlacing spirals, as well as with human figures and animals. Some of the dyes were imported from as far away as the Middle East, and the colors were oftentimes interspersed with gold, thus the term illuminated manuscripts.*

Next to the book was a diagram, explaining that the opened page was the Monogram Page, the most elaborate page in the entire Book of Kells. It explained that the Monogram Page contained the first three words of St. Matthew's account of the birth of Christ. The first word, "XRI", an abbreviation of *Christi,* was embellished with stylized angels and several whimsical animal motifs including cats, rats and moths.

As my eyes traced and followed every curvilinear spiral, I considered the terms given to Irish Catholics such as pagan Papists and renegade Catholics. Here was visual proof. The Celtic symbolism before me had little to do with traditional Christian iconography. I scanned the other page. Although I had studied Latin for four years in high school and college, I could decipher little of the beautifully rounded Celtic script with its brightly ornamented initial letters and human forms, which were used to decorate the end of lines.

I put the coffee table book back. Here was my chance to have a piece of the Book of Kells. I didn't care how much it weighed. I saw Mike waving frantically at me out of the corner of my eye. I grabbed a copy from a stack of cellophane wrapped books behind the Kells display and headed for the cashier. I could buy Brendan Behan or Roddy Doyle in Chicago. Mike was sure to love it. I paid for the book, stuck it in my oversized satchel bag and hurried back to claim my place in line.

"Have I got a surprise for you!" I said, while squirming into the line which was now three abreast.

"Let's see," Mike said.

"I'll show you tonight," I said. "It will be your last night in Malahide surprise."

"I bet it has nothing to do with Roddy Doyle," Mike responded.

We entered the exhibit area. The first room had large boards with larger than life photographs, explaining the history and significance of monasteries and illuminated manuscripts. The descriptions were written in an elementary fashion, which surprised me, as I was sure that anybody who came all the way to Ireland to stand in line for an hour to see a book would know what a monk, a monastery and an illuminated manuscript were. Now, not having to stay in line, I pushed forward into the crowd, past the placards and photographs in search of the real manuscripts.

We had read in our guidebook that the four books were displayed under glass. Each book was opened to reveal two pages, and the pages were turned each day so that one could view the entire contents of all four books. I wondered if anyone had ever accomplished this task. The guide claimed there were 340 sumptuously decorated pages.

It soon became obvious that the room we were now standing in and the next one were just ante rooms and the Book of Kells was in the third room, which, from what I could see, was jammed with people. I gestured to Mike that I was pushing my way through the crowd to get to the third room as soon as possible. He motioned that he would try to do the same.

When we got to the third room, I noticed there were only two waist high display cases, similar to jewelry cases, both surrounded by eager viewers. At first, this sight thrilled me with the idea that so many people were interested in this ancient Irish artifact. It soon became apparent, however, that I might not get to see it. We waited patiently for the people in front of us to get a good look. After twenty minutes of only being able to see other people gawking at the books, I got a little impatient. I walked over to the guard, who stood near the glass cases with his arms crossed, and expressed my complaint.

"Excuse me, I hate to be impolite," I began, "but do you realize those people at the case have been gaping at the manuscripts for twenty minutes? All I want is *one* minute. I have to get to the National Gallery after this!"

He smiled and uncrossed his arms. "No prob. I'll take care of it. It's just that people are so taken with The Book, they can't help themselves." He moved toward the crowd surrounding the case. "Could you nice people give some of the others a chance to see our Celtic masterpiece? They've been waitin' a long time to see them, probably longer than it took to write the four gospels."

This charmed the tourists. They murmured to each other and, took another look into the case and pulled themselves reluctantly away.

I stepped up to the case. The one-minute I thought I needed gradually melted into fifteen. We were running out of time. I saw the guard approach and he caught my eye.

"See?" he said as he pointed down and tapped on his wristwatch.

"They are mesmerizing," I said. "But I should let others have a chance." I moved back and let Mike take my place.

Now I was even more anxious to see the Celtic treasures at the National Museum. Mike must have felt the same way. As we left the exhibit, he suggested we skip lunch so he could see some of the National Museum before he went to the prison. I was starving but didn't say anything. We could eat in Malahide. Celtic art would be worth starving for.

When we got to the National Museum, the central entry was open, but the door was not. A small white index card was affixed to the door, and in manual typewritten script it read: *Due to excessive number of tourists, the museum is closed for remodeling.*

"Remodeling?" I yelled. I didn't know whether to laugh or cry. "When will we ever be able to get the chance to see it again?"

"This just means we'll have to come back," Mike said. Then, trying to cheer me up quipped, "Do you think there will be an excessive number of tourists at the prison?"

"I doubt it." I laughed, trying to mask my deep disappointment.

He tried again to lighten up the situation. "At least, we know if the Celtic artifacts have lasted since the Bronze Age, they'll last until the next time we're in Dublin."

My spirits picked up as I thought of returning to Dublin sometime. Besides, I felt that now I could return Mike's effort of trudging through medieval manuscripts with me by trudging through a prison with him.

"We'll just have an excuse to come back to Dublin just to see the National Museum. We can still see the Daniel O'Connell memorial on the way to the Post Office," I said with all of the enthusiasm I could muster. "We can give a quick wave to Cuchulainn in the window, head out to Kilmainham Jail and be there by three o'clock. We'll have *plenty of time*!"

"I'm betting that by the end of today's *Search For Something Celtic*, we're going to feel like we've *served time*." He threw his head back and laughed at his own joke. "Now let's go see a good Irish jail. How much difference could there be between a monk's cell and a prison cell?"

We walked down the museum stairs to hail a taxi.

"Look, as long as we're not going to see the Celtic jewelry until our next trip to Ireland," I said, "I have a little something that might make up for it. It's a little, no big, gem I found in the bookstore." I carefully removed the bulky Book of Kells from my satchel and tore off its protective cellophane.

"Wow!" His eyes lit up.

I rested the book in the crook of my arm and leafed through the pages until I came to an illustration from the first gospel according to St. Matthew, the same one we had seen on display at Trinity. "Look!"

The multi-colored drawings and scrolled gold-leafed lettering glistened on the page. Mike gently ran his hand across the page. Now he was mesmerized by its beauty, the way I had been looking at the original.

"I didn't really feel like I got a good look at it at the exhibit," he said. "Now I'll have all the time I need to look at it on the plane ride home."

"I bought it as a fitting souvenir of our year here together," I said. "All I need to do, is brush up on my Latin, and I can read you a page every night when we get back to the States."

Mike smiled and put his arm around my shoulder. "The year sure flew by…And what a beautiful and *illuminating* year it's been."

Serving Time At Kilmainham Gaol

Situated on a long, tree lined avenue that runs the length of the town of Kilmainham, the grim, gray bulk of Kilmainham Goal remains as bleak as the day it was opened in 1796. When we arrived, we discovered that the jail was turned into a historical museum, a shrine to Ireland's fight for freedom. It had been dedicated by none other than Eamon de Valera, President of Ireland, who had officially opened the Museum in 1966, exactly 42 years after de Valera himself left Kilmainham as its final prisoner.

Contrary to how I had felt this morning about choosing to visit the National Gallery over the prison, I was now fascinated with the whole idea of tracing Irish Independence through the history of a jail. Standing in front of its stony facade, a sudden rush of cold air blew against my face. It felt as if the ghosts of those political prisoners who languished here, who were tortured and killed for Irish independence, were still lingering inside the jail's steely walls. I moved forward to the enormous wooden-gated entrance as if in a trance like state. Vaguely, I could hear Mike's words fading in and out as he read from his guidebook.

"After being closed and falling into disrepair for over several decades, a group of dedicated volunteers, who were determined to make Kilmainham a memorial to Irish freedom, rebuilt the prison brick by brick," he read. *"It took six years to restore it, with all volunteer labor. That's pretty impressive."*

I murmured, "It looks like it could use a lot more work."

"It says here that the restoration is incomplete, but most of the prison has been restored to its original state."

We walked along into a dark, damp corridor. "This place is so scary looking," I said. "I'm surprised anybody would do anything to risk being thrown in here for one minute let alone several years."

"Pretty incredible, isn't it?" Mike asked. "How long do you think you'd last?"

"Not even a minute, if that," I responded.

"Look, there's a tour group gathering to go in." Mike said. "Let's try it. If we find he's not too good or he's moving too slowly, I can read to you from the guidebook as we make our way through. That way we could make the whole tour in half an hour and be on our way to Malahide. You look like you could use something to eat."

"I think I'm losing my appetite, just thinking about being shut in here," I said. "Let's do the tour and hope he has some juicy tidbits that aren't in the guide book. Don't worry about my eating. I have a candy bar in my satchel."

In a thick, Belfast accent, the guide introduced himself to our group of ten people as Eamon and then immediately asked for a donation to the museum fund, emphasizing that the project to rebuild the Gaol was strictly volunteer. I wondered if his namesake wasn't the one and only de Valera.

We tossed our Irish pounds into a plastic bowl, which sat on the floor next to his feet.

He leaned over and casually scooped the coins and bills into his hand and shoved them in his jeans.

"The Irish freedom fighters thank ye'," he said matter-of-factly. "If yas feel ya' need to *add* a little something to that at the end of the tour, please feel free to do so."

Was this an indirect way of telling us our donations were skimpy or did this intimate that he was going to give us the tour of our lives, and we'd be happy to double our contributions at the end of the tour. I decided to wait and see if he was worth it.

Eamon stood about six foot two and looked to be no more than a few years out of college. I figured if he were born in 1975, it would make sense that his namesake was indeed Eamon de Valera who died that same year. He leaned casually against the wall with one leg bent so his foot braced himself against the wall. He was dressed in worn but clean blue jeans and a blue plaid flannel shirt.

"Now, how many of ye have been inside a prison before?" he shouted, his voice reverberating through the corridor.

Mike and I were the only ones to raise our hands. We had been to Alcatraz prison in San Francisco Bay several years before.

"Visiting or serving time?" he teased.

"Both," Mike chided back. "My mother in law was with us."

This brought a chuckle from the group. At least their quick response proved they were sharp and attentive.

"May I ask which prison?" the guide asked politely.

Mike answered, "Probably the meanest prison anybody could see. Alcatraz."

"Alcatraz," Eamon repeated. "Cruelly facing San Francisco, surrounded by sharks and frigid waters. Nobody ever escaped alive. Although, obviously you two managed to. I think you'll soon learn there were plenty more people who died behind these walls than those of Alcatraz."

"How many tried to escape?" Mike challenged him.

"None," Eamon replied. They were tortured and killed before they had a *chance*. Many even starved to death," he said solemnly. Then he dramatically removed his foot from the wall and started down the corridor.

Taking this as their cue, the group followed quietly behind him. They formed a single file in order to squeeze down the gray stone lined corridor. The narrow space smelled musty and stale. We followed the group through the corridor, which eventually led to an enormous room, called the Main Compound. This large central room was open, with four stories of cells forming a huge rectangle. A single, open staircase, situated in the center of the compound was the only access to the rows of cells, which faced the interior of the room on each floor. A large skylight ran across the ceiling from which a dim, gray light filtered through.

Eamon led us through the Compound and stopped in front of one of the cells.

"Unlike Alcatraz and other well-known prisons," he began, "Kilmainham Goal was considered a modern, model prison when it was built in 1796. At that time, there were many indigent people living in Ireland, many who ended up living in public houses for the poor.

"The public houses were so ratty and degenerate, that indigents would often commit petty crimes in order to be placed into a prison where they would at least be provided with food and shelter. For this reason, the architects of Kilmainham were determined to create a prison that would be at least one step down from the most squalid public houses, a place where nobody could possibly choose to go, no matter how horrific their circumstances."

Eamon raised his hands up above his head and gestured toward the ceiling. He started, "Thousands of human beings were brought into Kilmainham never to leave its cruel walls. The intention of Kilmainham was to 'depersonalize' and 'dehumanize' anybody who was placed in here, to treat people no better than animals. This philosophy was perpetuated to 'discourage' people from ever doing anything that could cause them to end up in the worst hell hole that was ever designed by man."

Eamon cleared his throat and pointed to the rows of cells overhead. "As you can see above me, the architect designed the gaol so that all prisoners are exposed having no privacy whatsoever. All cells were designed exactly the same size and all faced into the interior of the room so that the prisoners could be observed by the guards at all times. Most modern high security prisons in existence today are based on this same model. Swill buckets were brought to and from the cells as well as the scant bread and water served twice daily to the prisoners. There was no heat.

A shiver went down my spine as I imagined how cold and damp it could be in the dead of winter.

Eamon walked from the center of the Main Compound and over to a cell on the main floor. He gestured toward the group. "Let's step into one of the cells, to get a real feel for what it was like."

The group quietly formed a line in order to take turns going into and out of the tiny room. The cell was narrow, approximately twelve feet deep by six feet wide. A small, narrow, rectangular window was located at the end of the room, about eleven feet up on the wall. Under it, on the floor at the far end of the room lay a thin mat. That was all. Each person walked into the tiny chamber looking up to the window, which was so far up the wall, there was nothing to be seen out of it. Each looked in earnest for something to fix on, but all there was to regard was the simple thin mat, which served as a prisoner's bed. A hush fell over the group.

Eamon continued, only this time he lowered his voice. I wasn't sure if this was done intentionally by him to create drama, although drama seemed unnecessary in this monument of man's inhumanity to man. "Now, you see how dark and claustrophobic this room is? If you're thinking that a criminal deserves to be treated like this, think about the famine years when hundreds of victims were placed here at Kilmainham, sometimes twenty to a room this size."

He made a grand gesture with his arms. "The men, women and children who were victims of the famine were forced into another humiliation by being placed with common criminals. If the starvation from the famine didn't get them, the squalor and disease, which followed them into Kilmainham took their lives. Ironically, most of the famine victims, who had come here to escape from the hunger, languished and eventually died *in here* from the same starvation from which they were trying to escape."

The group now peered into the cell again to get a second look, wondering how twenty people could fit into such a narrow, cramped space.

When we arrived on the second floor, he led us down another dark corridor off of the Main Compound to several cells, which faced each other across a narrow hallway. These cells were half the size of the others with no windows in the cells or in the hallway connecting them. Some of the cells had standing water on the floor.

When everyone was gathered around him, Eamon began. "Besides common criminals, indigents, and victims of famine, the rolls of

Kilmainham prison include the likes of many famous Irish rebels such as the Sheares Brothers who were executed for their part in the Rebellion of 1798. These were the types of cells where those prisoners who were eventually executed were held during their final days."

He pointed to the small plaques above the doorways of the cells. He read quietly, "Robert Emmet." "Robert Emmet," he spoke reverently, "led the Rising of 1803 in reaction to the Act of Union which had been passed just three years before, which made Ireland an extension of British soil."

He turned his face upwards to the ceiling and placed his hands together as if in a gesture of religious supplication. His voice continued to rise though he spoke evenly. "Robert Emmet, went from here to the gallows proclaiming that he would rather die than continue to *live* in a land where 4000 years of history had been carelessly and indifferently swept aside to rename Ireland a *mere province* of Great Britain!"

Then, Eamon, perhaps in an effort to awaken the ghost Robert Emmet himself, shouted out to the entranced group. "Sure, they tried to take his individuality away. They tried to dehumanize him. They tried to use the cruelty of Kilmainham prison to humiliate him and strip him of every ounce of pride left in him." Eamon's face was flushed red. He paused momentarily to catch his breath.

He then continued in a low voice, enunciating every word with an exaggerated Belfast accent. "But they didn't succeed. He *chose* death rather than life in a country he couldn't call his own. Robert Emmet *welcomed* death rather than submission. No, Robert Emmet didn't acquiesce. Robert Emmet didn't give in. No, Robert Emmet eagerly grasped the hangman's noose. He gratefully placed it around his own neck and cried out to his persecutors. *When my country takes her place among the nations of the earth*," Eamon stopped suddenly, and then proceeded to shout louder still, "*then, and not till then, let my epitaph be written!*" Eamon's voice reverberated through the hallway.

We all stood silently, in awe of this powerful and moving speech.

Exhausted from his own display, Eamon dropped his head and walked slowly to the next cell.

Another blast of cool air hit my face as Eamon opened the door of the tiny cell.

"Are there any questions so far?" Eamon demanded from his little audience.

We all stood dumbfounded. For a minute, he stared directly at us, and I avoided his gaze by earnestly trying to read the nameplate above the door.

Eamon read from one of the plaques. "Charles Parnell...Charles Parnell, as ye all probably know, directed the Land League boycotts of the 1870's and 1880's which eventually lead to Home Rule, which granted limited independence to Ireland. It wasn't until the end of World War I that Home Rule was reluctantly adopted by the British. Not too many people know that Charles Parnell strategized those boycotts from one of these cells.

Eamon's voice suddenly shifted to that of a typical tour guide. "There are also scores of Irish rebels who met their executioners here. For instance, the Invincibles of 1883, five of whom lie buried here where they were hanged."

"And now," he paused dramatically, "we will leave the building and go into the stone breakers yard. Besides dehumanizing conditions, an added cruelty of the prison was that all prisoners must perform hard labor. Please follow me down and out to the courtyard and gather at the wall."

We followed him down the uneven craggy stairway and out into the welcoming sunshine. The bright blue sky contrasted dramatically with the dull, brown gray of the thirty-foot stone walls enclosing the yard.

Eamon walked up to the group gathered at the wall. The stone breakers yard was approximately 50 x 120 feet. At one end stood a large double wooden gate. The ground was covered with gravel which prompted two bored little boys to pitch pieces of it at each other. Their father glared at them to stop.

"This is what is known as the stone breakers yard. What better way is there," Eamon asked, "to keep your prisoners in line, to keep them from becoming bored or too energetic? Work them to death! The stone breakers yard is where prisoners worked sixteen hour days cutting stone from raw blocks of granite which were hauled in through those doors on the other end of the yard." He pointed to the gates at the far end. "Workers had to lift the stone from the carts, cut the stone and then haul it to the other side of the yard where it was brought out." Eamon's voice rose. "Endless, day after day, back-breaking work. All work was done by hand. The men were used like enslaved animals."

I raised my hand timidly in schoolgirl fashion. "Is this the same courtyard where The Martyrs were shot after the Easter Rising of 1916?" I asked, eager to show an American could ask a decent question about Irish history.

"No, that will be next on our little itinerary." Eamon answered, seemingly a bit annoyed I was interrupting him.

He wasn't about to go on until he had made his point. He looked over at me and gestured me forward. "First, I'd like *you* to come over here and see if you can lift this one fifty-pound stone." He looked down at a solitary stone resting on the ground between his two feet which had obviously been placed there as a prop. It looked to be one cubic foot.

I walked over to him and the rock he was straddling.

"Oh, I'm sure I could barely budge it." I said, sorry that I had asked a question and was now singled out as part of his demonstration.

Mike came over to assist me. As I bent over and attempted to take hold of the rock, Mike grabbed the other end. I pulled at one end, he pulled at the other. After we managed to lift it only one inch from the ground, I dropped my end hopelessly onto the gravel.

Eamon said, "Can you imagine lifting that stone hundreds of times a day?"

"No," I said. "I *can't* imagine."

"Okay," Eamon said, smiling and knowing he had made his point as well as silencing his precocious student.

He started walking across the courtyard calling to us over his shoulder. "Now that you know what hard labor is, let's go into the next courtyard where the executions of the Martyrs took place in 1916." He nodded at me.

The second courtyard was much smaller than the first. Like the other one, it was surrounded by thirty foot gray stone walls and had a large wooden gate at one end. Two simple white wooden crosses stood at either end of the enclosure.

Eamon walked over to an engraved plaque, which was affixed to the courtyard wall. "Here are the names of the fifteen martyrs from the Easter Rising of 1916 who were executed in this courtyard."

Without looking at the plaque, Eamon rattled off the names of fifteen men, beginning with two of the most famous participants, Patrick Pearse and James Connolly.

"On Easter Monday, 1916 a poorly outfitted and ill-prepared band of less than 200 patriots, led by Pearse and Connolly, marched up Dublin's O'Connell Street to the General Post Office. After Pearse declared 'The Proclamation of the Irish Republic to the People of Ireland,' the rebels proceeded to occupy the building. Hundreds of Irish patriots zealously fought under the Sinn Fein banner of green, white and orange. After six days of bitter fighting, the battered but unbowed group finally surrendered.

"After the arrest, imprisonment and exile of hundreds of Irish Loyalists, Pearse, Connolly and fourteen others were executed by a firing squad. These Martyrs were summarily shot in cold blood at that end of this yard." He pointed to the far end of the yard where the white crosses stood. They appeared, too simple, too modest to mark such a dramatic event in Irish history.

"It was here, on this side of the yard, right where I'm standing," Eamon continued in an understated tone, "where political prisoner James Connolly was brought in by an ambulance through these doors. Connolly, who had been severely wounded in the Rising, was unable to stand for his own execution. Not to be deterred, his executioners strapped him into a chair, propped him up and then shot him to death."

Eamon walked over to the place where Connolly sat waiting to be shot.

"It was the bloodshed of these martyrs that fueled the fire for Irish independence. More importantly, it was from these courageous men's deaths that, in the words of Yeats, *a terrible beauty was born.*"

Eamon bowed his head reverently and put his hands together in a gesture of prayer. "Let's offer up a moment of silence for the courage and valor of these martyrs whose only escape from Kilmainham Goal was death."

Everybody stared down at the gravel beneath their feet.

A young voice broke the silence. "What happened to Mr. de Valera?" a young Irish girl asked, apparently too young to remember hearing about him.

"Good question," Eamon answered. "Eamon de Valera was spared from execution, apparently, because he was an American. He was eventually pardoned, but later returned to Kilmainham prison in 1921 for opposing the Anglo-Irish Treaty which permanently partitioned Ireland into two lands, the Republic and the North. After his release, he spent the rest of his life as a major political force in Ireland.

"He eventually became the Prime Minister of Ireland in 1926 and served as President of Ireland, off and on, until 1973 when he retired at the age of 92. He is probably considered the most important Irish leader of the twentieth century, albeit a controversial one."

I wondered how the course of Irish history might have changed had de Valera been executed like the rest of the Easter Rising martyrs.

Eamon continued, "Many people don't know there were a number of women who participated in the Rising. One of the most famous women who assumed a leadership position in the Rising was Countess Constance Markeivicz. She was sentenced to die for her role as a commandant in the Citizen's Army. Her sentence was later commuted. Like de Valera, she was eventually pardoned."

One of the young boys who had previously been throwing gravel at his buddy, called out to Eamon. "What's that big boat?"

Eamon answered patiently, "That's the part of the tour all of the young lads like. Let's go have a look."

The group followed Eamon to the end of the courtyard. It led to an open area, which displayed a large forty-foot boat, positioned at one end, covered by a protective canopy. It was a surrealistic sight to see this battered boat with its paint-pealing hull in a prison courtyard.

"This is the *Asgard*," Eamon explained. "This is the infamous boat which brought the guns and ammunition that were eventually used in the Rising of 1916. As you can see, it's a yacht, not a boat designed to carry armaments. The yacht had been a wedding present given to a wealthy revolutionary couple, Erskine Childers, and his American wife Molly. They were to deliver 900 rifles and 29,000 rounds of ammunition to the port of Howth."

"Unfortunately, as luck would have it, when it set out to sea, it was caught in a storm that was the worst to hit that area of Ireland in thirty years. Erskine Childers navigated the boat continuously for three days and nights until the boat finally reached Howth."

The boat looked as if it could barely stay afloat, let alone carry hundreds of rifles and thousands of rounds of ammunition.

"Despite the life-threatening gales and winds, the arms were delivered safely to Howth in 1914. These were the same arms used in the Rising, two years later."

The story about the *Asgard* seemed almost anticlimactic compared to the drama of the executions. However, the incongruous contrast between the personal yacht and a bloody revolution gave me pause. I considered Molly and her groom, and wondered why these wealthy people would, in the midst of their comfortable lives of luxury, choose to support a cause that could possibly send them to the world's most horrendous prison.

If they had been young, idealistic and poor, life-long rebels with nothing to lose, I could almost understand it. But these people could have floated around on their yacht, eating bon bons and reading a good book. Instead, they threw themselves into the fray, the fight for Irish Independence knowing the Goal could be the punishment for their passion. I wondered if I could ever feel that passionately about anything.

Eamon interrupted my thoughts by calling out to the group, "Thank you for your attention. I hope you have learned something from the tour." He placed the plastic donation bowl on the ground next to him.

We all walked up to the bowl and doubled the donations we had thrown in an hour before.

Mike turned to me as we all shuffled silently out of the courtyard, "You look like you could use something to eat, I mean, besides *bread and water*."

"Yeah, I could," I responded, "Even though, for the first time in my life, I can say I've lost my appetite. How can I eat thinking about so many people who starved here."

"Yeah, I know what you mean," he agreed.

"In the meantime, do you want to split my candy bar?" I reached into my satchel as we headed out of the Goal to the car.

"No, you eat it," he said. "I can wait until we get to Malahide. After a hearty dinner, a little pub hopping, and a little Irish jig, we'll forget all of this depressing business."

"That's what I'm afraid of," I responded, as I felt the hunger pangs come over me.

"That we'll forget *too* easily."

I looked back over my shoulder at the gray, grim wall of Kilmainham Goal and took a bite out of my candy bar. I hoped that at least part of me would never forget this place or those who died here for Irish Independence.

No Diddly Diddly

We took the R124 up to Malahide, formerly a sleepy seaside resort that had turned into a trendy night spot. This is where we could easily find the kind of Irish food, entertainment and ambiance that we wanted for our last night of revelry. Because of its ideal location just half an hour north of downtown Dublin, Malahide had always been the place where Dubliners could get away from the urban glut, enjoy the sea views, eat in one of its fine restaurants, and imbibe in one of its many pubs.

More recently, Malahide had attracted hosts of tourists and foreigners who, seduced by its panoramic views of the sea, often ended up buying vacation homes or condominiums in order to return to this beautiful retreat anytime they pleased. As we drove along its sandy shores, we were struck by the number of construction cranes silhouetted against the orange sky. It was evident Malahide was trying to keep up with the demand for condos. At least two blocks of shoreline were torn up with mounds of rubble, and stone and dirt were piled everywhere. Behind it, a huge blazing ball of sun was slipping slowly into the water seemingly unaffected by all of the building equipment.

"I hope they don't ruin this lovely spot with over-construction," Mike said solemnly as he searched for a parking spot, "like they've done in so many other places."

"At least it looks as if the builders considered the site," I replied. "Look how the condos are turned in toward each other, so it looks like an enclave. Although there must be hundreds of condos going up, the architects have cleverly constructed them to look like they fit in with the original architecture. See how they've kept the whitewashed walls and gabled roof lines?"

"They still look like a bunch of condos to me," Mike replied, unconvinced. "You can see how they're going to block the views of the water from the town itself."

For some reason, I continued to defend them, perhaps thinking that maybe we, too, might be able to own one of them and be able to come back to this enchanting town whenever we wanted.

"Look at the section that appears to be more than half complete," I countered. "It looks as though they won't be more than a few stories high. It's not as if they're going to be high rises, or anything grotesque."

"We'll just have to see about that," Mike replied.

"Maybe tomorrow morning, before we leave, we can visit the sales center and find out the story."

"And to find out the prices?" Mike asked.

Mike squinted out the window. "Now, as long as we haven't found a parking spot yet, I suggest we go right over to our bed and breakfast, get squared away, and then come back down here for dinner. Maybe by then, there will be a few spots. I don't know about you, but I'm starved. I didn't have a candy bar."

"Great idea," I said. "Maybe our B&B hostess can recommend a nice place to eat, something with authentic Irish food and a romantic view of the sea."

We found ourselves back on the road, which ran along Malahide's shores. The views in either direction, as we headed out of town, were breathtaking. Couples strolled hand in hand along a pathway, which separated the street from the sandy dunes and shoreline. We drove just a short way, Mike looking for a street name, as I enjoyed the sunset.

"Look, that must be Malahide Castle," I said, pointing out the passenger side window. "Can you pull over for a minute?"

The impressive castle stood staunchly on a hill overlooking the ocean. It's rounded towers gave it a fairy tale appearance.

Mike slowed the car as I leafed through my guidebook.

"Here it is." I found the page, which I had marked previously. "Malahide Castle stands on 250 acres of grounds. Its gardens are well known throughout Ireland and it has been occupied continuously from when its founder, Lord Talbot de Malahide, had it constructed in 1185 until 1973. It is now a museum, with 18th-century Irish furnishings, and an original portrait collection including such figures as Tom Wolfe."

Mike pulled the car to the curb and leaned over me trying to get a good look at the castle. "It's no condo, that's for sure," he said.

I read on. "It seems the most significant historical event attached to this castle is that on a morning in 1690, some 14 Talbot cousins sat down to breakfast together before leaving to fight for King James at the Battle of the Boyne. According to Irish legend, none made it back home for dinner."

"What happened?" Mike asked.

"They were all killed."

"Too bad we won't be able to see the inside," Mike said. "We'll just have to come back sometime."

"If we buy our condo here, we could visit it every day if you like."

Mike ignored my fantasy and considered the reality of finding our B&B. "We'd better get moving. It's getting dark. Now it's going to be harder to find our B&B." He pulled the car away from the curb and we drove along the beach.

"It should be one of these streets up here," I said. "The woman said it was walking distance from the castle."

"See if you can read this sign post," Mike said as he slowed the car.

There were four signs on the post, but only one of them was brown, indicating a hotel or B&B accommodation. I read it.

"'That's it, all right," I announced, happy. I was relieved to be able to decipher the sign in the near darkness.

Mike made a right, and we drove up a narrow street with stone walls flanking either side. We traveled for at least another two blocks, and then we came to an opening in the wall. A small, metal plate attached to the wall identified the place as *Ashton Manor.*

"Thank God we found it so easily," I said. "Now I'm so starving, I'm ready to faint."

"Me, too," Mike agreed. "Let's not fool around. We'll check in, bring the bags to the room and get back into town."

"Agreed," I said.

We pulled through the entry, which led to a long, curving driveway with enormous pine trees lining the drive. The trees were evergreens, which seemed incongruous for Ireland, which grew few pine trees. We continued down the drive until it turned into a horseshoe shaped strip of gravel that ended at a small cottage. Surely, this couldn't be it. I jumped out of the car and rapped on the red door of the tiny white house. A voice called from within.

"It's up the gravel part of the road," the voice said without waiting for a question. I returned to the car.

We continued slowly on the gravel road until it was so dark, I was sure we'd sideswipe one of the giant pines. Finally, we saw Ashton Manor. It loomed before us as if it had emerged from an English gothic novel. It was a classically Georgian design, only two stories high, but nearly eighty feet wide. As our eyes adjusted to the large mass of red brick, we could see a plump woman opening the wide door to greet us.

"Just pull it over there!" she hailed, pointing in the dark to a spot right in front. "That way you don't have to drag the luggage too far." She held the door open with one hip, trying to restrain a large black Labrador retriever by its collar.

I rolled the window down. "Thanks. We don't have too much though, just one small suitcase. We're the O'Briens!"

"Of course you are," she called back agreeably. "We've been expecting you! Welcome to Ashton Manor."

I felt guilty at the thought that I hadn't always appeared so chipper and welcoming to our guests all year at the Farmhouse. I felt a sudden pang of remorse, knowing how much I would miss the warmth of Irish hospitality. She *actually seemed* both happy and eager to see us.

"You're the Americans with the farmhouse in Castleconnell," she said, apparently wanting to make the B&B connection.

"That's us," Mike said. He pulled our suitcase from the trunk and escorted me over to her.

"Nice to meet you," I said, shaking our hostess' hand. She was what novels always called a handsome woman, pleasant looking, not beautiful, but graceful and feminine at the same time. Her shoulder-length hair was pulled back in a ponytail and she wore a loose fitting chambray jumper over a white cotton turtleneck sweater. She introduced herself as Shiela.

"Your American king sized bed is waiting for you," she said. "You can always tell people who are well-seasoned travelers. They are always very specific about what's important when they make their reservations. I saved the grandest room with the largest bed just for you, as you requested."

I felt a little self-conscious, knowing that this observation would embarrass Mike.

"I'm sure all of your rooms are spacious and lovely," I responded, trying to change the subject from the size of the bed.

"So this is your last night in Ireland?" she asked.

"Actually, no," I explained. "We're leaving Ireland in a few weeks, but this was our only weekend to see everything we hadn't gotten a chance to see all year. We spent all day running around Dublin."

"Poor dears. What did you see?" she asked politely as we entered the foyer together, as if she hadn't heard the litany of Dublin sights before. But she seemed as if she really did care about what we saw, even though she had surely heard this a million times before. Almost everyone who stayed with her had to be either going to, or coming from, Dublin.

"I'm afraid all we could get into was Trinity College and Kilmainham prison," Mike offered. "Unfortunately, The National Gallery was closed."

"I'm sorry," she said as if she were taking personal responsibility. Then she added cheerfully, "Well, all that means, is that you'll have an excuse to come back to visit. I'm planning on being here a long time."

Another thing I would miss about Ireland. Everybody seemed to stay in one place for awhile.

"How do you like Malahide?" Sheila asked.

"We really haven't gotten to see it yet," I said. "All we did was drive through it on the way here. It's a charming place. I can see why everybody raves about it. The castle with its dazzling setting on the sea is spectacular."

"Thanks," she said, as if my complimenting her town was a compliment to her.

"Let me show you to your room. It's a shame you can only stay the night, but I know how hard it is to get away when you're running a B& B." She led us up a flight of stairs.

A thick, wool carpet with an Oriental pattern ran up the center of the stairs, affixed to each stair with brass rods. The hand railings were painted white, as were all of the crown mouldings in the hallway, and the walls were deep burgundy red. Several oversized oil portraits hung from the walls, whom I guessed were important personages of their time. They gazed fixedly at us as we climbed the stairs.

"We were thinking about checking out those new condos going up on the water," Mike said trying to make small talk to the pleasant hostess.

"Oh, *condo* is a dirty word in this town," she said matter-of-factly. "We long time residents are all fighting them tooth and nail."

"I'm sorry," Mike offered.

"Ireland will be ruined if this condo craze keeps up," Sheila countered. "While we are doing everything to preserve what the tourists want to see, the developers are destroying it. For instance, take this house, which dates from the eighteenth century. As you can probably tell from the slightly listing hundred and fifty-year-old staircase, our family has done everything to keep it preserved for the enjoyment of our guests. I'm the fourth generation to inhabit it. Be careful that you don't fall on your way up!" she added with an attempt at Irish modesty after what she might have felt was grandiosity.

Although she was obviously proud of the elegant house and was pleased to have the opportunity to show it off to us, she felt more comfortable having fun with it than bragging about it.

"It's absolutely beautiful!" I exclaimed. "Did you have to do much restoration?"

"Maybe if you were staying a week, I'd get into that story," she quipped. "Just consider it a mini version of the Talbot Castle. It seems my ancestors and theirs were great competitors, and Ashton Manor was built as a more modest imitation of its grand model by the sea."

"Now I don't feel so bad that we didn't see the inside of the Castle," I said. "It couldn't be as lovely as this. You've done a wonderful job. I'm sure your ancestors would be proud that you're living here and maintaining it so beautifully."

"Believe me," she said, "I certainly wouldn't be able to if it weren't for the B&B guestrooms paying the bills. We spent $5,000 Irish pounds alone on this staircase, trying to level it so our guests could get to their rooms without killing themselves." She giggled. "We have ten guest rooms here. The best one, being this one, is ready and waiting just for the O'Briens." She opened the door to our room.

The room was painted deep royal blue. As guestrooms went, it was unusually large, perhaps 15 x 20 feet, with an enormous canopied bed in the middle of the room. The bed was covered by a fluffy, white islet comforter with several pillows propped up at one end. A Victorian marble fireplace, with a large crystal vase filled with fresh roses sat on the mantel which faced us from the far side of the room. At the other end of the room was a large, private bathroom with thick, royal blue towels draped over towel warmers and a white-laced shower curtain surrounding the tub. It felt like a room fit for royalty.

"Now," she said, "is there anything I can be gettin' for you? You're Americans, you'll probably be wantin' some ice or a Coke, or both."

"We'd really love to, but we're both starving to death," I gushed apologetically. What I really wanted was to fall into the fluffy bed and take a leisurely nap after the hectic day of running around. As I gazed around our enticing room, my eyes kept returning to the white islet comforter, which beckoned to me to collapse into it. The thick, white comforter was a marked contrast to the thin, straw mats lying on the prison cells at Kilmainham Gaol.

My stomach growled. "Do you have any recommendations for dinner?" I asked, trying to change the subject in an attempt to shake the depressing memory. "We were thinking of a romantic place overlooking the water. Hopefully, a place that has good old-fashioned Irish cooking."

She hesitated, rubbed her chin and then said, "You know, it's going to be hard to find a place with a good view *and* good food. That might be too much to ask. I have a bunch of menus downstairs in the parlor from all of the restaurants in town. I'd hate to recommend somewhere and have you not be happy with it. Why don't you take a look at the menus."

She seemed to be happier letting herself off the hook than making a personal recommendation. We walked down the staircase together as she told us how to get in if we came back after midnight, which we assured her would most likely be the case. Then she escorted us into the parlor, which was a double room, with a blazing fireplace in each room. In front of each fireplace were two sofas and two over-stuffed chairs with ottomans. The fires looked so warm and welcoming, that I wished we could relax, lounge in the comfy chairs and enjoy this fabulous setting for awhile.

"There you are," she said, as she handed me a stack of plastic laminated menus. "You know, Malahide is known for its restaurants. You can have your pick."

"There are so many to chose from," I said.

With that, Sheila excused herself to answer the phone. "Have fun!"

"Thanks," I said. I handed half of the stack to Mike. "How will we ever decide?"

"I don't know about you, but I'm way too hungry to go through all of these menus," he replied irritated. "Besides, how are we going to know which restaurants have a sea view? Isn't that what *you wanted?*"

"You're right. Let's just get in the car, go into Malahide, find the first restaurant with a view, and go for it."

We put down the menus on the coffee table and headed out to the car. We drove back along the route we had taken earlier, past the castle and into town. As we approached the intersection in the middle of town, we could see a log jam of cars in front of us. The streets were now teeming with people. It was beginning to look like we'd have the same problem as we had before finding a parking spot.

"Look at this mob scene!" Mike exclaimed. "We'd better grab any parking spot and start our restaurant search on foot."

"There's one," I yelled, seeing a car attempt to pull out of a parking spot that was entirely too small for our car.

"It's worth a try," Mike said. He turned on his turning signal, but a car coming toward us in the other lane responded by flashing his lights. Evidently, he thought he had seen the spot first.

"Every man for himself," Mike growled, and he turned our car head-first into the small spot. "He can't be as hungry as we are." He turned the steering wheel sharply, and threw the car in reverse. When he slowly stepped on the gas, the car eased backwards, causing the back end of our car to protrude into the middle of the oncoming cars. One of the startled cars honked at us.

"Yeah, I see ya, buddy," Mike yelled to the car as he tried to quickly maneuver into the parking place. Then he inched the car back and forth until it finally squeezed into the tiny spot.

"Why don't we try that restaurant on the corner, the one we just passed." I pointed down the block. "It looks like it has a nice view."

"I don't know what you're expecting to see in the dark anyway," Mike said half-heartedly. "Besides, don't you think that's probably a *seafood* place with a name like *The Captain's Table*? I thought you wanted Irish food, like shepherd's pie or lamb stew."

"I did…" my voice trailed off. "But now, I'm so hungry, I don't care what we eat.

How does seafood sound to you?"

"I could eat an entire whale!"

We rushed down the crowded street to *The Captain's Table*. As we approached the restaurant, we could see groups of people huddled out in front of the place and just inside the entry. A large, wooden mermaid, with faded peeling paint, lay across the top of the restaurant doorway. People spilled into the foyer of the restaurant, which led to a decrepit stairway. There were several people standing on the stairway, as well as at the top of the stairs.

"You wait here and I'll see how long of a wait there is." I gently eased my way through the crowded foyer and made my way up the stairs.

The dining room was small and stifling hot. A few booths jammed with people lined one wall. The far wall of the room contained several tables for two, but crammed so close together that their two-person occupants looked as if they were sharing in one big dinner party. It was noisy. Despite the uncomfortable temperature in the room, the windows were shut tight with several lit candles placed on the sills to insure that they would be kept closed.

Realizing our chances for a sea view were slim, all I could pray for now was to be seated anywhere.

A group of six stood pressing around the young hostess who was looking fervently over her reservation list on the podium in front of her. After a minute, she looked up and announced politely, "We're terribly sorry, but we're running a bit late. Although you do have reservations, we won't be able to seat you for at least a half-hour to forty-five minutes. Why don't yas get yerselves a drink and take it down to the foyer. I'll send someone down to get ya when your table's ready."

This was not a good sign. The group cheerfully accepted her explanation and squeezed past her to the little bar adjacent to the hostess station. I squirmed nearer, fingers crossed.

"Is there any hope for a table for two with no reservations?" I asked the hostess.

"I'm afraid not," she said. "We're totally booked, and backed up besides. Sorry. It's Saturday night in Malahide. Those people in front of ya had reservations for a month. Why don't you try the pizza place across the street?"

"Pizza place?" I repeated, bewildered. We were in the gourmet town of Malahide, our last night out on the town and she was suggesting *pizza*? And I thought I was settling for seafood instead of authentic shepherd's pie. I started for the stairs, regretting having to break the news to Mike.

He was waiting outside in a throng of people. When I caught his eye, I gave him the thumbs down sign and pushed my way through to him.

"How about that place across the street?" he asked. "It looks French, but at least it's food."

We crossed the street, carefully avoiding the cars, and walked up to the menu displayed in the window. *Roches Bistro*, it read. Today's specialties are *pate de fois gras, crudities, salmon en croute*. The menu had no prices.

My mouth watered as I pictured my plate covered with classic French cuisine brought to our table by handsome French waiters in red waistcoats. "Well, it's not what we were looking for, but it looks fantastic. I could handle some *fois gras* right now, even if it's served on soda bread!"

We walked in. A young man in a black dinner jacket greeted us.

"May I help you Madame and Monsieur?" I questioned whether we were still in Ireland.

"Two for dinner, please," Mike said.

"For tonight?" the young man asked.

"Well, of course, for tonight," Mike answered.

"Reservations?" the young man inquired.

"Why, no, but we'll wait if we have to," Mike replied, trying to control his temper.

"I'm sorry, Monsieur, but I'm afraid we're full."

"How about if we come back a little later?" Mike suggested.

"I'm sorry," the young man said in a firm and affected French accent. "We're completely full and besides, we only take people with reservations."

We left and, dejectedly, walked up the street. It was almost eight o'clock. I looked across at the pizza place, which was by now looking increasingly desirable. Mike loved pizza, even Irish pizza.

"Can't we try one more place before we settle for pizza?" I urged.

We walked up the street and turned the corner.

Halfway down the block, we could see a restaurant sign with scrolled lettering. It read, *Eastern Tandoori, authentic Indian cuisine.*

"Well?" I turned to Mike in desperation.

"We can try it," Mike said. "It says there on the sign, *flavors to suit all tastes.*"

We entered a large waiting area filled with people. I remained hopeful.

"Reservations?" asked a tiny, buxom Indian hostess dressed in a filmy turquoise sarong trimmed in gold.

"I'm afraid not," Mike said.

"Sorry," she said. "We are booked up solid." She pronounced the last three words with a distinct, schooled British accent.

"What if we come back?" Mike suggested again, sounding desperate.

"You could try that. If you try back in perhaps two hours, we might have availability," she allowed. "So sorry."

"Okay, pizza it is," I said. "No view, no shepherd's pie, but I just don't care anymore."

"Are you sure you don't want to keep looking?" he asked, still trying to please me. "Definitely not. It looks hopeless. Besides, we love pizza." I tried to sound encouraging.

We headed toward the pizzeria. By now *it* was overflowing with people. A short, stocky Italian looking man with a chipper grin and a white apron around his waist, greeted us at the door.

"Two for dinner," Mike said. "And we'd like to put our pizza order in immediately, if we can, to save some time."

"I'm sorry to tell you this," the Italian replied, "but there's over an hour wait right now, just for take-away. That's Saturday night for you," he said. "Why don't you try coming back in about an hour. Maybe things will quiet down by then."

Mike and I looked at each other in disbelief.

"I'd laugh, but I'm too weak from hunger," I said trying to stifle a giggle.

He laughed, too. "This is absolutely unbelievable!"

We continued down the street until we came to a tiny Chinese take-out place that was wedged in between two pubs.

"What do you say?" he asked. "You love egg *foo yung*!"

"Sounds great to me," I said.

Ten minutes later we were both balancing little white cardboard cartons on our laps. As Mike attempted to retrieve his chicken kow with his chopsticks, he called over to a young man seated at the counter. "Excuse me, could you tell us where there's a good place in Malahide to listen to Irish music or see Irish dancing tonight?"

"Oh, there's no diddly, diddly in Malahide," he replied with a recognizable Dublin accent.

"What do you mean *no diddly, diddly*?" Mike asked.

"You know all that fiddling and diddling," the Dubliner responded. "This is a *classy resort town*! We don't go for that sort of thing here. This is a refined place, known for our international restaurants and sophisticated wine bars, not *common* pubs with hokey music for tourists."

"Are you telling me out of all the pubs we've walked by tonight *not one of them* has Irish music or dance tonight?"

"Oh, there are plenty of pubs, but today's Saturday," the Dubliner explained. "People who come to the pubs in Malahide on Saturday night, come to socialize. They want chat bars. They are here to meet people. They don't want insipid Irish rebel fight songs or Irish jigs drowning out their conversations."

"Insipid?" Mike's voice rose.

"Now, lad, don't be getting excited," he replied nervously, regarding Mike's large frame. "Calm yourself."

"Calm myself? How can I calm myself with the thought of searching the rest of the night for Irish music?"

The Dubliner shrugged his shoulders, "So sorry, lad. I didn't mean to spoil your evening." Then he finished the last of his chow mein and walked out.

Mike scraped the bottom of his Chinese food carton with his chopsticks, pretending not to be disappointed. He turned to me and said, "Do you still want to go pub crawling if there are no pubs in Malahide with Irish singing or dancing? Chat bars...we could do a little chatting of our own back at Sheila's." He winked at me.

"I could go for that." I winked back, remembering how comfy that big bed looked.

Then he put his arm around my shoulder, knocking the empty carton off my lap.

We left the Chinese take out, passing the chat bars on the way back to our car.

Irish Good-byes

A large green helium balloon shaped like a shamrock hovered above the dining room table. The table was draped with an ecru Irish linen table-cloth and was set with place settings for a dozen people. Sparkling silverware flanked Beleek china, and Waterford crystal stemware graced the enormous cherry table. A splash of fushia colored roses stood in a Waterford cut glass vase at the center of the table. I wondered whom the special guests were that Mary had gone all out for?

Tethered to the end of the balloon's long, curly red ribbon was an over-sized greeting card with the names "Pat and Mike" written across the back of it in calligraphy. As I picked up the card to examine it more closely, voices rose up all around me. "Surpriiiiise!" A dozen familiar faces emerged out of the corners of the room. While their bright eyes gazed happily at me, I began to walk around the room giving all of them a heart-felt hug. So this was it. A farewell party…for us.

There was Mike standing in the middle of the group. He was grinning. He looked smug. He must have been in on the planning. I reflected on all of the hour-long good-byes we had had over the year in people's doorways, foyers and front steps. The Irish had a hard time letting you out of their sight. They found it difficult to let go. They would hang onto your every parting word. Often, the saying of good-byes took longer than the visit itself. We would be leaving for America in a few days, and we had been saying good-bye for over a month, proving to be one of the longest Irish good-byes on record.

"Are you surprised?" Mary made her way through the crowd. "I had a heck of a time trying to keep my mouth shut for the last month. Do ya remember when I reminded Mary McGurty about our little get together

on the phone that morning? I was sure you heard me and were pretendin'
not to!"

"No, honestly, I don't remember that at all," I said. "Was that the day
the owners called to tell us they were coming back earlier than expected?
I was in a complete panic that day. I never dreamed we could have all of
our things organized and packed in just one month. It made me get
organized a lot sooner than I would have. It's just a shame it went by in
such a hurry."

Mike bent over and kissed me on my cheek. "I know you're surprised.
Didn't you notice we were all avoiding you so we wouldn't let the cat out
of the bag?"

Kevin chimed in. "Yeh, we were afraid you'd think we were snubbing
you, and now it turns out you didn't even notice!"

Mary held the envelope to me. "Now go on and open yer present, so
we can get started with your farewell dinner party," she urged.

I took the envelope from her eager hand and thought how much I
would miss our Mary. "Oh, you really mustn't have." I protested. "But
I'm sure glad you did! You know how I love surprises! This has been the
most wonderful year of my life, thanks to all of you." My throat started
to close on the last two words. I looked around the room at all of our
beloved friends.

Mike handed me the letter opener from the sideboard. I sliced the top
of the enormous envelope from side to side. I knew I'd want to keep it as
a remembrance, a cherished memento of our year in Ireland. "I love things
that come in envelopes." I tried to act more cheery than how I really felt.
"Usually, one size fits all!" The small crowd chuckled at my feeble attempt
at humor in what was, to me, a sad situation.

I tugged at the card, removing it from the envelope. The Balloon above
bobbed gaily with each of my tears and tugs at the card. Finally, the card
slid out and on it were large, scrolled letters, writing out the salutation,
"Good-bye and Good Luck!"

The reality of our leaving now struck me as weighty as a stone. "Do we really have to say *good-bye?*" I managed to whisper. "You know we don't want to!" Mary and Kevin placed their arms around my shoulders for solace.

I was barely able to read the words with the tears blurring my vision.

The inside of the card was blank except for the signatures of all of our friends, each with a one-line note wishing us luck or farewell. I lingered on each one, hoping it would show my appreciation for the effort which must have gone into this good-bye get together. I noticed what undoubtedly must have been Kevin's signature. All that was written was "Love, from your favorite farmhand. K." I smiled at him. A folded paper that was enclosed with the card, fell out onto the floor.

Mary bent down to pick it up and handed it to me. "If it takes ya that long to open one measly card, we're sure glad we didn't give ya thousands of presents. We woulda' been here all night!"

I took the paper and unfolded it carefully.

"Read it out loud," someone called from the group, "so we can all year ye!"

"Dear Pat and Mike," it began. "We will surely all miss you and cherish the time we had together. We feel like we hardly got to know ye! We'll think of you often as we hope you will think of us. Come back as soon as you can only next time stay forever. We love you! Signed, Your Friends. P.S. For your farewell gift, each couple will provide a story from the past year to reminisce about over the farewell feast we have prepared for you."

This is why I loved Irish dinner parties. The guests always felt obligated to do the entertaining at the table, so the host and hostess could finally relax after their daylong preparations for the meal.

"Will yas all take your seats?" Mary ushered everyone to the table. "Read your little place cards to be findin' where ya belong!"

We all obliged her and took our chairs. The dinner group was arranged in a boy-girl alternating fashion with Mike and me at either end of the table. Kevin and Mary sat in the middle of each side of the table so they could orchestrate.

Kevin stood up. "I'd like to propose a toast to the Yanks who stole our hearts. In case yas wouldn't be knowin', that would be you two." He nodded down to each end of the table to reassure us. Everyone giggled self consciously, happy that Kevin had taken the lead at speaking. "Seriously, we all don't know what we'll be doin' without yas now that we've finally gotten used to yas," Kevin teased, good-naturedly. "We hope yas will be keepin' us in your minds as well as your hearts, for you both will always be in ours." He was strikingly eloquent. The group applauded politely. Then we all lifted our glasses, now brimming with champagne, and took a sip.

Kevin continued, "Now before we hear from our honored guests, we want to thank all the ladies for organizin' this gourmet meal and Mary who set this gorgeous table, a table the kings of Munster would be proud of!" As he said this, Mary tried to hide behind her dinner napkin. "Now, we'd like a word or two from the Yanks, themselves."

Mike and I both stood up. I waved to Mike to go first, as I was having a hard time composing myself.

"We are very happy and honored for this beautiful dinner party," Mike said. "Unhappily, the cause for the event is our much regretted departure. We know we will be back to see all of you, so we refuse to say 'good-bye' and will only say 'until we meet again.' Now, let's have a toast to all of *you*, our new found friends who made our year here so memorable." He held his champagne glass up and we all took another drink.

"If you'll allow me," I said, trying to keep the tears from my eyes. "I'd rather save my toast until the end of the dinner. You're probably getting tired of all of the blather going around this room already. Thanks. I sat down before my voice cracked, giving them no time to protest.

"Cheers!" the group all yelled in unison.

Everyone unfolded their napkins and looked around the table at the extravagant feast. Platters of piping hot roast lamb, pork and mashed potatoes appeared and the dinner guests began loading up their plates with healthy portions.

"There won't be any talk of diets, tonight, please!" Mary ordered from the center of the table.

After the prayer, Kevin stood up. "I'm going to start this evening's entertainment portion with one of my favorite stories about the Yanks from Chicago who couldn't tell a rooster from a hen or a cow from a bull." He looked over at me, smirking the whole time. He then related the story about introducing us to Nettie, the cow, and Tarzan the cock on our first day at the Farmhouse. Nobody but Mike knew this story, so the whole group howled with laughter and incredulity. Kevin relished the telling of it. He pantomimed the young bull reaching for the cow's teat with his mug and mimicked Tarzan chasing the rattled hens around the chicken coupe. When the laughter subsided, Kevin took a bow and sat down, proud of his performance.

"It seems like it was a hundred years ago since that first day." Mike stood up to take his turn. "I'd like to tell the story about how my wife made me climb out onto the roof to retrieve a two-liter bottle of Coke she left to cool out on the window sill."

"I didn't make you," I protested.

"Okay, then you tell it!" He sat down.

"It looks like I'd better, if you're going to hear the correct version. One night, the first month or so that we lived here, I kept a bottle of Coke outside on our window sill, so if I got thirsty in the late evening or the middle of the night, I wouldn't have to get dressed to go down to raid the frig. I also didn't want to disturb the guests, as one time one of them sneaked up on me in the kitchen and we almost scared the bejessus out of each other. We both screamed so loudly, I was sure we woke everyone else up!

"So I got into this habit of putting the Coke out on the sill. Mike would warn me that if it ever fell off, it could kill somebody, but of course, I just ignored him and put it out there anyway. Then late one night, I got up to adjust the shutters, as there was a gust of wind rattling through the room. As I was reaching for the shutter to close it, the wind got hold of it. It banged backward and hit the bottle of Coke off the sill. It fell down onto the roof below, which had to have been ten feet down. It broke the slate tiles but the bottle, miraculously didn't shatter.

"Of course, the noise woke Mike up, and he gallantly offered to go out onto the roof to get the Coke. Before I knew it, Mike was easing himself out through the window, eventually hanging by his fingertips from the sill. When he finally let go of the ledge, he landed easily onto the lower roof. He retrieved the Coke and handed it up to me. I reached out, hanging way out over the sill, and grabbed the bottle.

"After asking him how he planned on getting back through the window, he reached up his arms to me and said, 'Why, you're going to pull me up!'

"'Yeah, like I can pull up over two hundred pounds. What's your other idea?'

"Mike walked over to the edge of the rooftop and came back again. 'This roof is too high for me to jump down from. It must be twenty feet. I'll have to try to jump straight up, grab the sill and hoist myself up.'

"Mike jumped straight up, and miraculously got a good handful of window sill the first try. He inched his fingers around the sill and tried to walk up the side of the wall. He suddenly lost his grip and fell backwards and landed on his backside. I giggled. I couldn't help myself.

"Then, he stood up, brushed off his bruised pride, and tried it again. This time instead of walking up the wall, he tried to drag his body straight up, grabbing tightly to the sill. He got far enough up to pull his shoulders and upper chest up to the window frame. He was panting heavily. I continued to giggle. It looked as comical as a Three Stooges routine. He raised his hand to admonish me for laughing. This threw his balance off and he tumbled backward out through the window and back onto the lower roof again. I stopped laughing only long enough to see if he was actually hurt. He sat sprawled on the smashed roof tiles.

I called down to him. "Let me go fetch Kevin to get a ladder," I offered trying to suppress another fit of laughter.

"You're not calling Kevin!" he whispered back up to me. "If you'd quit your giggling, I'd be up there by now.'

"Okay, suit yourself. I'll try not to laugh this time. I'll try and get hold of you when you get half of yourself through the window."

"Mike tried to jump straight up again, but he was losing his strength and he couldn't get enough height. He tried another two more attempts. The third time, he was finally able to grip the sill. With all of the strength he had left in him, he dragged himself, grunting and groaning, halfway through the window. As I approached him to give him a hand I burst out laughing and so did he. He continued to grip the sill and balance his body so that he wouldn't fall back out. Then he became very serious and admonished me to leave the room immediately. I had to leave without helping to pull him in, doubled over with laughter.

"I listened from the other side of the bedroom door, then heard a tremendous thump as Mike's body fell into the room. He had gotten the Coke."

"Now speaking of being locked out," Mary said, and stood up to tell her anecdote. "Remember the British gent Mr. Redhead, who locked himself out of *his* room? He was an upper crust English chap who was some kind of international ambassador or the like. He was extremely high brow and even acted a bit snooty to our other guests. He told them stories of bein' friends with Royalty and meetin' people like Henry Kissinger. I remember wonderin' if he was makin' it all up to impress us.

"That evenin' I was at the registration desk, doin' a bit of paperwork and I heard a little commotion up on the second landing. I paid no heed to it as I was busy and I figured it was just one of the guests sleep walkin'. I remember, I was lookin' for a paper clip in the top drawer of the desk when I looked up and saw my man Mr. Redhead standing naked as a Jay bird before me. I swear," she continued trying to keep herself together, "all he had on was his smile and a Ghandi-like diaper covering himself!"

The room came down with laughter.

"You see," Mary went on, "our Mr. Redhead had locked himself out of the room with only his birthday suit, so he took one of our Irish lace curtains down from the second hallway window, wrapped it around himself and marched up to me askin' for an extra key, as easy as ya please!"

"What did you do?"

"I just handed him the extra key, he politely thanked me, and he sauntered up the stairs in his ill-fitting drapery. You should 'ave seen 'im, acting as grand as ever. He didn't even flinch!" Mary took her seat.

Everyone giggled.

"I, myself," said Kevin, "would have liked to have been there to see the expression on Mary's face, let alone his."

"Oh, go on." Mary said.

Our neighbor James related his story about the busload of tourists stranded by the side of the road with a flat tire. "Remember how we divvied the group up amongst ourselves, each selecting the ones we thought could fit most easily on our sofas? They all nodded, grinning and remembering when we put up thirty instant overnight guests in our living rooms.

Each of the group tried to top the other with an unusual or funny story.

"How about the World War II enemies who almost went at it over breakfast?" Mike asked. "I thought there'd be a food fight, at least."

"Mike, tell us my favorite," Mary said. "About the German who insisted on usin' his own towel, the one he kept in his suitcase for a week."

"How about the American couple who stayed here thinking they were leaving from Shannon and found out at breakfast they had return tickets from Dublin and had to high tail it back to Dublin to catch their plane on time!"

"Better yet," I tried to top them all. "What about the couple whose luggage never caught up to them? We offered to loan them clothes so they wouldn't have to go out and buy any until their bags arrived. The first day, they didn't look all that bad wearing what we could come up with. By the fourth day, they looked pretty comical decked out in the outlandish outfits we selected just to see if they would actually be *polite* enough to wear them. And they did! Remember how they looked getting into their car wearing that getup of Mike's plaid shorts and Mary's sweater? Talk about The Emperor's new clothes!"

Mary stood up. " Should we ladies start the dishes while the gents have a smoke?"

I jumped up. "I'd sincerely appreciate it if you'd allow me to do all of the cleaning up. You've all have been so gracious tonight. It would be my pleasure while relishing all of the wonderful stories you have all shared with us tonight. Please, I really want to!"

"I'll have none of that!" Mary protested hotly. Go on, now, all of yas…into the parlor. I'll be bringin' the coffee and desserts into ya."

As we gathered in the parlor to drink our Irish coffees and taste the many delicious looking deserts, the telephone rang. Mike got up to get it. The group continued with their string of stories. After several minutes, Mike returned to the room. He looked flushed and had a bewildered look about him.

"Is anything wrong, Dear?" I asked.

"No," he hesitated, searching for the right words. "I think something is very right." He added, slowly, enunciating every word, "You are *not* going to *believe* this." Then he turned to the group. "Well, we might just be getting the gift we were wishing for after all. That was the owners who telephoned. It seems they have changed their minds and want to stay on sabbatical for another year. I guess they are beginning to realize that tending to twins while running a B & B might not work. They wanted to know if we'd be interested in staying on indefinitely. Otherwise, they're going to start interviewing other couples."

I collapsed on the couch. "You're joking! You're all in on this!"

"Nobody would joke about a thing like that!" Mary said. "After you've packed everything up and gotten the tickets? Would we have thrown you this great party if we didn't think you were really leaving?"

"I don't know what to say." I looked at Mike. "What should we do?"
Mike shrugged his shoulders.

"Well, like I always say, 'what's the worst that could happen?'"

My heart pounded wildly. I looked around the room at our dear friends, the friends that we might not have to leave after all. "And, we already *know* the *best* that could happen!" I exclaimed. "Tell them we'd be delighted to stay another year."

About the Author

Patricia O'Brien was born the middle of seven children in an Irish Catholic neighborhood on Chicago's South Side. At the impressionable age of nine, Ms O'Brien and her family squeezed into their 1951 Buick and took a month long odyssey across the United States, their destination displayed by a cardboard sign taped in the back window: "California or Bust." By the time they reached the West Coast, Ms. O'Brien was hooked on travel and adventure.

Since then, she has lived and traveled extensively in The Republic of Ireland, Great Britain and Europe. Ms. O'Brien spent one year in Vienna, Austria where she studied at the Institute of European Studies and later, she and her husband, Michael, spent two years in Paris, France where Patricia studied at the Sorbonne while Michael played professional basketball.

After receiving her bachelor's degree in history from Rosary College in River Forest, Illinois and her Master's degree in art history from Northern Illinois University, Ms. O'Brien taught history and humanities for twelve years on the high school and college levels while writing her travel adventure novels. Ms. O'Brien and her husband currently reside in a southwest Chicago suburb.